The Dalai Lama
A Biography

Claude B. Levenson

Translated by Stephen Cox

OXFORD
UNIVERSITY PRESS

OXFORD
UNIVERSITY PRESS

YMCA Library Building, Jai Singh Road, New Delhi 110 001

Oxford University Press is a department of the University of Oxford. It furthers the
University's objective of excellence in research, scholarship, and education
by publishing worldwide in

Oxford   New York

Athens   Auckland   Bangkok   Bogota   Buenos Aires   Cape Town
Chennai   Dar es Salaam   Delhi   Florence   Hong Kong   Istanbul   Karachi
Kolkata   Kuala Lumpur   Madrid   Melbourne   Mexico City   Mumbai
Nairobi   Paris   São Paulo   Shanghai   Singapore   Taipei   Tokyo   Toronto   Warsaw

with associated companies in Berlin Ibadan

Oxford is a registered trade mark of Oxford University Press
in the UK and in certain other countries

Published in India
By Oxford University Press, New Delhi

© Oxford University Press 1978

First published 1988
Oxford University Press 1999
Oxford India Paperbacks 2001

ISBN 019 565650 4

Printed at Rashtriya Printers, Delhi 110 032
Published by Manzar Khan, Oxford University Press
YMCA Library Building, Jai Singh Road, New Delhi 110 001

My sincerest thanks to all those
without whom this book would be
only a dream, but above all to the
Precious Master who made it possible.

THE DALAI LAMA

THEKCHEN CHOELING
McLEOD GANJ 176219
KANGRA DISTRICT
HIMACHAL PRADESH

I have known Mrs Claude B. Levenson for some years now. She has always shown sympathetic understanding of the Tibetan issue. This is deeply appreciated because the problem is very complicated, much misunderstood and little known.

Mrs Levenson has dealt with the Tibetan issue with clarity and sincerity in her book *Le Seigneur du Lotus Blanc*. I am confident that this English version will be as successful as the original French.

17 August 1988

If you cross the mountain, you will see the palace of the King
of the Land of the Lotus.

(*Drowazan-mo*, Tibetan folk mystery play)

Contents

Illustrations

Between pages 174 and 175

Preface

Since the 1987 publication of this biography in French to which His Holiness the Dalai Lama had actively contributed, some things have remained the same while others have changed. The book was rapidly translated into English, German, Danish, Romanian, Thai and Spanish and widely distributed in paperback, especially in France and Germany. This biography is still essentially valid even if the Dalai Lama has written a beautiful autobiography and several other authors have recently published biographical works.

During the past decade or so, I have been lucky enough to continue accompanying the Dalai Lama during many of his activities: his travels throughout the world in support of his people's cause, his other meetings and talks which have gathered momentum in recent years. Besides, I was able to meet him on several occasions during these years and have discussions about the future. Since the first publication of this book I have returned to Tibet, under Chinese domination, on several occasions and from one trip to another I have been forced to note with great sadness the substantial degradation of the situation due to calculated and heartless sinocization.

Nevertheless, the Dalai Lama remains hopeful and pursues steadily the political road he chose years ago, known as the Middle Path. Twelve years is negligible and yet a great length of time in a human life – a complete cycle from the Buddhist point of view. For whatever may happen, the wheel does turn. However a few events should be underlined as landmarks of memory.

To begin with, during a deceitful lull which encouraged the

unusual presence of numerous Western tourists, there were recurrent peaceful protests in Lhasa during 1987 and 1988. As a result, in the wake of Losar, the Tibetan New Year which marked the passage of the Year of the Fire-Dragon to that of the Earth-Serpent (6 February 1989) and in anticipation of eventual uprisings around 10 March, the anniversary of the people's anti-Chinese uprising in Lhasa in 1959, the Chinese authorities decided to take no chances and decreed a state of emergency in the principal cities of what they have baptized as the Autonomous Region of Tibet. The day before the fatal date, martial law was imposed and maintained until May 1990, that is to say until over a year later and much later than in China itself.

Meanwhile Gorbatchev made his historic visit to Peking in order to reconcile the rivals of now shattered communism, under the inquisitive eyes of the television cameras from the world over. But above all there was Tien An Men, the rebellious wave of new generation Chinese demanding more liberty at the foot of a statue baptized the Goddess of Democracy in imitation of the Statue of Liberty. There was also the emblematic image of an unknown civilian in dark socks and white shirt, forcing the leading tank of an armoured column to deviate from its path so as to avoid crushing him, before he disappeared forever and thus allowed his unforgettable gesture to melt into the heart of collective memory. And then the end of illusions, the return to the routine-ness of silencing and oppression.

In the same year the jury of Oslo chose as the Nobel Laureate for Peace, the Dalai Lama, honouring in this manner the tireless non-violent struggle of his people. His Holiness commented: 'It is a pity that the prize was not shared with Deng Xiao-ping; it would have provided an occasion to meet and perhaps begin a dialogue'. And further added: 'I am essentially a mirror of the hopes, the fears and the aspirations of the Tibetan people. Neither more nor less.' However that Tibetans themselves consider that this distinction which at last recognizes the exceptional calibre of their spiritual and political leader as, 'a *puja* of long life from the Occident to the Dalai Lama.'

The Dalai Lama's message had been clear since his 1988 speech before the European Parliament in Strasburg. Disclosed publicly in Washington in September 1987, the famous 'Five Point Plan' developed at that time was conceived as the foundation of a serious background to discussion. The propositions suggested the transformation of the whole of Tibet into a zone of peace; the immediate cessation of the massive transfer of the Han population (or those of Han origin); the respect of human rights and the fundamental liberties of the Tibetan people; the restoration of the natural environment and its protection through, for instance, putting an end to the disposal of nuclear wastes or of the construction of atomic weapons on Tibetan territory; the beginning of valid negotiations concerning the status of Tibet and the future relationships between the two peoples.

The fundamental, non-violent approach has never been abandoned by the Dalai Lama who has always managed, at least until now, to dissuade the Tibetans, in particular the youngest and most ardent, from the temptations of violent action. These concepts have been received and judged to be perfectly sensible by international opinion, as also among responsible politicians. However Peking has maintained its implacable position; to the Chinese leaders these propositions constitute 'conditions', and negotiations are not to be considered if there are such preliminary conditions. This attitude is perhaps a quick way of establishing a dead end for an assertion made by Deng Xiaoping himself who, in 1979, assured an older brother of the Dalai Lama that 'all was negotiable, except independence'.

The small war of words continues its sly course all the same. The Dalai Lama's people remain suspicious of official propaganda. However, repressive measures weigh heavily. Arrests and imprisonments multiply among the stubborn and resistant, torture and abuse are the daily lot of the prisoners who are subject to the whole scale of humiliations which the authorities inflict. The long list of breaches and violations of human rights continues to lengthen and more of the young, born since the change of government, are slipping away on the road to exile, often at the risk of their lives.

Bit by bit in Tibet, over the years and after many changes, the Tibetans' spontaneity is withering as they remain confined to their own country and are reduced there to the rank of second-rate citizens. In the exiled communities, dissensions appear as impatience grows due to the prolonged period of limbo. A dialogue with the Chinese remains indispensable but hopes of it are fading with them, rebellious at the idea of the slightest concession. Meanwhile the Tibetan cause is slowly gaining acceptance among dissidents and young democrats in pursuit of a remodelled and modernized China.

In the wake of the Nobel prize this complex issue has been attracting considerable attention. Curiosity about an inaccessible culture, the discovery of a civilization which has remained marginal, the fascination inspired by the high, deserted lands, the crystallization of unformulated dreams around the myths born of legends, the encounters with charismatic personalities inspired research thus enriching humanitarianism, culture, relationships and politics.

However there still remain unanswered questions. Why should the Chinese version be more credible than the Tibetan one when the debate concerns, in truth, a historical disagreement between two neighbouring countries whose relationship has never been particularly cordial? Sovereignty, suzerainty and independence are concepts that are constantly evolving and the protagonists and specialists are perpetually debating over subtleties. The Tibetans want nothing to do with them: they know who they are, are jealous of their identity next to a powerful neighbour, and they intend to remain different, conscious of their traditions and original knowledge.

Slowly but surely, this aspect of their nationalist claims has been imposed upon the world thanks to their torch bearer, the Dalai Lama. Some have realized that, in fact, the forced annexation of Tibet by the Popular Armed Liberation Forces in 1949–50 had all the characteristics of a colonial expedition despite the peaceful liberation terminology and that the transferring of populations which followed was a real act of colonization, behaviour which evidently tarnishes the image of a liberated and liberating nation in the service of oppressed people.

Tibet had remained closed to foreigners for many years; the limited access allowed since 1980 has made it possible to go and assess the change. Lhasa, the divine city, the historical and religious capital has become unrecognizable. Under the pretext of cleaning up and modernizing, the traditional neighbourhoods have been methodically demolished and replaced by outrageous buildings of glass and concrete which are totally inappropriate for the climate and have signed the death warrant of an original architecture which was perfectly symbiotic with its surroundings. In just a few years the now Chinese style city has been marred and corseted by military barracks. In front of Jokhang, the most sacred sanctuary in the heart of the ancient city, a space has been created, supposedly to clear the way for the view. In fact, this now allows closer surveillance with cameras on roof tops to check the movements of potentially hostile crowds. As for the great square at the foot of the Potala, not only does it appear ridiculous facing the majestic, ancient winter palace of the Dalai Lamas, it is further marred by the appalling lampposts topped by clusters of shattered light bulbs. True, at night the light does tempt bearers of the fearsome, Tibetan catapults .... And so it is with everything else: each of the heavy, ultra-realistic socialist monuments, placed at crossings, snubs the elegance of the horsemen on the lofty steppes or the good-natured gait of the yaks. Karaokes, soldiers' bars and brothels are only trivial features of the modernistic kitsch of the city, violated, yes, but where a rebellious heart continues to beat and refuse the systematic desire to wipe out even the memory of history and the past.

Forty years later many Tibetans still have trouble being used to the foreign presence. They barely survive in menial jobs and feel frustated and helpless. And they still secretely hope for recovered liberty. A local form of apartheid has been introduced: the Chinese colonists continue to feel as though they were somewhere else, silent while in service, nostalgic for home when they accept to talk, impatient to return to their country as soon as they've earned some money. Some even admit that if the military shield disappeared they would not feel secure and would prefer to leave immediately.

Over the past twelve years public opinion the world over has moved in favour of Tibet. The flag is now well recognized ever since a French association made one so large that it has been inscribed in official books of records as being the largest in the world. Marches have been organized in many countries in favour of the Tibetan cause: annual rallies, growing steadily larger, mark the anniversary of the uprising of 10 March 1959. Tibetan bouddhism is in vogue in the United States, Europe, Australia, Chinese colonies overseas and the visit of the Dalai Lama in Taiwan drew huge crowds. People of all age groups gather to listen to his teachings from Mongolia, which has returned to its traditions; it has travelled to France, Italy or Germany where some have discovered in it a path leading to serenity, as it has through Kalmouki or Bouriati in Russia. India too remains supportive of the Dalai Lama and his cause.

Aspects of the Tibetan drama – from the flight of children and young adults from Tibet in a quest for the future to the sharing of the spiritual quest of the XIVth Dalai Lama – have been receiving extensive coverage. Overwhelming testimony relates the before and after of the invasion of 1949 which is matched by Chinese propaganda to justify the 'battle to life and to death' against what they have qualified as 'Tibetan separatism'. University graduates and historians from all over the world have met and debated; famous lawyers have cited the legal, international standards which regulate the notions of country and sovereignty, independence and the application of the fundamental right to self-determination.

Their future belongs first of all to the Tibetans, colonized or refugees. The age of colonialism is over as should be the age where solutions are imposed through coercion. The currents forming the global community demand innovative solutions to historical, even ancient, antagonisms. Several examples seem to indicate that however relentless they may be, opponents in a conflict end up realizing that negotiations are necessary. Non-violence may reveal itself to be a useful path as long as it is not underestimated as being a way to passive fatality, but understood as one of assumed and shared responsibility. Far from being simple, this road exacts perseveration, imagination and rigour in a world which seems to have lost even the perception of these qualities. However, Tenzin Gyatso, XIVth Dalai Lama of Tibet, never tires of repeating: 'Tolerance, patience and courage are the signs not of failure, but of victory ... .'

PART I

Setting the Scene

1

Mönlam in Bodh Gaya

Everything leads us to believe that there is a certain point at which life and death, real and imaginary, past and future, communicable and incommunicable, cease to be contradictorily perceived.

(*André Breton*)

The maroon and saffron colours of the monks' robes set off the opaque whiteness at the foot of the Bodhi tree whose broad foliage almost rivals the venerable stupa which stands on the place of the Buddha's Awakening. Rising from deep within them, and intensely alive, the prayers of thousands of monks weave a lattice of sound; they create a dimension of sacredness, an untouchable but invulnerable space, on human ground.

The ground was in Bodh Gaya, in the impoverished north Indian State of Bihar, and the time was December 1985, when thousands of Buddhist pilgrims converged on a remote little village, travelling on foot, in trucks and buses, and in ox-carts. Some of them had spent weeks along their road, and crossed the great barrier of the Himalayas from the far corners of Tibet, with or without official permission, through empty wastes and high plateaux, just to see and hear their spiritual guide and to share a moment of intense communion. After braving hostile weather and unfriendly authorities, the faithful kept pouring in to swell the ranks of a motley, eager crowd, full of both gravity and joy, in the strength of its union around the latest in an immemorial line embodying a way of being which is both serenity and wisdom.

According to the elder guardians of tradition, with their parchment skins and youthful eyes, you had to go a long way back in time to find mention of any similar gathering. Some ageing lamas recalled how the Great Prayers were held in Lhasa every year, following the New Year ceremonies and praying for the well-being of all living creatures, when for a whole week the town became one great monastery. That was in the days when Lhasa was still a fabulous forbidden city, the home of the divine.

In the December sunshine, through the glinting dust raised by the millions of footsteps of the thousands of the faithful, Lhasa loomed over Bodh Gaya, and, if there were no mountains, the surrounding temples blurred into hills. All around the Tree of Life a fantastic living mandala was organised, a wine-coloured tide with lines of orange breakers between sun and shade, thousands of shaven skulls turning towards a small platform standing only a few yards away from the sturdy trunk; the Throne of the White Lotus was surmounted by a broad yellow parasol, the symbol of royalty.

A breeze passed like a shiver through the waiting silence. Clustered prayer-flags spread a rainbow of colours. A bell chimed quietly, to be echoed by the trilling of a bird, and a trumpet sounded gravely in the distance. Another wait, and then in silence four grand lamas, the heads of the schools of Tibetan Buddhism, slid on to their seats that flanked the throne, halfway between the ground and the sofa occupied by the master of ceremonies. Novice monks and young reincarnations of venerated wise men looked on wide-eyed; never before had they taken part in such a gathering out of time.

A sound of shawms and drums came nearer, and the melody emerged, to the beat of rapid footsteps slipping over stone polished by centuries of ritual circumambulations. The familiar silhouette of the Fourteenth Dalai Lama appeared at the top of the stair and he hastened down it, preceded and followed by half a dozen musician monks, the parasol bearer hurrying to keep up, and a handful of alert bodyguards. The supple walk, athletic build beneath the maroon robe, bared right shoulder, muscular arm and powerful hand, all conveyed an impression of harmony; and the spiritual strength which is focused in his eyes was also expressed by the easy movement of the physical body and the flesh-and-blood perception of a solid footing on the earth.

Incarnation of the Buddha of Infinite Compassion, god-king, sovereign of the high Land of Snows, Buddhist monk, Ocean of Wisdom, Tentzin Gyatso walked on, with his luminous smile. With hands clasped before him he bowed towards the statue of the Great Compassionate, lowered an eyelid in a wink of recognition, turned away, greeted the privileged people along his path, and walked to the seat covered by a heavy drape of shimmering damask silk. First he bowed down before the throne, to honour the teaching of the Buddha, then he sat comfortably cross-legged, smoothed the folds of his robe with a swift movement, and answered the expectant goodwill of the audience with the radiant sweetness of his smile, with his eyes already looking inward. The scuffling and jostling faded, and the silence throbbed.

A deep, barely audible note sounded at the threshold of perception, resonant with power, and slowly rose. Without the sight of that standing monk, an upright pillar in the midst of a seated, watchful congregation, you would have thought that this swelling, rising, spreading voice, charged with every potential and accompanied by the faint and then broadening murmur of the thousands of bonzes and novices, was emerging from the earth itself, this earth of Bodh Gaya consecrated by the uninterrupted devotion of generations of the faithful. Time was abolished. This controlled power, invoking other worlds and all worlds, recreated the origin, the awakening or illumination, and in the subtle interplay of invisible but perceptible connections, only a single voice remained to raise its deep, modulated reply to the call of that countless crowd whose hearts were beating in unison. It was the voice of the Dalai Lama.

For hours the prayer pursued its lengthy ceremonial as the chanting rolled on between the tree and the temple, with one brief interval for tea, drunk the Tibetan way, with ghee and salt, and poured from big pot-bellied teapots held by a troop of smiling novices delighted by an excuse to stretch their legs. Another surprise in the midst of that magnificent Tibetan ritual was the interweaving of a Zen melody from Japan, a blessing from Korea, and an offering from Burma. At the foot of the Lotus throne the yellow robes of the Theravada bhikkhus (monks) stood out from the dark purple wave of the adepts of the Great Vehicle, the Mahayana.

Finally the sun grew tired, and darted its last rays through the dust-filled air as if in tribute to the litany reaching upwards to the sky in the heat of an inner flame. One beat of a muted, incredibly sonorous gong threw a cloak of silence. Thousands of faint candles were lit in the falling dusk, and suddenly it was night. Sculptures in butter gleamed in the half-light, and the grand master of ceremonies melted into the rustling tide of monastic robes for a moment, then slipped into the crowd, and, as he passed her, greeted Tara, protectress of Tibet since the dawn of Buddhist times, before leaving with a smile to return to the monastery.

The Great Prayer for the happiness of all beings, the exceptional prelude to the initiation of the Wheel of Time in Bodh Gaya, was at an end. From high on the outer walkway of the temple I was left with the vision, at the heart of a corona composed of leaves of the Bodhi tree, of a monk with a contagious serenity. Timelessness coexisted with a feeling of changelessness and completion in space, an extraordinary convergence between yesterday and tomorrow, in that focal point of the moment prolonged until it suddenly contains the brightness of eternity. In my dream there was a boat, a ferryman and a river, but no opposite bank. Only the motionless horizon on the edge of infinity – and something like the recall of a path sketched into the memory, a passing life, a mirage, a sign or a reverie. A presence.

2
Of Myth and History

Life is not a problem to solve, it is a reality to experience.
(*Buddha*)

The institution of the Dalai Lama sums up in itself not only
the appeal and audacity, but also the profundity, of a rare
civilisation in which myth and history accompany, support
and interpenetrate each other so thoroughly that they become
more than legend and pass into reality. It is a disconcerting
reality, at least at first sight, because it compels the observer to
take account of dimensions which are usually given over to
poets, artists, dreamers and mystics, and sometimes to scholars and seekers of every variety of the impossible. Yet it
happens that on the Roof of the World the notions of time,
space and infinity, timelessness and eternity, and hence reincarnation, are knitted into the flesh of a spiritual and intellectual heritage generally claimed and valued as such.

This means accepting, with no further ado, that the very idea
of reincarnation is perceived as perfectly natural; not simple
transmigration – the passage of souls from one body to
another and one life to another through all eternity until the
fulfilment of time – but the deliberate decision to return, and
to be re-embodied, with the purpose of helping the immeas-
urable myriad of beings.

In its true foundations, so-called Tibetan Buddhism – it
would be more accurate to speak of the Buddhism practised in
Tibet – is rooted in the direct line of the great Indian

philosophical tradition. However, like any living principle, it
has followed its own development, evolved at its own individual tempo, and adapted to an exceptional environment. In
order to enter into its mysteries with no danger of instant
vertigo, it is enough to leave preconceived notions behind and
be without fear, ready for whatever adventures lie ahead.
They are not hard to find.

People of every climate and complexion have always
sought the secret of immortality. Some have sensed it, others
have almost touched it, and the Tibetans may have found it.
The line of the Dalai Lamas gives a glimpse of it, and chance
encounters with other men's eyes occasionally reveal looks
that come from such a distance, from so manifestly different a
continuum, that the mind of the viewer is suddenly seized by
the idea that it takes lifetimes to achieve such clarity. History,
real history, as the records describe it, probably begins in the
mists of time. The history of the wise, the greatly wise, begins
a little later, in the dawn of modern times, about six centuries
ago.

Like all the peoples of the world, the Tibetans lived inside
their natural ramparts – theirs are especially formidable – and
within the defences created by the sheer passage of time. If
their history appears so unusual, no doubt it is partly because
it has been lived in isolation, and sheltered from the eyes of the
people of the plain, who came increasingly to believe that
gods lived somewhere up above them. And now and then the
gods were fond of meddling in human affairs, and did not
hesitate to descend among them, taking the most unexpected
forms while remaining themselves. In the image of the gods,
beings also come and go, in an ageless succession of worlds,
until they free themselves from the mirage of illusion and
fulfil themselves by crossing the threshold of death, knowledge or wisdom.

For centuries the human imagination has dwelled upon
Tibet, the forbidden country. Misunderstood, half understood or simply unknown, it was seen as the ultimate enigma
by those who dreamed about it, and to set out in search of
Tibet meant braving the inaccessible and challenging the

mystery. Occasionally the seeker would return to report such fabulous tales that they verged upon legends, and kindled a curiosity tinged with dread by evoking the land's enchanting beauty, solitude and awesome majesty. At the heart of these fumbling approaches, one vital thread led unerringly to the lord spiritual and temporal, the man known as god-king, living Buddha, the Wish-Fulfilling Gem, the Precious Master, who so symbolises his land and his people that they have become indissociable.

Coming as the culmination of a long historical development, with all sorts of ups and downs, contradictions and periods of transitory balance, the institution itself was forged in the course of a few generations around the sixteenth century. Yet, curiously, the impression persists that the Dalai Lama so absolutely personifies a mode of being and a way of life, a conception of the world, that he has always existed high in the Land of Snows, if only at the level of potentiality, coming into bloom at the exact moment when the metamorphosis proved necessary. From then onwards the spiritual and the historical view run together.

A Buddhist country, brought to that vision of the world following the reign of the thirty-third great king, Srongtsen Gampo in the seventh century AD, by the power and glory of masters such as Padmasambhava and Atisa, Tibet has been shaped by the Good Law, the *Dharma*, just as much as the law has moulded itself to the character of its rugged inhabitants. As the quintessential place of magic – and how could it be escaped at those breathtaking altitudes, bristling with overwhelming mountain chains and peaks? – Tibet has been propitious to the boldest ventures of the spirit. These have been manifested in the rise and fall of a number of alternately complementary and rival schools, struggling for temporal power and political dominance from age to age.

As elsewhere in the world, kings and princes often made war on one another, attracting the favour or the wrath of the fortress-monasteries which are spread across most of these vast expanses. Inside the *gompas*, which combined the functions of stronghold and secular town or village, lay existence went on under the immediate protection of the lamas, great or small, literate or illiterate, some of them experts in magic, black or white, and in the shadow of tutelary divinities of whom it could be said that it was better to win their goodwill for the key events in life than to suffer their thunderbolts. Meanwhile, however, in the silence of their cells or in distant hermitages, monks were in constant search for different goals, and tirelessly, quietly – sometimes, it is said, by the sheer power of thought – they transmitted their astounding discoveries to their disciples. But it was up to the disciples to continue along the way.

So lines of transmission grew up from the remotest past to the rational enlightenment of our own day. Knowledge lends perspectives of unfailing surprise. Reincarnation does not explain everything, but it is the cornerstone of the extraordinary sovereignty of the Dalai Lamas of Tibet; in a world governed by the law of energy and its transformations, it appears as one possibility among others, and has an utterly logical place in a time which has gone beyond the conventional old western notions of life and death.

At the beginning of Buddhism in Tibet was Guru Rimpoche, the Precious Master Padmasambhava, who came from India to spread the Teaching. He proved to be so convincing, so astute and powerful, that the inhabitants of the high plains put down the sword in favour of the prayer wheel. Following the building of Samye, the first monastery founded by the great Padma himself, other monasteries sprang up and exerted a growing ascendancy over the population.

Gradually distinct schools emerged and divided into four main branches: the Ancients, or Nyingma, the direct heirs of Padma; the Kagyupa, those of the 'whispered tradition', tracing their origins to the translator Marpa and his famous disciple, the poet Milarepa; the Sakya, so called after the monastery where they began; and lastly the Gelukpa, or 'they who practise virtue', descended from the reformer Tsong-kha-pa. The Dalai Lama belongs to the latter school, as well as being the spiritual guide of all Tibetans

Here it is worth while to point out that there is no rivalry among these various modes of expression of a single faith; the schools complement one another and derive from the same basic teaching, which is Sakyamuni's, the historic Buddha.

As well as wearing the yellow hat, to distinguish themselves outwardly from the red hat of the ancients, the Gelukpa maintain a strict insistence on monastic celibacy and a total ban on alcohol. By his reforms in the early fifteenth century, Tsong-kha-pa strengthened the discipline in monastic communities and discontinued the practice of certain rites taken from Bon, the native religion rooted in shamanism and sorcery, which had distorted the original meaning of the Buddhist precepts.

As well as his unusual erudition and a brilliant intelligence acknowledged far and near and preserved in the collective memory, Tsong-kha-pa bequeathed to his disciples one of the most extraordinary monasteries in the Lhasa valley, Ganden – whose name means 'land of joy' – which he had founded in 1409. In 1949 the Italian Tibetologist Giuseppe Tucci wrote:

> As far as the eye could reach, an ocean of peaks hove into sight. Against that grandiose background, Ganden was set off in the trim spruceness of its freshly whitewashed walls framing the blazing red of the temples and the garish gold of the roofs. It was a sight out of this world.[1]

Up above, the sky is still as blue as Tucci saw it, but of Ganden – so called after the paradise where Maitreya, the Buddha of the future, awaits his hour – little remains today except ruins. The Chinese Red Guards destroyed everything in their path. And patiently, humbly, the Tibetans are rebuilding.

At that time, in the fifteenth century, Tsong-kha-pa's fame had spread far and wide, into the remotest valleys of the Roof of the World. The reformer was wise, and his disciples numerous, and the closest among them was Gedun Truppa. The son of transhumant stockbreeders from the high plains of western Tibet, his first contact with the outside world was out of the ordinary. According to the Tibetan chronicles, one cold dark night, in a howling gale, a band of brigands burst into the hamlet. The terrified inhabitants scattered out of sight, and the frightened young mother only had time to conceal her newborn son behind some stones. When the danger was past and the villagers returned, they found to their astonishment that the baby was smiling in his hiding place, under the guard of a crow. They concluded that there was something unusual about the boy.

To prove them correct, Gedun Truppa soon displayed a clear inclination for the study of religion, and distinct abilities. On the death of his father, when he was only seven years old, he entered a monastery not far from Shigatse, in the service of a monk, before taking the robe himself. Much to the amazement of his peers, he lost no time in starting to write philosophical treatises and religious texts. At the age of 20 he met Tsong-kha-pa and became one of his most assiduous disciples. He was taught the subtle mysteries of the tantras by another of Tsong-kha-pa's loyal colleagues, Sherab Senge.

While Jamyang Shojay was founding the famous monastery of Drepung, on the outskirts of Lhasa, Gedun Truppa had the Tashi Lumpo monastery built in Shigatse, supervising every detail in person. In time it was to become a factor of considerable political importance in Tibetan history. But is a single lifetime even the 82 years that Gedun Truppa lived, enough for the completion of such a project? Not in the view of Tsong-kha-pa's disciple, who declared on his deathbed that he would return to continue his task. His only testament was to adjure his pupils to 'remember the teachings of the Lord Buddha and meditate upon them with the utmost religious fervour'. When the spirit left the body, the scribes noted meticulously that the physical remains began to glow without decomposing, and that their colour turned to gold.

The exceptional qualities and exemplary wish of this peerless monk supported the idea that he had been well and truly a reincarnation of the tutelary god of the high country, Chenrezig, Lord of Infinite Compassion. For the first time, at least officially in that form, the concept of the *bodhisattva* made its appearance in Tibet. A bodhisattva is a 'being of enlightenment', one who helps and teaches. Through thought, daily discipline, meditation and unceasing effort, it is therefore possible for the human being to reach liberation, nirvana – to come to 'buddhahood' – in the space of a single lifetime. But instead of entering the joy of infinite bliss for ever, the bodhisattva deliberately chooses to resume human shape and return to earth, in order to guide and comfort all beings suffering along the path of supreme fulfilment.

Is this a symbolic view, the raving of a fevered brain, or a reality so self-evident that it compels a natural recognition? The fact remains that the Buddhists of Tibet still cling to the tradition; the bodhisattva is part of their conception of the world, like *karma* – the law of cause and effect – or the powers of the great sages considered as supernatural in other parts of the world. In any case, the notion of the bodhisattva is only one of the logical implications of reincarnation, and long before Tsong-kha-pa and the Gelukpa, Tibetan history already contained exceptional ascetics whose achievements, not to say exploits, are so many white pebbles strewn along the long path leading to wisdom.

If the very idea of the bodhisattva took hold so quickly among the great masters of the Yellow Hat school, it is because, unlike the ancients, its adepts obeyed the law of celibacy and there could be no question of transmitting their knowledge in a hereditary way. Hence it was essential to institute another line of descent, and that could only be a spiritual one. This kind of reincarnation is not the exclusive prerogative of the Dalai Lama, and many masters, ascetics and wise men continue to return from generation to generation, for the benefit of the faithful. These are the men known as *tulkus*, they are not rare, and various western travellers have met them.

This is how the Reverend Father Huc describes his first encounter with a 'living Buddha' returning from Lhasa to his monastery in the country of the Khalkas, not far from the Russian border:

His body was of average height, and quite stout. His deeply tanned face conveyed an astonishing good-heartedness, but in his eyes, when one considered them attentively, there was something wild, a strange expression that made us afraid.

This impression obviously haunted him, because a little later on he adds:

> The words and manners of this grand lama were always full of affability, but we could not accustom ourselves to the strangeness in his gaze: in his eyes we seem to see something devilish and infernal.[2]

Be that as it may, some years after the departure of Gedun Truppa, the high dignitaries of Drepung proclaimed that he had returned to the monastery under the name of Gedun Gyatso. A generation later the line thus established was to become that of the Dalai Lamas, and it continues to this day in the person of his 14th representative. During the 67 years of his life, Gedun Gyatso concentrated on completing the projects left unfinished during his previous stay on earth; and the Drepung monastery enjoyed particular benefits, and carved out a special position in the life of the country, one which it did not lose in practice until the Chinese invasion of 1950. Perhaps more often than expected, it came to play a predominant role in politics, and consolidated a reputation – not entirely outdated – as a strong-minded member of the monastic community. But its philosophical and spiritual fame did not lag behind, and together with Sera and Ganden, Drepung became one of the 'three pillars of Tibet', constituting a fundamental part of the very backbone of society.

In the twilight of his life, reckoning his task still incomplete, Gedun Gyatso is said to have expressed his wish to return and continue it. Thus there need be no surprise that in 1543, a year after his departure, another young monk, Sönam Gyatso, was proclaimed the reincarnation of Gedun Truppa in his turn. He marks the official beginning in the Tibetan records of the Dalai Lamas – or the Dalai Lama, if one accepts as the Tibetans do the unchanging nature of his deeper personality, his superior essence and spiritual reality. Only his physical body alters from one generation to the next. He is perceived as being the temporal personification, one lifetime long, of an emanation of the divine; it is always the same being who continually returns to sit on the throne of the gods and point those who suffer along the way to Enlightenment.

In parallel with the religious development, another progression, this time of power and people, played out its intrigues and internal quarrels on the Roof of the World. Relations eventually stabilised among the different Buddhist schools, which alternately gained and lost the ascendancy by virtue of the secular protection they slowly built up, both inside and outside the country. For all that, the fundamental process was a slow harmonisation and delimitation of their spheres of influence between the Buddhist clergy and the lay nobility. In the last instance it was religion that emerged supreme, but by attaching the temporal power to itself; despite the various ups and downs, eclipses and unpleasant surprises, the course of centuries saw the Dalai Lama concentrating all effective power into his hands. Although he may exercise it with discrimination, and perhaps with some reservations too, for Tibetans he remains the holder of supreme power. After all, how could it be otherwise, for a god-king?

However, the relative isolation of Tibet, though it generally brought a *de facto* independence, did not entirely protect it from the ambitions of its neighbours. With the exception of the great era of Srongtsen Gampo, when the military power of Lhasa was feared even by the Sons of Heaven, the Chinese, the contacts with the outside world have often been antagonistic – with China in particular, but also with the Mongolia of the conquering khans.

After the turning point of the year 1000, medieval Tibet saw Buddhism reborn from its own ashes, after its persecution by the apostate king Lang Darma, under the influence of the great Indian sage Atisa. In those days the Mongol empire was at its height, and the rivalries among the Tibetan monasteries were shrewdly exploited by the neighbouring sovereigns. In the thirteenth century, Godan, son of Ogedei and grandson of

Jenghiz, the Supreme Khan of Mongolia, appointed the leader of the Sakya vice-regent of the high country; thus for the first time a religious leader became the foremost dignitary in Tibet. A hundred years later the power of the Sakya declined and bowed to the supremacy of the Kagyupa. But in theory the church continued to uphold the civil power, incarnated by the king, and now its principal protector. The reforms of Tsong-kha-pa altered these shifting balances and brought about the irresistible rise of the new school of the Yellow Hats.

With Sönam Gyatso the experiment came to an end and changed into an institution. Once again Tibet had thrown up an outstanding figure, happily combining deep erudition with unusual persuasive gifts. Invited to visit Altan Khan of Mongolia, then ruling in Amdo, near Lake Koko Nor, he arrived in the royal capital of Khar Ngonpo preceded by a brilliant reputation. According to the stories, during the long journey he did not hesitate to give the measure of his talents by using his supernatural powers to impress the Mongol nation, which was soon talking about his miracles. Nevertheless, history also records that Altan Khan was more impressed by the depth of his learning, his modesty and immense piety, so much so that he embraced his illustrious guest's conception of the world. With consummate skill, and by explaining his views on reincarnation, Sönam Gyatso convinced the Mongol sovereign that he had once been the great Kublai Khan in person, while he himself, the simple Buddhist monk, had been his spiritual teacher.

As a token of his veneration and a clear display of his gratitude, Altan Khan honoured the Tibetan sage with the title of Ta-lai Lama – *ta-lai* (or *dalai*) meaning 'ocean-wide', a reference to the breadth of his wisdom. He also bestowed on Sönam Gyatso a seal inscribed with the title of *Dorje Chang*, 'Holder of the *Vajra* (thunderbolt)'. Many of the Khan's kindred and courtiers followed the royal example, so much so that the Buddhism reformed by Tsong-kha-pa took permanent root in Mongolia. (The present Dalai Lama was able to observe this fact at first hand during his visits there in 1979 and 1982, when senior members of the Communist Party hierarchy came to ask for his blessing.) These events strengthened the ties between the two countries, with everything such links imply, both on the spiritual and temporal planes. The date was 1578.

Clothed in his new dignity and endowed with a title destined to become famous, Sönam Gyatso subsequently travelled the length and breadth of eastern Tibet, where he founded the monastery of Lithang in the pursuit of his untiring activities. At the pressing invitation of Altan Khan's son and heir, he set out again for Mongolia to continue the education of the faithful. On the way, not far from Koko Nor, on the spot where Tsong-kha-pa was born, he began to build the monastery of Kum Bum, 'the Ten Thousand Images', in 1582. A miraculous tree which grew from some of the reformer's hair and whose leaves bore sacred letters in Tibetan is revered there to this day.

Sönam Gyatso was on the point of setting out for Tibet again in 1588 when he fell ill and shed his mortal remains on the steppes of central Asia. His ashes were returned to Drepung. According to the chronicles, in keeping with a promise made on his deathbed, he chose a Mongol family in which to return among his new disciples. And it was no ordinary family; Yonten Gyatso, a grandson of Altan Khan, was to be recognised by the Buddhist dignitaries as the fourth reincarnation of Gedun Truppa. He briefly bore the title of fourth Dalai Lama since Sönam Gyatso had decided to honour his two predecessors by retrospectively bestowing that privilege on them, and hence on his successors.

Although the reign of Yonten Gyatso was brief – only fifteen years from his enthronement, at the age of 12, till his death in 1617 – it was also decisive, a turning point. He considerably reinforced the ties between Tibet and Mongolia and that was to prove a crucial development in the following generation.

A troubled period of instability and uncertainty followed, and created circumstances that called for a firm hand. Bloody antagonisms erupted between the declining Karmapa and

Kagyupa and the rising Gelukpa sects. The Mongols were
occasional arbitrators, while the kingdom of Tsang, around
Shigatse, and of Ü, in the heart of the country around Lhasa,
fell into rivalries embittered both by misunderstandings
between grand lamas and by the intrigues concocted by their
respective protectors. This period saw the advent of the man
who is considered as the unifier of Tibet; so striking were his
character and personality, and so deep the mark he left upon
his country, that he has gone down in history as 'the Great
Fifth' Dalai Lama. He was the first to establish himself not
only as a master of wisdom and an accomplished teacher, but
also as a politician of the highest level, a wise administrator
and a builder for the future. Many of his reforms were to
endure all the way to the Chinese invasion of 1950, adjusted
and adapted in the early twentieth century by the Thirteenth
Dalai Lama.

Duly recognised and verified by the highest-ranking dignitaries of the Gelukpa, the rebirth of the Dalai Lama, fifth in the
line, took place in 1617 in Chögyas. The new-born incumbent
was called Ngawang Lobsang Gyatso and, because of the
uncertainties that brooded over the Land of Snows, the
announcement of his discovery was postponed and the child
kept in concealment before being brought back to Drepung in
1622 to receive the education appropriate to his rank and
destiny.

In 1625 the grand lama of the monastery of Shigatse
sponsored Lobsang Gyatso's solemn entry into the *sangha*, the
monastic order. It was to the Fifth Dalai Lama that the master
of Tashi Lumop owed his title of Panchen Lama, 'Great
Scholar', which has been passed on to all his subsequent
reincarnations. As a student at Drepung, Lobsang Gyatso was
his pupil, and he honoured him in recognition of his priceless
teaching. This was another initiative later to prove pregnant
with consequences, not all of them happy ones for Tibet.

In the days when the young Lobsang Gyatso was learning
the duties of his position and taking instruction in religion,
outside the walls of the monasteries battles raged between the
zealots of the ancient and the new sects. The struggle grew so

violent that, fearing for the life of the reincarnated Precious Master, some of the advisers and high officials in his entourage took the precaution of calling on the Mongol leaders for help. The bloody quarrel between Karmapa and Gelukpa, backed by the lords of Tsang and Ü, was settled in the end by Mongol intermediaries; the Khoshot chief Gushri Khan, under the banner of the Dalai Lama, challenged the chief of Chogthu, whose son Arsalang, supposed to defend the cause of the Karmapa, had pledged allegiance to the Dalai Lama in the venerable sanctuary of Ramoche. It was the death-knell for the temporal power of the Red Hats, and ushered in the irresistible rise of the Yellow Hats.

A series of skirmishes and pitched battles between 1637 and 1642 almost turned to tragedy when Gushri Khan decided to be finished once and for all with the arrogance of the sovereign of Tsang, who was trespassing on the authority of Lhasa. Reluctantly involved in a situation which he privately deplored, the Dalai Lama intervened as a mediator to prevent a general bloodbath. Having defeated, but not eliminated, his enemy, Gushri Khan bowed to the will of the lord spiritual, and in the great hall of Tashi Lumpo, conquered by force of arms, after the customary offerings, the Mongol khan solemnly proclaimed the Dalai Lama the supreme authority over all Tibet, from Tsa-tsien-lu in the east to the borders of Ladakh in the west. For the first time, the Dalai Lama thus officially became the spiritual and temporal leader of the Land of Snows. At the same time his steward and close collaborator was granted the title of *desi*, or regent, and put in charge of the political administration of the country. But in the last resort it fell to the Dalai Lama to take the vital decisions, and it was also the Dalai Lama who appointed the *desi* of his choice.

Back in his own city after the ceremonies in Shigatse, the Dalai Lama decided to make Lhasa the capital of Tibet and to build himself a palace there on the remains of the one built in the seventh century by Srongtsen Gampo. So the Potala, or seat of the gods, was reborn out of its own ruins, eventually to become one of the most imposing symbols of the Tibetan theocracy.

Yet nothing came really easily to the Fifth Dalai Lama, and if he did achieve his goals, it was chiefly because of his iron determination and political foresight. Troubles flared up sporadically, on the frontiers with Ladakh, Bhutan and Sikkim, but they were quickly extinguished. And when he responded to an invitation from the Manchu sovereign sitting on the throne of the Middle Kingdom, the Dalai Lama was received with great pomp and unprecedented honours in Beijing, where the Yellow Palace in the Forbidden City had been built especially for him.

The unifier of Tibet was also able to surround himself with loyal and competent officials and administrators, specially trained for their positions. It was through their agency that he carried out the first census ever undertaken on the Roof of the World. He also set up a system of taxes which were fairly assessed and scrupulously collected, and recorded in secular registers. Although courteous to all comers, and to his subjects, his justice was stern and, in the case of rebellion, inflexible. All these qualities contributed towards making him one of the greatest figures in Tibetan history.

But other virtues enhanced the distinction of this unusual enlightened monarch. With his deep devotion to study and philosophical speculation, throughout his lifetime Lobsang Gyatso displayed a rare open-mindedness and remarkable tolerance towards those who did not necessarily think as he did. He took a keen interest in schools different from his own, and did not hesitate to enlist scholarly lamas of other persuasions as his advisers. During his reign there was a considerable rise in the number of cultural exchanges, particularly with India; many students of religion and men of learning made the journey to Lhasa, while great strides were taken in the translation of Buddhist texts.

For his lay and ecclesiastical officials, the Fifth Dalai Lama created two academies where, as well as the traditional administrative and religious disciplines, the students learned Mongol, Sanskrit, astrology, poetry, archery and horsemanship. Its religious activities were no less thorough, and he himself wrote several works, ranging from spiritual commentaries to temporal precepts and even a treatise on poetry. It was the Fifth Dalai Lama who officially confirmed that he was the reincarnation of Chenrezig, Lord of Infinite Compassion and patron deity of Tibet, elsewhere known as Avalokitesvara. He added that his predecessors in the line had also been reincarnations of the same bodhisattva.

After the successive deaths of two regents and the resignation of the third, the Dalai Lama belatedly chose his own spiritual disciple, a young man of 27, Sangye Gyatso, the nephew of one of his closest stewards, to be his regent, and entrusted him with the country's secular affairs. Whether selected by chance or premonition, the fact remains that the blameless and cherished young regent was to play a very special part in the years to come. In 1682 – or in the year 2226 counting from the Buddha's departure to nirvana, or the twenty-fifth day of the second month of the year of the Water Dog by the Tibetan calendar – the Great Fifth Dalai Lama left his physical envelope, worn out by 68 years of an eventful strenuous life. But a veil of silence descended over the Potala; for fifteen years (some say thirteen, others only nine) Sangye Gyatso managed to conceal the god-king's death from the world outside.

The fact is surprising, and in more than one respect. Discounting the idea of a bid for personal power (which seems not to have been the case), a number of different theories have attempted to explain the astonishing decision taken by the young regent. Fear of an unstable situation deteriorating beyond repair is one; distrust of a possible foreign intervention, always possible during the interregnum, is another. The wish to complete the literally gigantic task of rebuilding the Potala in accordance with the earnest intentions of the Fifth Dalai Lama is a third, and officially it was also the argument put forward by Sangye Gyatso himself. But imagine the wealth of inventiveness that he must have expended in pulling off the deception, with hardly a stumble along the way!

It is true that the Dalai Lama always lived a life removed from inquisitive eyes, and surrounded by the most rigorous ceremonial and protocol. There was nothing unusual, either, about announcing that he had decided to undertake a period of protracted and indeterminate meditation – Tibetan monks and ascetics commonly withdrew from the world for months, even years, in order to conduct their own experiments with certain practices that required the utmost solitude. In itself, this alleged withdrawal from public life was not at all exceptional. But it is one thing to have announced such a decision, and another to have kept the secret for so long, when after all it concerned an ultimately public figure.

In order to maintain the impossible pretence, Sangye Gyatso drew quite unsparingly upon his own reserves, simultaneously pursuing his own administrative activities while also performing the tasks which were supposed to fall to the Dalai Lama. By being everywhere at once, by his astute management of official ceremonies and constant interest in all aspects of everyday life he succeeded in allaying the worst suspicions. Certainly there were times when rumour was rife in Lhasa, as when Mongol envoys or foreign emissaries sought audiences with the sovereign, or when young lamas were supposed to receive his blessing or certain particular instructions. Suitably disguised and duly rehea.sed according to circumstance, the chosen double made the most of the shrouded half-light of the audience rooms to remain hidden from prying visitors, and would cut short these interviews if they looked like getting out of hand. Only three people were in on the secret of the gods.

This strange conspiracy did not prevent the regent from conducting a clandestine search for the new incarnation of the absent leader. Taking all the customary precautions, in 1685 he found a child just over three years old, in the region of Monyul, who satisfied the demands of tradition and destiny. However, he chose to keep his momentous secret to himself, and in 1688 the child was smuggled into Nankartse, where his education began under the desi's watchful eye.

Here too, it is not easy to disentangle the threads of the legend, woven as they are into the gleaming fabric of a shifting reality. To this day, Monyul remains one of the most sequestered regions of India, on the poorly-defined borders of Tibet and Bhutan, in a frontier area closed and inaccessible to outside curiosity. Yet the Monpa tribe that inhabits the Tawang valley preserves the precious memory of the mysterious child born in 1682 into a lama family of the Kagyupa tradition which traced its descent far back in the Buddhist line, directly to the famous 'finder of treasures' Pemalingpa.

Apparently the ancestral home can still be seen in Urgelling, about fifteen miles from Tawang, not far from a monastery distinguished by the presence of a tree several hundred years old, with a majestic crown. According to local tradition the child, then secretly recognised as the reincarnation of the Great Fifth, showed some reluctance to leave his native hamlet. Before leaving, while the caravan was preparing to set out, the little boy is said to have stopped in front of a frail sapling and said the strange words: 'When the three branches of this tree are of equal height, I shall return.'

He did not return to his village, at any rate not in that lifetime, not as the child prodigy who grew up to be a romantic poet whose subtle quatrains hover between mystic raptures and the double meaning of a different, more carnal, nostalgia. But later, so long afterwards that it was almost lost in the mist of oblivion, there were those who suddenly remembered it. It was on an April day in 1959, the three branches of the tree had grown to the same height, and the Fourteenth Dalai Lama with his faithful escort of tough Khampa warriors had crossed the frontier at Chutamghu on his way to Tawang, in Monyul, at the beginning of his exile in India.

Later, when the Potala had been completed and the death of the Great Fifth publicly announced, the Panchen Lama came in person to Nankartse to hear the adolescent's preliminary vows. He conferred on him the name of Tsangyang Gyatso, and in 1697 the Sixth Dalai Lama was installed, according to the rites, on his predecessors' throne. It was from that time on that things began to go wrong, and to take an unexpected turn.

To the surprise of his subjects and the dismay of his

entourage, the new sovereign of the Roof of the World
behaved in ways apparently not compatible with his status
and duties. While manifestly uninterested in the spiritual
quest, he adored archery and loved to take part in the archery
competitions still very much in fashion among the Tibetans.
Worse, at night he would leave the red palace to make merry
in the nearby hamlet and flirt with the girls there. The popular
amazement grew still further when rumour declared that he
had had private rooms built, and elegantly but profanely
decorated, for his amorous pursuits. The Tibetans were
neither prudes nor puritans; they may have been taken aback,
but their faith in their leader was undiminished. And everybody acknowledged his poetic gifts and unequalled genius for
dashing off love poems, still well known in the high country
today.

A controversial and unexpected figure he may have been,
but in Tibetan eyes the Sixth Dalai Lama was none the less the
authentic reincarnation of the Great Fifth and the one man
entitled to occupy the sacred throne. At any rate he was also a
character; when he decided not to pronounce his full monastic
vows, and even to renounce the partial vows which he had
earlier assumed, there was nothing to be done about it. The
regent, the master of Tashi Lumpo, the superiors of the three
great monasteries and the lords of Mongolia tried in vain to
argue him out of his decision, but in 1702 Tsangyang Gyatso
went to see the Panchen Lama in Tashi Lumpo to return his
monk's robes and to be released from his vows. Dressed like a
layman, he returned to the Potala and, to the despair of
Sangye Gyatso, continued to sing his drinking songs and go
gallivanting about with an officer of his guard.

But a situation like this could not last long when China was
watching and looking for a means to gain a footing in Tibet,
especially when a new menace was growing from the direction of the Mongols of Dzungaria. The Ming dynasty had
given way in 1644 to the Ch'ing, or Manchu, occupation,
while in Mongolia inter-tribal quarrels had intensified. On the
pretext of these rivalries, and of the deception finally revealed
in Lhasa, the Emperor K'ang Hsi took his chance to interfere

in Tibetan affairs. In 1703 the regent Sangye Gyatso, had resigned, although behind the scenes he kept his hands on the administration of the country. Talks between the Mongols and Tibetans about the conduct or misconduct of the Dalai Lama had already begun to turn sour. Around 1705 Lhazang Khan raised troops, attacked Lhasa, took control of the town and government, had Sangye Gyatso killed and decided to seize the Dalai Lama.

Taken prisoner by treachery, Tsangyang Gyatso was taken under escort to the Mongol camp and given a severe lecture by the Khan, who upbraided him for all his failings and informed him of his dismissal – this in full accordance with the Manchu emperor – and his imminent departure into exile. The Dalai Lama nevertheless succeeded in sending a message to one of his lady friends, the true significance of which did not emerge until some time later:

> White crane, fine bird,
> Lend me your wings.
> I will not go far
> I will return from Lithang.[3]

The Tibetans were outraged, because for them, despite his incomprehensible behaviour, Tsangyang Gyatso was the utterly legitimate incarnation of Chenrezig, and that was that. After a show of rebellion by the monks of Sera and Drepung, soon quelled by the Dalai Lama, the fallen god-king was taken eastward – either to China or Mongolia, according to the different versions of this historic episode – but he never arrived. To the south of Koko Nor, near the little lake of Kunga Nor, the Dalai Lama died – or so the official chronicle relates. Whether it was murder or illness, no one knows. Unless he had disappeared, swept up by a sudden whirlwind – some said that afterwards he spent long years in meditation on the steppes of central Asia. Some even assert that he met his successor, the Seventh Dalai Lama, in person in Mongolia, where he allegedly had numerous disciples. For according to tradition, since the Dalai Lama is in fact a Buddha, he may take as many physical forms as he wishes for the purposes of the moment. His mortal remains were never found, which explains the absence of his tomb in the Potala, whereas the cenotaphs of his predecessors and successors are to be found in the west wing of the palace.

In the view of Tentzin Gyatso, the present Dalai Lama, there is no question that the subtle poet and lover of pretty girls was the true sixth reincarnation of the protector of Tibet. The state oracles were categorical on this point, and there are no grounds for doubting the validity of their predictions. His Holiness will point out that the way of being of a spiritual master, no matter how strange in appearance, is not to be judged by the common yardstick, and that his powers undoubtedly entitled him to adopt such a line of conduct. Suppose it was done to put the faith of his people to the test? Both in India and Tibet, tantric ascetics are reputed to have carried out actions that count as miracles elsewhere, and Tibetan folk traditions abound in heroic tales in which the wildest marvels vie with the crudest realism. Then why not the Sixth Dalai Lama? As for his decision to discard the monastic robe, perhaps it had come to him that in those days a powerful monarch had become necessary, to safeguard the unity and sovereignty of the Land of Snows. Tsangyang Gyatso may have considered taking a wife and thus installing a genuine hereditary monarchy. People and circumstances decided otherwise.

After the ten-year interlude of a usurper's rule, when Lhazang Khan proclaimed Yeshe Gyatso Seventh Dalai Lama, another Mongol chief captured Lhasa, killed his rival and deposed his protégé. Not that the latter had ever been accepted by the Tibetans, who call their sovereign *Chamchad Khenpo*, the All-Knowing, whereas Yeshe Gyatso only qualified for the title of *Kushab* – Mister. Betrayals and vendettas continued among the Mongol tribes until 1720, with spectacular switches of alliances and unexpected reversals. Undermined from within, the Mongol influence faded into permanent decline, supplanted by that of the Manchus, who sent an *amban*, a representative, to Lhasa for the first time.

Already the seventh reincarnation had appeared. Kelsang Gyatso, a young lama born in 1708 near Lithang, had drawn attention by displaying particular qualities recognised as unmistakable signs. As a precautionary step, with an eye on the future, he was first brought to Derge, then to the Kum Bum monastery, where he received his first teaching. When his discovery was announced, Tibetans realised that Tsangyang Gyatso's enigmatic promise, 'I will return from Lithang' had been fulfilled.

These turbulent years also saw some strange pilgrims venture to the city of the gods. A handful of Capuchin monks arrived, led by Giuseppe d'Ascoli and François de Tours, took up residence, and laid the foundations of a mission which ended in 1745, partly for lack of funds but mainly because of the growing reservations of the lamas. A famous Jesuit, Ippolito Desideri – a man of the calibre of Matteo Ricci in China or Roberto de Nobili in India – won his way to Lhasa in 1716 and threw himself headlong into the study of the language, customs and morals of the high country. He found himself compelled to leave after five years, under combined pressure from the Capuchins, determined to be the only source of the propagation of the faith, and the monks of the great monasteries. Nevertheless he did have time to draft the outline of a detailed refutation of the Buddhist doctrine, written in Tibetan; this bold initiative was greeted with kindly curiosity, though naturally it made not the slightest impression on the convictions of those for whom it was theoretically intended.

As if to efface the mixed recollections of the Sixth Dalai Lama, the Seventh proved to be an undoubted scholar, subtle and profound, but with limited political power, especially at the start of his reign. He came to the throne in 1720, and seven years later he had to face a serious rebellion which signally inflamed relations between the Tibetans and the Manchus. A series of intrigues broke out in the god-king's entourage, and culminated in a civil war in which the Manchu Son of Heaven naturally seized the opportunity to try to re-establish his own order among the mountain heights. Unwilling to provoke

popular anger, however, he invited the Dalai Lama to come
to Beijing, seeing that his absence would give the Manchus a
free hand with their own policies. Since in those days the
imperial wish was the equivalent of a command, Kelsang
Gyatso set out, but in the end he went no further than
Garthar, near Lithang, in Kham, where he was held under
ceremonious surveillance and a well-armed guard for seven
years. After that he was allowed back to Lhasa, but on condition that he should play no part in politics.

During this eclipse of the Dalai Lama temporal power,
there was quarrelling among rival lords and petty kings. A
new rebellion broke out, and was bloodily put down, while
disagreements among the ministers of the lay cabinet set fire
to another powder keg – this time it was the turn of
Manchus and Mongols to settle their own disputes through
Tibetan intermediaries.

An ambitious but able man now emerged on to the political scene. Pho-lha-né had begun his political career by
siding with Lhazang Khan while still a young official. A
native of Tsang, he became an ardent supporter of rapprochement with the Manchus, and he did not hesitate to
change alliances according to changing necessities, and to
ride into battle, sword in hand, to tip the scales towards
himself. His tactical skill, both on and off the battlefield,
and ruthless determination earned him the nickname of Miwang
Pho-lha – Pho-lha the Mighty. He never relaxed his constant
opposition to any prospect of restoring political influence to
the Dalai Lama, and proved to be a scrupulous administrator
of his country's affairs, both honest and efficient. But
whereas Tibetans acknowledged these qualities, they also
blamed him for having become the mainspring of Chinese
penetration on to the Roof of the World. On the other hand
he certainly brought his country a period of eighteen years'
tranquillity, distinguished by improvements in social life,
since the sphere of deadly rivalries was limited to a few noble
families directly concerned with power. Upon his death in
1747 he was succeeded by his youngest son and, by an
intelligent but not too conspicuous participation in the

country's life, the Dalai Lama regained a fraction of his temporal power.

The god-king had been well aware that Pho-lha-né would never permit the slightest infringement of his personal power. He therefore devoted the greater part of his time to study and meditation, occasionally intervening as a mediator to cool the tempers of embattled political rivals. He encouraged the creation of a cabinet of ministers, or *kashag*, to replace the function of desi, for fear of too great a concentration of power into one man's hands. He also decided to build a summer palace near some hot springs where a great open-air feast had traditionally been held in early autumn for all the lay and ecclesiastical officials. And so the Norbu-lingka, the Jewel Park, was created, and became the summer residence of the Sovereign of the Land of the Gods.

But the scholarly Dalai Lama's health had always been delicate, and he left the earthly scene in March 1757, in his fiftieth year. Three months later, far away on the plains of Bengal, Robert Clive's decisive victory in the battle of Plassey crippled French ambitions in India and strengthened the British hold on the subcontinent for a few decades. But the news gave little concern to Tibet at that time.

With Jampal Gyatso the pre-eminence of the Dalai Lama subsided for nearly a century, as against the increased powers of the regent, supported by the kashag, while the Panchen Lama saw his power augmented, in step with the growing links between Tashi Lumpo and Beijing. From that time onwards the successive masters of the Forbidden City set about playing off the two grand lamas against each other, by exploiting the latent rivalries among their entourages without being seen to be meddling. Their designs were further promoted because of the utter lack of harmony between the kingdoms of Tsang and Ü, feudal fiefs whose lords did not hesitate to call on their neighbours for support when they felt threatened.

Such was the position during the minority of the Eighth Dalai Lama. On the death of the Seventh, a grand lama of Drepung, Jampal Delek, was appointed to the regency. At once he embarked on the customary search to find the new incarnation of Chenrezig: the child was discovered in Tsang, in Thopgyal, and brought to Lhasa in 1762, at the age of four. Tibet was then going through troubled times, partly because of occasional clashes with British troops in Bhutan; Warren Hastings, the governor of Bengal, had turned his attention in the direction of Tibet and took the opportunity of the Panchen Lama's offer of mediation to enter into contact with Shigatse. Two emissaries from His Gracious Majesty George III were received with courtesy at Tashi Lumpo, but disagreement with Lhasa forced them to retrace their steps after a few weeks, having been refused permission to travel to the city of the gods.

On the death of the regent in 1777 the Eighth Dalai Lama declined the kashag's offer to assume the responsibilities of government in order to enable him to complete his studies. Another regent took the helm. At this juncture the emperor invited the Panchen Lama to Beijing, where he was very much in favour. At first the Dalai Lama and his advisers considered a refusal, particularly because the master of Tashi Lumpo was not at all eager to make the journey, and because there was news of a smallpox epidemic in China. In the end the Panchen Lama bowed to religious necessity and left for Beijing, where he contracted smallpox and died.

There followed a bitter dispute over the inheritance between the Panchen Lama's two younger brothers, one of whom lived in Nepal. More and more skirmishes erupted on the most futile of pretexts, heated commercial quarrels broke out over trifles, ancient resentments were revived, sporadic insurrections were staged against the authority of Lhasa, and, while the Manchu power in China went into its slow decline, a series of military clashes with Nepal came finally to an outright Gurkha invasion of Tibet. To recover its captured provinces Tibet was compelled to pay tribute to its temporarily all-powerful neighbour.

In an attempt to contain, if not to quell, these opposing currents, in 1781 the Dalai Lama agreed to take the reins of temporal power. However, this did not prevent the general situation from deteriorating further; and all the while the Chinese and British watched carefully but refrained for the moment from intervening. Amid this whirl of events, which meant very little to him, the Eighth Dalai Lama died in 1804. He had taken hardly any interest in the affairs of the world, obviously preferring his contemplative existence inside the sheltering walls of the Potala.

In the years that followed, a regent went on governing, the Fourth Panchen Lama was found, high officials and lesser kings vied for spheres of influence, and a blazing row broke out between two families – one from Kham and the other from Amdo – on the subject of the due recognition of the new Dalai Lama. The decision went to the child from Kham, born in 1806, but he only lived until 1815, after catching a chill during the New Year ceremonies. In response to the growth of inner tensions and of outside threats, Tibet began to close its doors against foreign travellers, encouraged by the Chinese *ambans*, resident officials, who had their own reasons for favouring the isolation of the high country.

The Tenth Dalai Lama was chosen from among three candidates, all of them from Kham. The ambans pushed the Buddhist dignitaries into using a golden urn, specially dispatched for that purpose by the Imperial Court, to decide among the claimants, the lamas had already made their choice, and only went through the staged charade so as not to antagonise openly the Chinese emissaries. But the lamas' choice, Tsultrim Gyatso, did not live past 20. Despite his poor health, he appears to have been very well informed about his subjects' lives, and according to some Tibetan sources the unceremonious complaints that he is said to have addressed to the authorities who governed in his name were not unconnected with his premature death. Khedrup Gyatso, the Eleventh, born in 1838, and Trinley Gyatso, the Twelfth, born in 1856, had no better luck. Is it possible that court intrigues and monastic plots inside Tibet itself, together with the constant frontier conflicts, may have led some powerful members of the Dalai Lama entourage to prevent him at all costs from asserting his presence on the political scene? Many historians make this supposition, arguing from the naked ambitions and shrewd manoeuvres of lay or religious dignitaries more given to politics than to the search for the absolute.

The Tibetans themselves did not take kindly to the sight of their spiritual guide playing hide-and-seek in such abnormal circumstances, while regents and officials squabbled for power. One legend tells how certain lamas were particularly expert in casting spells, that some were skilled with poisons, and that others may have succumbed to the profane temptations of easy wealth. But another folk belief alleges that one of these four ill-fated reincarnations had woefully offended Palden Lhamo, sole protective goddess of the Dalai Lamas, who dwells in the sacred lake of Lhamo Latso. Otherwise how was it possible to explain that series of sudden exits by a being so far above the level of mortal men?

This long period of uncertainties, expedients, rivalries and wars, a disastrous era for the country, had lasted far too long. It seemed to be time to leave this chaos behind and to restore the unity necessary if Tibet was to regain at least some fraction of its former glory. But who could take up such a challenge, if not a Dalai Lama of real weight and stature, one who could call a halt to the bad fortune which seemed to have descended on his line? Circumstances were to change at last, and to open the way for the thirteenth reincarnation of the Lord of Infinite Compassion.

At Chökhorgyal, about one hundred miles south-east of Lhasa, lies a lake which is particularly sacred among all the lakes of Tibet – the Lhamo Latso. No doubt it would be necessary to look deep into the past to find the origin of the veneration which surrounds it, for it is said that when it is questioned in the proper way by emissaries duly prepared, it will consent to reveal the future in the clear mirror of its waters. Be that as it may, when there were great decisions to be made, the Buddhist hierarchy and highest government officials never failed to consult it. So it was that after the death of the Twelfth Dalai Lama a member of the group sent in search of the new incarnation announced that they should make their way to the south-east region of the country, to a place called Thakpo Langdun, and when the seekers got there they discovered a child born in May 1876. But the boy was only ten months old, and obviously it was impossible to subject him to the usual tests straightaway.

A year later, when they returned to the place, the worthy emissaries were quick to arrive at an opinion; the child unerringly chose the personal belongings which had been his in his previous life, as distinct from exactly similar objects which had not. He carried various definite marks on his body, in the proper places, and certain purely religious points confirmed the first indications. The return of the Dalai Lama was proclaimed without delay, and the child was taken somewhere close to Lhasa. In 1888 the Panchen Lama gave him the name Thubten Gyatso, and a year later the new sovereign of Tibet was solemnly enthroned in the Potala.

Until his coming of age the reins of power were to remain in the hands of the regent, Demo Trinley Rabgyas, assisted by the ministers of the kashag and the advice of a few lamas. During these years the boy-king had all the time he needed to refresh his memory, complete his education and extend his religious studies. His teachers watched over his development, even though they were sometimes surprised by their pupil's knowledge and maturity.

At this late stage of the nineteenth century, great events were brewing which were to produce fundamental upheavals both in Asia and in Europe, but since the tell-tale details were taking shape on the periphery of great empires, in the corridors of chancelleries and in gracious drawing rooms, only a few rare local observers could perceive them, and it was much later, with hindsight and often too late, that the principal interested parties realised their full implications. The people of Tibet are well placed to see the pattern today, since unwittingly and almost unawares they found themselves at the geopolitical intersection of two voracious appetites – the British crown's and the Tsarist empire's.

Great Britain was methodically consolidating its presence in the Indian subcontinent by means of alliances, treaties and agreements with rajahs, maharajahs and other local nabobs, thus cheaply securing allies who may not always have shown their exemplary loyalty but who were often very useful all the same. Step by step, sometimes by threats and sometimes by flattery, and by brute force too when other methods proved ineffective, the good and loyal servants of the British Queen advanced to the foot of the Himalayas.

With consummate skill and remarkable pragmatism, the British robbed Peter to pay Paul, remaining perfectly prepared to anger some Singh or Khan for the sake of mollifying yet another party. Thus the little hill states of Tehri, on the borders of Ladakh, became British protectorates, while the splendid valleys of Spiti and Lahul were incorporated into Kangra, to be generously offered to a Kashmir tailored to measure for the benefit of Gulab Singh. The Darjeeling district, and its future tea plantations, came under the British wing, as did Kalimpong a little later on, as a result of 'arrangements' made with Sikkim and Bhutan. Similarly, the British protected their rear in the even more inaccessible country of Assam by agreements with hill tribe chieftains. But Tibet remained stubbornly closed, despite the growing interest being shown by missionaries, traders and state servants, sometimes disguised as pilgrims or messengers of good will.

Meanwhile Russia was steadily pursuing its march across the Asian continent, and the tempo of events quickened noticeably in the mid-nineteenth century, with the first Afghan War, and the progressive Russian occupation of territories from the Caspian to Turkestan, by way of Tashkent, Samarkand, Bukhara, Khiva, Turkmenistan and Pamir. So the Tsar of All the Russias, whom the Mongols sometimes called Tsagan Khan, 'chief of the White Horde', slowly pushed his pawns as far forward as the banks of the Amur, where the Manchus of China still stood guard. Through these nomadic peoples, with their stubborn resistance to assimilation, the Russians managed to maintain fairly loose and sporadic links with Tibet, where Buryat and Kalmuck traders made intermittent visits. While British emissaries were at their wits' end to gain permission to cross the passes leading to the high plateau, in 1880 Aguang Dorji performed his first pilgrimage to Lhasa. This Buryat lama, whom Tibetans call Ngawang Lozang, or Tsenyi Khenpo, was to play a major role some years later, under the westernised name of Dorjiev.

During these years the influence of the ambans continued to dwindle in the holy city of lamaism, in step with the decline of Manchu power in Beijing. The Sino-Japanese War of 1894–5 left the Manchus weaker still, and dealt an unprecedented blow to the morale and arrogance of the Sons of Heaven. Tensions rose between Tibet and the British as a result of clashes in Sikkim. A series of petty misunderstandings resolved themselves into a general lack of mutual understanding, and this in turn involved misinterpretations which gave rise to lapses of judgement, especially when both sides were stand-offish enough in their own way to be ready to stand on principles mostly unknown to the other party.

When Lord Curzon became Viceroy of India in 1899 the Thirteenth Dalai Lama had already been enthroned for four years. Thubten Gyatso was not yet 19 when he first took full spiritual and temporal powers over his country. He was a brilliant young monk with a sharp intelligence, a fiery temperament which he kept under careful control, and unusual gifts of political intuition, although he also had his enemies, even among his own people.

In an atmosphere of intrigues, if not outright plots, within his entourage, the oracle at Nechung twice gave warning that the life of the Dalai Lama was in danger, and in Lhasa nobody made light of the oracle's words, for it spoke on behalf of Dorje Drakden, the guardian spirit of the high country, and possessor of fearsome powers. Summoned to Lhasa, the medium in trance revealed that an evil spell had been cast against the Dalai Lama by the former regent, vexed by the loss of his privileges, through the agency of a lama by the name of Sögyal. The lama was commanded to give an account of himself, and readily admitted having received the gift of a pair of shoes from the ex-regent Demo Trinley Rabgyas. A servant went to fetch them, and at first sight they seemed ordinary enough, but closer examination revealed that hidden in one heel was a magic charm bearing the name and date of birth of the Dalai Lama. The lama then reported that he had twice made attempts to wear his new shoes, and twice been compelled to take them off again, because each time he had started to bleed from the nose. The ex-regent was sent for, and confessed to his crime; he was sentenced to prison for life. In the annals of Tibet this conspiracy is given the evocative title of 'the affair of the enchanted shoes'.

But the young Dalai Lama quickly found himself up against some altogether more alarming influences and more compelling pressures. On the political chessboard of the early twentieth century the expansionist ambitions of Great Britain, Russia and China were more and more in open conflict, and Tibet was in the middle of the cross-fire. The common suspicions were all the more intense because London, St Petersburg and Beijing were all three hunting on the same ground.

In 1898 the Buryat lama who had been chosen as one of the Dalai Lama's religious tutors had travelled to Russia, not in any overt official capacity but to collect funds on behalf of Drepung, the monastery to which he was attached. Then, in 1901, goaded by the ever more prying eyes of the British hovering around the high plateau, and spurred on in his initiative by Dorjiev, the Dalai Lama dispatched a first official mission to the Russian court. The visit drew a great deal of comment, and it goes without saying that it sounded the alarm in British India. Persistent rumours began to circulate about the existence of a secret treaty between Russia and Tibet. Although nobody really contemplated any genuine threat from the Land of Snows, British observers nevertheless feared that a possible rapprochement between Lhasa and St Petersburg would eventually lead to friction all along the Himalayan frontier. In order to put a stop to what he believed he detected as stirrings of independence, and at the same time unwilling to provoke the tottering Manchus, Lord Curzon sent Colonel Francis Younghusband to assess the dangers at first hand.

When the advance of the British army turned into a punitive expedition by the time it reached Lhasa in August 1904, the leading officials of Tibet took the precaution of moving their Precious Master to a safe place. With an impressive retinue of some hundreds of people, the Dalai Lama sought temporary refuge in Urga (now known as Ulan Bator), the capital of Mongolia, where he was received with open arms, and with all the pomp and ceremony proper to his rank. The people paid him unprecedented homage, and kept bringing money and gifts to heap at the foot of his throne, so that eventually Jetsun Damba Hutuktu, the superior of the lamas of Mongolia, took umbrage against the presence of a god-king five years younger than himself, and the darling of his own people. To avoid a direct clash between these two exceptional personalities, Khanda Dorji, the reigning prince, wisely decided to invite the Dalai Lama to take up quarters just outside the town, in his own official residence.

After a year the famous guest was ready to leave. He visited Kum Bum in particular, as well as various other monasteries, and at this point received an invitation to visit the Imperial Court. He accepted, and went as far as Beijing, but refused to appear at an audience with the Emperor when he learned that protocol required him to bow the knee before the Son of Heaven. Obviously the god incarnate was bound to refuse. Nevertheless an interview was arranged with the Dowager Empress. On the way to Beijing the Dalai Lama received a visit from William Rockwill, the American representative in China, and probably the first United States citizen ever to have met so high a dignitary from Tibet. The Dalai Lama stayed long enough in Beijing to attend the funerals of the Emperor and his mother, and the enthronement of the last Manchu sovereign in 1908, before returning to his own Himalayan lands.

The British expeditionary force to Lhasa had withdrawn as soon as the Anglo-Tibetan treaty of 1904 was signed. Colonel Younghusband had brought with him clear instructions on this issue, and he had achieved his objectives: an arrangement over the frontier with Sikkim; trading posts and British agents at Gyantse, Gartok and Yatung; promises to renew trade agreements; an indemnity of about half a million pounds sterling; but above all a clause excluding any other foreign influence over the policy of Tibet. The most noteworthy feature of this agreement is that it had been negotiated, concluded and signed without the slightest participation or intervention from a single Chinese representative.

Indeed, by then the Manchu presence in Lhasa was a mere fiction, with the ambans reduced to the status of figureheads, while in Beijing the declining Chinese empire was disintegrating in its own corruption. It goes without saying that the British played their own game with characteristic pragmatic ambiguity, so that conventions agreed with China in 1906 and then with Russia in 1907 may leave the impression that the British Crown more or less accepted some sort of implicit Chinese suzerainty over Tibet – a suggestion that the Tibetans themselves have always utterly rejected. But neither in 1906 or 1907 did the British see fit to consult the Tibetans, or even to keep them informed of their negotiations with Beijing and St Petersburg. Furious with the liberties taken by the British Raj, in a final burst of outraged dignity the Chinese imperial government sent troops to restore order in Tibet in what it persisted in considering as an outlying vassal province. The Dalai Lama appealed in vain to 'Great Britain and the foreign powers'. The Chinese army behaved as if given free rein in conquered territory, descended on Lhasa in the midst of the New Year ceremonies, and earned a reputation that the Chinese were never to lose in the hearts of all Tibetans.

General Chung Ying, with an army of 2,000 thugs, burst into the capital in 1910 and seized power, but was unable to capture the Dalai Lama, who just had time to reach Kalimpong, and then Darjeeling, where he remained in exile once again, this time for two years and under the protection of the British. During this period he built up a relationship with Charles Bell, the then political resident in Sikkim. The friendship they began was to prove invaluable for its contribution to outside knowledge of Tibet, and to a lesser extent for the country's political development.

The imperial Chinese government proclaimed the deposition of the Thirteenth Dalai Lama and quite ingenuously ordered a new incarnation to be chosen to replace him. The Raj made a formal protest, but left it at that, since the agreements reached with Beijing were not revoked. Meanwhile in Tibet no one would collaborate with the occupying power, and passive resistance spread; when the Panchen Lama was approached to take temporary charge of the administration, he refused to play the Chinese game, and for the first time the Chinese realised that without the Dalai Lama, Tibet is ungovernable.

Things were moving fast at the imperial court in Beijing. Manchu power was only a shadow of its former self, and the revolution broke out in 1911, soon to be followed by the proclamation of the Republic. Throughout this period, bands of Tibetan irregulars kept harrying the Chinese troops, some of whom eventually mutinied. The Dalai Lama came back to his country, but did not return to the capital until 1913, when not a single Han soldier remained in Tibet. Meanwhile a treaty signed in Urga between Tibet and Mongolia affirmed the full sovereignty of both countries and their total freedom from China. In addition, the Dalai Lama officially proclaimed the independence of Tibet in a solemn proclamation drafted and published in Lhasa on the eighth day of the first month of the year of the Water Buffalo (1913).

It is hardly surprising that in these critical times the Thirteenth Dalai Lama had to assert and prove himself mainly in the strictly temporal sphere of political affairs. Because his enforced stay in India had put him into closer contact with the modern world, it also gave him the opportunity to weigh up its cynicism and to observe its methods of government, which obviously had very little in common with the rules officially respected in a theocratic society. He likewise came to know about the hollowness of promises and the ephemeral reliability of the signatures appended to treaties. The experience only sharpened an already penetrating mind, and the eyes that now looked out on the surrounding world contained an understanding of society seldom previously found among the

sovereigns of Tibet. Participants in the Simla Conference of
1913–14 testified to his shrewd instructions and unbending
views.

For a while, calm seemed to have returned to the heart of
the Asian highlands, especially in contrast with the confrontations soon to flare into full-scale war in Europe. Of course
these years were punctuated by all sorts of incidents, and there
was a slight growth of links with the outside world – particularly with Great Britain, thanks to Charles Bell's mission
to Lhasa in 1920 – although contacts declined with Beijing. A
timid process of modernisation was begun under the aegis of
the Dalai Lama: the first banknotes appeared; a modest army
took shape; a telegraph line was constructed to link the capital
with Gyantse; a geological survey of natural resources
conducted; a small hydroelectrical plant built in Lhasa; a
Sikkimese officer organised a police force; and in 1924 a small
English school was opened in Gyantse.

Another source of future troubles broke out again on the
occasion of a falling out with the Panchen Lama, who went
into exile in China and was royally received there, following a
dispute about the costs of maintaining the infant Tibetan
army. The Dalai Lama also had to balance his modernising
ambitions against the conservative instincts of the powerful
Buddhist clergy. The monks of the great monasteries, particularly in the valley of Lhasa, had always played upon their
influen. e in Tibetan society, and as the Thirteenth Dalai Lama
would brook no compromises on the strict respect for monastic rules, the overriding respect owed to the god-king was
sometimes underlaid by deep-seated grudges. For a considerable number of lamas, politics ought to consist in upholding
religion, and therefore their own privileges, and for some it
was unthinkable to pursue any other social concerns. But
Thubten Gyatso seems to have been acutely aware of developments in the outside world, and to have realised that it was
impossible for Tibet to continue its more or less tranquil and
hermetically sealed existence indefinitely, and that certain
basic changes were urgently required.

In any case, judging by several of his writings, and in particular by what is commonly called his testament, there is no doubt that the keen eyes of the Dalai Lama saw a long way into the future – perhaps a very long way. To the very end of his life, in 1933, he kept a firm hand on the reins of power, striving to keep as stable a balance as possible between Great Britain and China, and demanding in others what he demanded from himself, not afraid to reprimand those lamas who were sometimes tempted to abuse their position in collisions with the common people over land rights. Under his influence, and with all due caution, the doors of Tibet were re-opened to foreign travellers, in spite of what were sometimes grave reservations among the monks, and of intrigues among various noble families jealous of their old prerogatives.

Perhaps the most striking thing today is the almost prophetic nature of some of his analyses. A year before his death, the Thirteenth Dalai Lama wrote:

As for myself, at my age it would be better to renounce ecclesiastical and temporal power so as to dedicate the brief span of life which still remains to religious devotion. Many are my future lives, and I would like to be able to devote myself entirely to spiritual affairs. Nevertheless, because of the guardian Divinities who repose in me, and by virtue of my Root Lama [master to whom the disciple is attached by a very special tie, in this case the Lord of Infinite Compassion], people do come to ask for my teachings, or to have their disagreements settled, and they profoundly hope that I will not give up my secular ministry. Until now I have carried out my task to the best of my abilities, but soon I shall be 58 years old, and then it will be harder for me to continue to perform my religious and my secular activities. Who will not understand that?

The government of India is close to us and it has a large army at its disposal. The government of China too has a large army. Therefore we must maintain firm friendships with both countries, for both are powerful . . . .

Further, these are the days of the five kinds of degeneracy in every land. The gravest is the behaviour of the Reds. They are not allowing searches to be made to find the new incarnation of the Grand Lama of Urga. They have seized and taken possession of all the sacred objects in the monasteries. They have forced the monks to become soldiers. They have broken religion, so that even its name is obliterated. Have you heard all these things which have happened in Urga? And they are continuing. It may be that some day, here, in the heart of Tibet, religion and the secular administration will be simultaneously attacked both from within and without. Unless we ourselves watch over our country it will happen that the Dalai Lamas and Panchen Lamas, father and son, the guardians of the Faith, the glorious Reincarnations, are overthrown and their names doomed to be forgotten. The monastic communities and the clergy will see their lands destroyed. The administrative practices of the Three Great Kings of religion will be weakened. The religious and lay officials will see their estates seized and their other goods confiscated. They themselves will be reduced to slavery by the enemy or compelled to wander like vagrants. All living beings will sink into poverty and terror, and darkness will slowly fall over the suffering of the world.

Do not be traitors to Faith or State by working for another country than your own. Today Tibet is happy and enjoys a certain well-being. The rest lies in your hands. Everything must be arranged with full knowledge of the facts. Work in harmony with one another, and do not aspire to do what you can not.

Consider what it is proper to do and not to do, and carry out your task without doubts, as the All-Knowing Master wills, as if every thing was happening under his eye. Act in this spirit and all will be well . . . . Those who turn away from law and tradition to take a false path, those who care for nothing but their own interests, helping only those who please them, and not the rest, those who are unworthy of trust today and who do not keep to the good, they will not reach their goals and will be punished by the Protectors . . . . Consider seriously what I have said, irrevocably reject the bad and abide by the good.[4]

For a few months longer the Great Thirteenth laboured to strengthen what he had undertaken, but on the evening of the thirteenth day of the tenth month of the year of the Water Bird, that is on 17 December 1933, came the end of that incarnation. While history focuses on his political stature and his skill in keeping his country outside the invasive orbit of

China by declaring it sovereign and independent, those who knew him point to his qualities of openness, intelligence and friendship, while others preserve the memory of an accomplished religious hierarch. On a more profane level, his sense of justice was unanimously praised; he abolished not only the death penalty, except for treason, but also degrading punishments. Timid though they were, his reforms showed a genuine will to bring his country up to date, and at the same time not to push the pace too fast.

Coming as it did in a particularly sensitive era and an explosive international context, his death left the field open to greeds which had not dared to express themselves too loudly during his lifetime, and to the settlement of vendettas long held in check among family and political clans. His wise warnings were completely ignored and it was years before Tibetans came to recognise the full implications of what some do not hesitate to see as a prophetic vision.

Once the Chinese had been driven out of Tibet in 1912, no official Chinese representative had been allowed to set foot in Lhasa. Beijing jumped at the pretext of the Thirteenth Dalai Lama's death to ask permission to send a mission of condolences. The offer was difficult to decline, and a delegation led by General Huang Mu-sung arrived in Lhasa in April 1934. This was an opportunity for China to re-establish contact, but the Tibetans stubbornly refused to make any concessions about their independence, instead proclaiming it loud and clear. The struggle between the Communists and Nationalists within China had already begun, and around this time it intensified. The Long March started in October 1934, when about 90,000 soldiers led by Mao Zedong were forced to retreat from superior forces under Chiang Kai-shek. A reduced number of tattered and ill-equipped soldiers passed through the Tibetan regions of Horkhog, Lithang, Nyarong and Derge in 1935, but were at once escorted back on to Han territory by the Tibetan army.

In spite of sporadic clashes and brief localised confrontations, until 1950 Tibet went on living more or less on the fringe of the world's development, although not without undergoing its own upheavals and domestic quarrels, some of them fiercely contested. Because of the growing rivalry between Tashi Lumpo and the Potala, the breach between the Panchen Lama and the Dalai Lama was cleverly exploited by the agents of foreign powers, with the aim of reducing the prestige of the two great masters in the eyes of the faithful and consequently making them easier to manipulate.

For the moment, however, in the half-light of the holy shrines and the secrecy of the sacred books, it was time for the traditional preparations for a process vital to the future of the Land of Snows – the careful search for the fourteenth incarnation, the new avatar of Chenrezig on the high stage of gods and men.

PART II

Portrait of a
Tibetan Monk as
Dalai Lama

3

One Life, and Many

Human freedom never consists in being spared from hardships, but in facing them for one's own good, and making them an element of joy.

(*Rabindranath Tagore*)

The curtain of history had hardly fallen on the Great Thirteenth Dalai Lama before a corner was raised again as if to remove possible uncertainties and to throw light on the direction to be followed in the search for the next incarnation. At any rate, that was the interpretation laid upon several unusual signs which appeared with a curious persistence in the month of December 1933.

First came a series of strange clouds in the shape of elephants or dragons, suffused with rainbows, which kept floating above the north-eastern side of the city of Lhasa – so strange that they gave food for thought to those monks and laymen who were accustomed to examining signs. Another out-of-the-ordinary event occurred in the chapel of rest where the dead man's body was laid; a kind of giant fungus grew up overnight on a supporting pillar carved out of a tree trunk. The most extraordinary thing was that the cryptogam was shaped exactly like a star, and that it appeared – but was it purely a chance appearance? – on the north-east pillar of the room. Not to be outdone, the late Dalai Lama himself made his own fantastic intervention. As custom required, he had been awaiting his burial seated cross-legged in the Norbulingka and facing towards the south, the traditionally auspicious direction, while the faithful came to pay their final homage. So imagine the astonishment of the monks, servitors and dignitaries one morning when they discovered that by an imperceptible movement the head had turned and that the face was now looking towards the north-east.

Disconcerting though they may seem to orthodox minds, these signs were encouraging for the Tibetans, who were engrossed by the urgency of regaining the Precious Master and in particular of bringing him back safe and sound to the city of the gods. Threats were amassing along the frontiers of the high country, and though the regent might be doing his duty perfectly, the Lion Throne that symbolised the supreme spiritual and temporal power had to be restored to its legitimate occupant as soon as possible. In the interregnum the Chinese intrigued, a new British mission led by Sir Basil Gould visited Lhasa, and once again the talk revolved around the situation of the Panchen Lama. His religious role was not in question, but his political contacts were bound to rouse some apprehensions among the Tibetans.

Less directly affected by purely political commotions, the lineage of the Panchen Lama, the second highest dignitary of Tibetan Buddhism, is less prolific than the Dalai Lama's; since the institution of the title, the throne of Tashi Lumpo has been held by seven incarnations, and is still in theory held by the seventh, who returned in 1938. In fact, however, Chökyi Gyaltsen Tinley Lhundup, whom the Chinese call Pechen Erdeni, spends most of his time in Beijing where, under the strictest surveillance, he is supposed to oversee Buddhist affairs in the whole of the People's Republic.

But before coming to the present situation, it is worth while recalling that relations between the two great lamas have often suffered from adverse outside conditions. Thus as early as 1728 the Manchus tried to play them off against each other and offered full sovereignty over the territory of Tibet to the Panchen Lama, who declined it. It is sometimes said that history does not repeat itself, but in this case it at least stammers, and it practically caricatures itself over succeeding generations, when we find a similar offer being made in 1910 to the Sixth Panchen Lama, Thupten Chögyi Nyima, and much the same ploy being used by today's Chinese government in its dealings with the Seventh Panchen Lama. And the latter's predecessor was caught up in a compromising involvement, and went into more or less voluntary exile in China in 1923 after a disagreement with the Great Thirteenth, no doubt fuelled by the machinations of both their entourages. He ventured back to the high country after the death of Thubten Gyatso, but the Tibetans were not endeared to him when a quantity of grenades were found in the baggage he sent in advance, and a Chinese military escort also turned up to accompany him to his monastery.

Sometimes the Panchen Lama is credited with what is alleged to be a spiritual superiority, according to a tradition which sees him as always being a consummate master and eminent scholar. This is explained by the fact that the sage of Tashi Lumpo is considered to be a reincarnation of the Dhyani Amithaba Buddha, the original Buddha of the sphere of meditation, whose projection in the world of forms is none other than the bodhisattva Avalokitesvara – himself reincarnated, remember, in the person of the Dalai Lama. While it is true that the masters of Shigatse have often been distinguished by their marked leaning towards study and religion, they have never played a paramount role in politics, in spite of repeated Chinese manoeuvres to that end. Nor has there ever been any ground for doubting the spiritual and temporal supremacy of the Dalai Lama over all of Tibet and its people, whatever the vicissitudes of his successive reigns. Today, as always, it is out of the question for Tibetans to accept that they should alter their customs and traditions at the beck and call of the leadership that happens to be installed in Beijing.

Because the two great lamas have always walked in and out of each other's footsteps down the centuries, and through the gales of history, they have interchanged the roles of master and disciple between their respective successions. Before leaving the earthly scene the Sixth Panchen Lama was consulted about the search for the Fourteenth Dalai Lama. His spiritual qualities and knowledge were a welcome guide for

the lay and religious dignitaries in carrying out their most
difficult of tasks and coming to the proper conclusion; above
all they had to be sure that they made no mistakes, and did
not arouse the suspicions of their meddling Chinese neighbours, always alert to the slightest excuse for interfering in
Tibetan affairs. At the time of the search, the Panchen Lama
was living in Jye-kundo, on the Tibetan border, and the
Chinese governor of the province was a Muslim general
called Ma Pu-feng.

To an outside eye there is something extraordinarily
colourful about the events surrounding the discovery. But
although they seem exotic, the details nevertheless form part
of a shimmering fabric whose quality of wonder is all the
more moving because it belongs to the daily reality, the
everyday magic, of the Land of Snows. In accordance with
tradition and his responsibilities, the regent, Reting Rimpoche, gave the requisite instructions to begin the search.
While prayers and ceremonies went on throughout the
country to ensure the swift return of the Great Protector, the
main oracles were consulted, in particular those at Nechung,
Gadong and Samye, and their predictions recorded under the
seal of secrecy. Premonitory dreams and portents were duly
examined without publicity, some special signs were interpreted, and early in 1935 the regent himself, together with a
few grand lamas and some members of the kashag, set out to
consult the sacred lake of Lhamo Latso. Near the monastery
of Chökhorgyal, founded by the Second Dalai Lama, the
little band halted and set up temporary quarters in order to
purify themselves, to meditate in deepest silence and to
prepare for their encounter with the higher powers.

According to the Tibetan historian W. D. Shakabpa, the
acting secretary of that very special mission, he himself saw
nothing in the blue mirror of the lake, in spite of all his
efforts. On the other hand the regent had a vision of remarkable clarity, in particular of three letters of the Tibetan alphabet – *A*, *Ka* and *Ma* – while other dignitaries saw an
unmistakable view of the gold and jade rooftops of a monastery, a little hamlet nestling in a secluded valley, and a

simple farm with turquoise tiles. A brown and white speckled dog was frisking in the yard.

All these indications were carefully noted down and sealed in their turn, before being communicated to the relevant authorities. Some days later, Reting Rimpoche once again dreamt of a farm with a turquoise roof. After further consultation of the oracles, still with the utmost discretion, three missions were dispatched in three directions: Purchok Rimpoche left for Dagpo and Kongpo in the south-east; Khangser Rimpoche was instructed to enquire in Kham and Jang to the east; while Ke-Tsang Rimpoche went further, towards Amdo and Arig in the north-east. With hindsight, some tiny details turn out to be more significant than they first seemed; thus the Nechung oracle suggested that the third mission should be given a certain mirror, a symbol of wisdom or omniscience. These unusual pilgrims carried gifts and official letters of introduction to all those authorities who might be of assistance in their researches, and in particular the Chinese governor of Sining, the abbot of Kum Bum and the Panchen Lama.

Ke-Tsang Rimpoche's little group made ready to leave Lhasa in September 1936, under a sudden early snowfall, but as they set out, all at once the sky cleared and the sun lit up the city of the gods. It was a good omen. And when, three months later, the caravan came in sight of the Kum Bum monastery, the vision of the sacred lake was confirmed; the roofs of gold and jade were definitely those of the famous eastern lamasery. As if to validate their intuitions a magnificent rainbow arched brilliantly above the monastery by way of a ceremonial greeting.

All the same, the greatest possible care was still required, and the emissaries enquired for confirmations, listened to the advice of the abbots and the Panchen Lama, and informed themselves about fresh clues. Secret discussions of the portents soon produced the rudiments of an itinerary to be followed; it led to Taktser, in the region of Koko Nor, in Amdo. Monks took the searchers there, disguised as traders, since it was essential for them to be able to arrive at a verdict without any interference. Ke-Tsang Rimpoche put on extra camouflage by acting as a servant, while the other members of the mission pretended to be the leaders of the caravan.

As usual in Tibet, the travellers were made welcome and allowed to prepare their tea in the kitchen. While the hosts exchanged words with the visitors the lama made a leisurely examination of the neighbourhood. He spotted some details that gave him a thrill of pleasure, but gave no sign. Pleased with his exploration, he was on his way to the kitchen when a little boy about two years old tagged along beside him, and as soon as he sat down the child climbed straight on to his lap and without more ado began to examine a string of beads which he wore around his neck. The beads had belonged to the Great Thirteenth. 'They're yours if you tell me who I am', the lama promised, and back came the unhesitating reply: 'You are a lama from Sera.' The boy went on in the same breath to add the correct names of two other members of the mission. Still more surprisingly, Lhamo Dondup – that was his name – spoke in the elegant dialect of Lhasa, which few people spoke in the Amdo region.

Judging this first contact, if not conclusive, at least extremely suggestive, but giving nothing away, the dignitaries decided to leave again at dawn to bring their preliminary findings to the attention of the government. Great was their surprise when they saw the child resolutely waiting for them. He begged to be allowed to go with them to Lhasa, and it was no easy matter to explain that the time had not yet come; only the promise of a prompt return disarmed the boy's impatience.

Some months later the emissaries returned. At the crossroads of the hamlet a young Chinaman pressed them to take the lower footpath, which was the slightly longer way round. They followed his advice, and soon found that the path led straight to the front door of the farm with the turquoise tiles, whereas the other, shorter, path would have brought them to a back door of the building. It was another omen; the front entrance was the more auspicious.

Meanwhile the findings of all three missions had been minutely compared, and only two candidates were still in the running, no doubt with the choice inclining towards the eager little boy from Taktser. The second visit was decisive; it brought the child a series of tests which he passed with flying colours. He walked through the trials of former memory, recognising a number of objects which had to be selected from among various false but sometimes finer-looking alternatives. And his occasional hesitations proved convincing rather than negative, as when he hesitated between two walking staffs, and chose one of them – to the chagrin of the experts – before changing his mind and deciding on the other. That was a relief, but the near-mistake was soon explained, because while the Thirteenth Dalai Lama had carried the second staff until he died, the first had remained in his possession for a while before being given to a venerable lama. Picking up a *damarū*, a small ritual drum with dangling balls attached on the end of short thongs, he played it with such control of rhythm and tone that the searchers were amazed. A physical examination revealed the eight major distinctive marks which are the attributes of Chenrezig's incarnation. Now the Lhasa envoys were thoroughly convinced, and the last doubts had been removed. The next set of difficulties were of a different order.

Despite all precautions, it was common knowledge that several missions were searching for the future sovereign of Tibet and that investigations were under way to determine which of the candidates would finally be confirmed. Both the religious and the lay authorities were agreed that the choice had better not be announced too hastily, so that the child could be taken to Lhasa without interference. In the case of the one from Taktser this was not the easiest of tasks; the province of Amdo was certainly an integral part of Tibet, but the Chinese administration had arrogated a right of inspection there, and the governor, Ma Pu-feng, had already expressed his intention of having a say in the hierarchs' choice.

Representatives of Kum Bum and Ma Pu-feng demanded proof that the little boy from Taktser was truly the reincarnate god, and they learned that only the final trials to be conducted in Lhasa would yield an unequivocal answer to the question.

The lamas of Kum Bum were satisfied with that, and the child – who was not yet four years old – was taken into the monastic community there, to meet his first teachers and to begin the hard apprenticeship of discipline.

But the governor was not easily taken in, and he demanded a 'departure duty' of 100,000 Chinese dollars in the currency of the time. As soon as this ransom was paid he tripled his demand. Finding a sum like that in a hurry – the equivalent of 92,000 US dollars – was practically a conjuring trick, and yet they managed it. A caravan of Muslim traders on their way to Mecca agreed to advance the sum until they reached Lhasa, where they would be paid cash on the nail. The lamas breathed again, and keeping a constant vigil over the child, who they were inwardly convinced was the Fourteenth Dalai Lama, the mission started back to the city of the gods. In July 1939 the assembly met to hear the details of the investigations and the results of the tests, while several accomplished lamas and the oracle of Nechung confirmed the return of the representative of Chenrezig to the people of Tibet. After that, it was a matter of making the traditional preparations for the enthronement. Messengers were sent to the government of British India, to Beijing, to the king of Nepal and the rajahs of Sikkim and Bhutan to announce the great news and to invite them to the ceremonies.

Questioned about that period today, Tentzin Gyatso says, with a smile in his eyes, that he does not remember all the details of the tests he underwent to establish the connection with his previous life, for, he explains,

> the new memories tied to this body are stronger. The facts of the past have faded and grown vaguer. I no longer remember whether or not I was capable of these acts of recall when I was a child. The best time for remembering that sort of thing, those previous memories, comes between three and four years old, when you are starting to talk. It is the most favourable moment for memories of the past. After that, the ability diminishes the more the new physical structure develops. It depends on the sharpness of mind and mental development of the individual – some remember one life, or two, or three, or hundreds, or even an infinite number of previous lives.[5]

Nevertheless the Fourteenth Dalai Lama does admit that he
had always shown a wish to go to Lhasa and that he had been
waiting for someone to come and take him there. He would
straddle a piece of wood and imagine himself prancing down
the long dusty road, and he kept telling his mother that he
must leave. So he was not surprised when the emissaries from
Sera arrived at his home; it was in the logic of things. He also
recalls that a pair of crows used regularly to perch on a cornice
of the house, and it is accepted in Tibet that there is a special
relationship between the Dalai Lama and these birds. Traditionally, it was a crow that protected Gedun Truppa during
the bandit raid on the night he was born, and later on his
spiritual practices were to enable him to make direct contact
with the fearsome divinity Mahakala (Dark Lord of Transcendental Wisdom, and also of Time). The god had confirmed that he was under privileged protection, and since that
time similar anecdotes punctuate the lives of the Seventh,
Eighth and Twelfth Dalai Lamas. So it is no surprise to find
the crow associated with the Fourteenth Dalai Lama too – not
that this prevents him from remarking in a confidential tone
that he does not really like the bird, because 'they are too cruel
to the smaller ones'.

Others have retained very clear memories of those days.
Tentzin Gyatso's mother, who died in 1981, remembered a
difficult pregnancy. Her husband, who died when the
god-king was 12, had to take to his bed at that time, and no
one could discover the source of his illness. But as soon as the
baby was born he was up and about again, none the weaker
and ready to resume his many tasks around the modest
farmstead without delay. On the night before the birth, she
had had an odd dream; two blue dragons came to greet her in
the most formal manner.

There were some in the village who had not forgotten that
as he was returning from a pilgrimage to a small hermitage in
the district, the Great Thirteenth had stopped in a nearby
meadow. He had even left a pair of worn-out boots there,
which according to the folk wisdom of the high plateau
plainly meant that he was going to return. Certainly the

villagers were flattered that the incarnation of Chenrezig should have chosen their hamlet for this return, but now they also knew why fate had come down so hard against them during the years before; with no obvious meteorological reason, and in spite of propitiatory ceremonies, hail and drought had destroyed several harvests. Does tradition not affirm that such events clearly herald the arrival of exceptional beings?

It is hard to imagine the greeting and welcome kept in store for the young sovereign who from now on would be subjected to the strictest rules of living and rigorous discipline – even though it was less than fifty years ago. Members of the government came to meet him with great pomp and circumstance, soon followed by the chiefs of the great monasteries and even the few foreign representatives resident in Lhasa. It is thanks to their accounts that it is possible to achieve some vague idea of the splendour and majesty of the ceremonies. After halts at Nagchukha, the monastery of Reting and the hermitage of Rekya, the procession traversed Lhasa on the twenty-fifth day of the eighth month of the year of the Earth Hare (8 October 1939). Before going on to the summer palace of the Norbu-lingka it stopped while a ceremony was held in the Jokhang, the holy of holies of Tibetan Buddhism.

As all accounts are unanimous in confirming, what struck the participants and observers was the stunning poise of the little boy, his controlled vitality, and the innately knowledge-able manner of his bearing and ritual gestures. Already the gaze he directed at the world was extraordinary for its depth, tinged with mischief, and the attention he paid to others evinced a kindly curiosity, open to every approach. Despite the strictest of protocols, the child's charm and appeal were self-evident, yet at the same time he displayed his unassailable patience; it was a true character, firmly founded, which years of adversity would temper still further, while also smoothing down a few of its rough edges. But the seeds of a fierce determination were already there, and as time went by they grew to an exemplary strength and cultivation.

A few weeks later, before the statue of the Buddha in the

Jokhang, the regent Reting Rimpoche personally conducted the ritual ceremony of shaving the boy-monk's head. From now on he would bear the name of Tentzin Gyatso. After the oracles and astrologers had been consulted, the enthronement was set for the fourteenth day of the first month of the year of the Iron Dragon, or 22 February 1940. The magic of the Orient displayed itself in all the profusion of its inexhaustible resources for a rite whose splendours engraved themselves for ever after in the memory of all who took part in it. Here, too, what stands out is the natural nobility and impeccable behaviour of the god-king throughout the lengthy ceremonial.

The years that followed were studious, and no doubt irksome too for a boy bursting with energy and compelled to follow the meticulous apprenticeship in the duties of his position. Today the Fourteenth Dalai Lama confines himself to recalling that 'I never felt ill-at-ease in my role'. For all that, he remains reticent about this period, for as a good Buddhist monk he feels that he has nothing special to say on the subject; the rules require that the monk's knowledge and personal achievements are never to be put on display. It is his manner of being and the daily report to others that attest to the extent of his progress along the Way. The true wise man has no need to advertise himself; he simply is. Religion as understood by the true masters is a very private, almost secret, domain which requires no long explanations.

When he occasionally consents to speak about his own experience, the Dalai Lama does so in very general terms – if he does so at all – to clarify an idea whose essence he wishes to convey to the other speaker:

I studied Buddhism in my own language, and became a monk very young. That is to say that the environment was favourable to me. In terms of personal development, when I was 15 or 16 years old I started to show a real enthusiasm for practice. I have never stopped practising since then – now I am 50 years old . . . . Inner development happens a step at a time. That is why the will to practise without relaxing the effort is very important. Progress comes from the constancy of daily effort.[6]

Although he was later to be hardened by the turmoils of his life, the Fourteenth Dalai Lama was also shaped by his various teachers, and above all by his two tutors – two exceptional figures whose (temporary) loss was keenly felt by the entire community of Tibet. The younger tutor, Kyabje Yongdzin Trijang Rimpoche, came from the Ganden monastery and was reputed to be the most eminent lama of the Gelukpa school of that era. Born in 1900, he was a monk of the purest scholarly tradition, whose personal achievements were universally valued. He went away in 1981, and his new incarnation has appeared among the Tibetan refugees in India.

Originally attached to Drepung, Kyabje Yongdzin Ling Rimpoche, His Holiness's senior tutor, had discharged the duties of Ganden Tripa, abbot of Ganden, since 1965. As such he was the ninety-seventh successor of Tsong-kha-pa the reformer, and considered as the leader of the Gelukpa tradition. An accomplished master, experienced in the monastic disciplines and well versed in the rites, he passed on all the initiatory rites he knew to the Fourteenth Dalai Lama, whom he had loyally served since 1937, first as assistant tutor, then as junior tutor and after 1949 as senior tutor. It was he who took Tentzin Gyatso's vows in 1954 and ordained him as a full monk on the occasion of the annual celebrations of the Great Prayer, the Mönlam Chenmo.

Between them, Kyabje Trijang Rimpoche and Kyabje Ling Rimpoche made a pair of reliable guides, friends and protectors for the lord of the Land of Snows; if the Dalai Lama is what he has become, he acknowledges that he owes it in large part to the care of these two masters of the most exalted stature. The Tibetans say that in any case these two had travelled side by side in several previous lives, and that in earlier existences they had worked together to pass on the Buddhist teachings. The direct predecessor of Ling Rimpoche had also been tutor to the Thirteenth Dalai Lama. Eyewitnesses say that at the moment of leaving this world, on 25 December 1983, in Dharamsala, Ling Rimpoche gave a peaceful smile to his weeping disciples before entering 'the clear light', the state of deep meditation at the threshold of the other world, where he remained until 7 January. Various revelational signs appeared during this period for all to see, while the master's mortal body suffered none of the usual deterioration.

As soon as he was entrusted to his tutors the Fourteenth Dalai Lama buckled down to his apprenticeship and to memorising the many and difficult texts required. Like all novice monks he began with the easiest disciplines – the alphabet and calligraphy, reading and reciting the most common sacred texts. At the beginning he was a little overawed by the stern manner of his first master, Ling Rimpoche; a mere reprimand from him felt like the supreme punishment. Nevertheless it was this great scholar and shrewd observer of human affairs who was to become and remain one of his closest companions and advisers.

As he passed through the many stages of the studies which are in fact a lifetime's work, Tentzin Gyatso learned by heart dozens of treatises on the five major branches of Buddhist knowledge – Sanskrit, dialectics, logic, religious philosophy and metaphysics – essential for acquiring the title of *geshe lharampa*, the Buddhist doctor of law. Most of these works come down from Indian sages, and over the centuries Tibetan masters and scholars have produced thousands of pages of commentaries, analyses and expositions. The five minor branches consist of the theatre, music and dance, astrology, poetry and composition; it goes without saying that all artistic activities are intimately bound up with spiritual knowledge.

These subtleties do not stop there, of course; religious philosophy, for example, branches into transcendental wisdom (*prajna paramita*), the middle way (*madhyamika*), the canon of monastic discipline (*vinaya*), metaphysics (*abhidharma*), and logic and dialectics (*pramana*). Unlike the ancient masters of India, the Tibetan sages devote special attention to logic and dialectics, whose foundations in solid reason are laid by strenuous debates, lasting for hours, between masters and disciples in private, or sometimes in the presence of hundreds of monks, when the debate is fought between students of more or less equal strength, under the teachers' attentive eyes.

These debates improve the depth and speed of memory, and also call for agile thinking and quick wits.

This daily preparation, interspersed with hours of intense meditation, essential for understanding and assimilating texts, nevertheless leaves room for a few moments of leisure. The rigorous protocol that surrounded the Dalai Lama did not allow him to mix freely with other children of his own age, and only his brothers and sisters were permitted to play games with him – in particular Lobsang Samten, two years his elder. While he may sometimes have felt the effects of this near-exclusion from the world of ordinary people and things, the Dalai Lama nevertheless remembers high times spent with old lamas who let their childish souls revive for a while to share the fancies of their famous charge.

Sometimes a snatch of childhood surfaces through the strict rigours of those years, and brings a burst of laughter, a brief mood of nostalgia or a happy memory. Thus the heroic story cycle of Ge-sar of Ling, a chronicle of legendary deeds and exploits from deep in the folk memory of Tibet, reminds the Dalai Lama of an old bard who would spend hours with the god-king reciting thrilling episodes of the myth:

> Might Ge-sar return one day, as some people say and others believe? It is true that he promised to, and some believe and assert that he could play a vital part in Tibet. Alexandra David-Neel is not the only one to have reported this version, which has been told for many years on the high plains. Besides, isn't it said that Ge-sar is an incarnation of Avalokitesvara, the Buddha of Infinite Compassion? So he too is a master, and masters have great power .... I don't know exactly, because I haven't made any serious study of the king of Ling, and I don't know any more about him than any average Tibetan.
>
> All I can tell you is that in the old days, in the Potala, a marvellous story teller sometimes used to come and tell me those fabulous tales. I loved to listen to him. He made a great impression on me, and do you know why? Not only did he know any number of details and variations, even though he may have made some of them up as he went along, but he also had a huge bowl of tea, enormous! He kept it constantly filled up with prodigious

quantities of tea, and drank it in surprising amounts. It was his salary, and certainly his pleasure too; to drink tea from the kitchens of the Dalai Lama! I don't know very much more about him, although . . .[7]

And the unfinished sentence, full of unspoken implications, is lost again in the mischievous ring of a burst of laughter.

Much to the despair of the three monks in charge of supplies – the Zimpön Khenpo for clothing, the Supön Khenpo for food, and the Chöpön Khenpo for ritual objects – who followed the young monk like shadows, he soon turned out to be made of quicksilver. His boisterous energy impelled him into all sorts of escapades and caused him to poke his august nose into the most out-of-the-way corners of the summer and winter palaces. For instance, he and his brother used to haul a little pony which they used for their games up on to the roof of one of the residences in the Norbu-lingka, just for the pleasure of gazing at the surrounding valley. The two of them also loved to borrow a small boat and sail it on the lake in the Jewel Park, while the good servant monks stood rooted on the bank, since there was no room for any one else in the boat, praying to heaven and the gods for no harm to come to their unruly young masters.

Another feature of the young sovereign's character was his absolute passion for machinery. Whenever he got hold of anything that could be taken apart it was quickly in pieces, whether it was an old cuckoo clock or a valuable music box given by the Tsar to his predecessor and kept in a treasure chamber, or even one of the three fair-sized motor cars brought to Lhasa in pieces on muleback, for the exclusive use of the Great Thirteenth. Sometimes he would reassemble the object with remarkable dexterity, as if he had been doing it all his life.

On other occasions the scrapes were more awkward. The first time the adolescent Dalai Lama sat at the wheel of one of the vehicles he had repaired by himself, naturally unsuper-vised, he came out of the situation quite honourably – except that an unexpected collision broke the smoked glass of one of the front head-lamps. Without getting the least bit flustered, the god-king found and cut another piece of glass, and smeared it with cane syrup, using a brush and a toothpick. It seems that the innocent deception worked. Even today the Dalai Lama continues to take a keen interest in the most advanced technological achievements, and if he is no longer surprised by railway locomotives or aircraft, he is fascinated by machines like the body scanner or the cyclotron.

To help satisfy his thirst for knowledge, the young Dalai Lama took advantage of the presence in Lhasa of Heinrich Harrer, a European with a chequered past. He was an Austrian who had escaped from the camp at Dehra Dun where the British had interned him. Posing as a simple mountain lover, he managed to introduce himself into the entourage of the semi-reclusive sovereign, and told him all sorts of details about the countries he had seen. These unknown names caught young Tentzin Gyatso's imagination when he turned the pages of old atlases unearthed from a shelf in some antique bookcase in the Potala. It was from the Austrian that he learned the first rudiments of English and began to discover what was happening across the Himalayas. Despite the reservations of the monks and civil servants, the god-king was tremendously interested in photography and the cinema, and he gave the visitor permission to make some films which have now become invaluable evidence about life in Lhasa before the Chinese invasion.

In the meantime, while the young monk went on dutifully preparing for his future tasks, beyond the walls of the Potala and the Norbu-lingka other events whose importance was not always recognised in the city of the gods were changing the face of the world and paving the way for subsequent upheavals. These masters of omens and powers were terribly far from understanding the barbarous customs and standards prevailing in the lowlands, or from being able to detect the very real dangers whose reverberations rose so faintly towards the Roof of the World. Yet signals had been sent and duly recorded in the fat registers of the local administration. During the Second World War, and the Dalai Lama's minority, Tibet managed to keep clear of the general agony with relative ease; its natural and traditional isolation preserved it from the direct consequences of the battles that were fought, but unwittingly it became a factor in the longer-term ambitions of the warring powers. No doubt it is also worth mentioning that there were only a handful of people in the outside world who realised the genuine strategic importance of Tibet; it was the advent and spread of aircraft that revealed it, and later the presence of orbiting satellites. From the heights of Tibet, the resident power dominates not only the plains of India and China but also the eastern republics of the Soviet Union, not to mention the corridor into Afghanistan. And the greatest rivers of Asia flow down from these snow-covered heights.

. For the time being, but even inside Lhasa, the British and Chinese manoeuvred behind the scenes, and the small closed world of local politics observed the changes through half-closed eyes. Certainly the Tibetans had been concerned when the tattered columns of Mao's partisan forces entered their territory for a while during their Long March, but they imagined that the contest between Chinese Nationalists and Communists did not involve them – let the Han kill one another, it was that much more peace ensured for the people of Tibet. The Sino–Japanese War had also aroused some alarm, for in Lhasa perhaps the greatest fear was of a threat from Japan, but there too the ferment did not last. The resignation of the regent in 1941 – the oracles had predicted that he did not have long to live if he did not devote himself from then on to meditation and spiritual improvement – greatly upset the Chinese, who had seemed to have found a sympathetic ear in him and there were those who claimed that various small gifts may also have helped the Chinese cause. He was replaced by Taktra Rimpoche, who was regarded as a conservative. His powers of discernment and government would very soon be put to the test.

Late in 1941 political competition and the struggle for influence closed in around the Roof of the World. First, Lhasa was taken off guard by the reversal of alliances between Great

Britain and China, following the Japanese entry into the war.
Wary, and too far removed from the theatre of events to see
what was at stake, the Tibetan government confined itself to
playing a waiting game, unlike the Great Thirteenth, who
had shown sympathy for the allies at the time of the First
World War.

For some months, the *kashag* had stood up to heavy
pressure from Chiang Kai-shek, who was threatened by the
uncertainties that lapped around the mountain barrier and
anxious to build new roads over the high plateau to safeguard
his ground supply lines – the Burma route had been cut by the
Japanese advance and it was imperative to find alternative
ways. From promises to threats, compromise to raids, and
provocation to blackmail, in the end Tibet agreed to allow
goods to be shipped across its territory between India and
China, though excluding military supplies.

Meanwhile an official delegation from the United States
had arrived in Lhasa. It consisted of Captain Ilya Tolstoy and
Lieutenant Brooke Dolan, and carried a personal message
from Franklin D. Roosevelt to the Dalai Lama; its mission
was to investigate conditions along the supply routes to
Nationalist China. The two American officers were received
with all due consideration and decorum, and a month later,
when Tibetan soldiers escorted them to Sining, on the
Chinese border, after a meeting with the young sovereign,
they were thoroughly convinced that Tibet was an independent, viable well-run country, and proud of being so.

In their baggage the American envoys took away precious
gifts for their president and a reply from the Dalai Lama
addressed to 'the Honourable Franklin D. Roosevelt, President of the United States of America – At the White House,
Washington DC – USA'. After the usual thanks and com-
pliments, the text went on to say:

We are happy to learn that you and the people of the United
States of America are interested in our country. It is particularly
significant that the American people, with twenty-seven other
countries, should at present be engaged upon a war for the

preservation of freedom, a war forced upon it by nations bent on conquest, with the aim of everywhere destroying freedom of thought, religion and action.

Tibet too sets a high value on the freedom and independence which it has enjoyed since time immemorial, and placed at the heart of the Buddhist religion, despite my youth I strive to uphold and promote our religious precepts, thus continuing the pious labours of my predecessors. I sincerely hope and pray for a speedy end to the hostilities, so that the nations of the world may enjoy a just and lasting peace, based on the principles of freedom and goodwill . . . .

Dated on the nineteenth day of the first Tibetan month of the year of the Water Sheep, or 24 February 1943. Under the seal of the Dalai Lama of Tibet.[8]

Perhaps this very official message is not entirely the work of a boy of eight; nevertheless it goes to show that its signatory already took his role very seriously, and that the fourteenth incarnation of Chenrezig would have a special contribution to make, not only to his own country, but perhaps in the world beyond.

Another American, Lieutenant R. E. Crozier, found himself on the Roof of the World the following year, only his was an unplanned visit – he literally dropped in out of the skies. His cargo plane on the India–China run had flown off course, run out of fuel and crashed not far from the big monastery of Samye. The pilot and crew were welcomed, looked after, and then very ceremoniously escorted to the frontier with India. After that the United States gave an undertaking not to allow any American aircraft to overfly Tibetan territory.

One unexpected consequence of these incidents was that the Tibetan government saw that they had better make provision for the future and decided to open an English school in Lhasa straight away, for a number of hand-picked pupils in the service of the authorities. Strenuous protests from the monks over the next few months compelled its closure, and some Tibetan students were therefore given grants to go to school in India, so that they could learn English and get to

know something about the outside world. The school
established in Gyantse in 1923 had survived for three years
before meeting the same fate for the same reasons, namely
the fear among the lamas that foreign influence would
subvert religious beliefs. Perhaps they were not altogether
mistaken, but in the last instance this conservative reflex was
to have dire consequences for Tibet.

In any case, the end of worldwide hostilities landed Tibet
in a critical situation which it could neither fully grasp nor
control. With a characteristic blend of caution and persistence, it decided that it needed to assert its own authority and
autonomy, and yet one gesture intended as friendly was to
go severely amiss. It was decided to send an official delegation to India and China with a message of goodwill and
congratulations to the victors in the Second World War.
Whether because they were too honest or too ingenuous, too
trusting or too ignorant of the pitfalls of high international
policy, the emissaries from Lhasa walked into a Chinese
trap.

These Tibetan moves towards self-assertion were naturally unwelcome to Beijing. On this point both Nationalists
and Communists were united in their refusal to do anything
that might amount to recognition of the independence of
Tibet. In India, the Tibetan mission went off well, and the
envoys from Lhasa were received by the Viceroy, Lord
Wavell. Some Chinese officials did their best to chaperone
and shadow them, but were put smartly in their place.

It was in China itself that things went wrong. Although
Hugh Richardson, then officer in charge of the British
mission in Lhasa, had made every effort to warn the kashag
against putting in any kind of appearance in the Chinese
National Assembly, the Tibetan envoys were held in Beijing
to attend it. Certainly they did not sign or initial a single
document, but the harm was done; despite their protestations of good faith, the Chinese exploited the situation by
informing all and sundry that the Tibetan people were
Chinese. The Lhasa authorities were rather uneasy and very
annoyed about these proclamations, but not particularly

alarmed; in their innocence, they considered that since they were lies, no one would give them credence or take them seriously.

In 1947 the free and sovereign nation of Tibet sent delegates to the Asian Conference organised by the Indian Congress Party. They had talks with Mahatma Gandhi and Jawaharlal Nehru, but how could either of these spare much attention for the future of Tibet when the burning issue was the end of British rule, partitition and Indian independence?

Meanwhile in Lhasa seething dissatisfactions rose and boiled over into a rudimentary coup d'état, or putsch at least. In the beginning, difficulties over unpaid interest and overdue taxes caused grumblings among the monks at two religious colleges in Sera, which degenerated into brawls and eventually to the suspension of both abbots, who were replaced out of hand by the civil power. A few months later, rumours began to circulate about the imminent resignation of the regent and his replacement by his predecessor, Reting Rimpoche, who was not remembered with universal affection. Obscure rivalries surfaced between the two men, mysterious ambushes were laid, parcel bombs sent, meetings cancelled at the last moment, suspicious cables exchanged – in other words an intrigue full of new twists and turns went on inside the city of the gods, while the struggle for political power behind the scenes grew more intense. Reting Rimpoche was arrested, his accomplices made confessions, and the plot was unearthed. The monks in the two colleges in Sera did not relish its discovery and broke into open rebellion against the government, even fighting the soldiers sent to restore order, before they realised that the cause was lost and returned to their cells to pray and do penitence. Thereupon the former regent removed himself permanently from the scene by dying. After three weeks of acute crisis the episode was closed, and there would be no civil war around the Potala.

In any case these incidents are minor compared with the griefs in store. Slowly the Tibetan authorities saw the scale of what they were facing and the need for urgent action. Thus they sent a trade delegation to India, Great Britain, the United

States and China in October 1947, barely two months after
Indian independence. Its four members travelled on Tibetan
passports and were received in New Delhi as the representatives of a sovereign power. When they visited Beijing they
met Chiang Kai-shek and turned down a new invitation to
take part in the sittings of the National Assembly. The
Communists were already starting to gain the upper hand
over the Nationalist government, which was soon to collapse.

At about that time in 1948, as if some strange force was
working to raise the alarm, Lhasa witnessed an outbreak of
evil omens, or at any rate of unusual indications which were
interpreted as such and which only exacerbated the underlying tension. At the height of the dry season, with not a
single raindrop able to fall from a uniformly deep-blue sky, a
gilded gargoyle on the roof of the Jokhang, the holy of holies
in Lhasa, kept up a constant, irritating drip. For some weeks a
comet was visible in the sky at night. The older inhabitants
recalled with dismay that a similar phenomenon had been
recorded in 1910 on the eve of the Chinese invasion. The birth
of monsters was reported, and one night the capital of an
ancient stone column dating back to the year AD 763 somehow
broke loose and went crashing down to the foot of the Potala.
Special ceremonies and major rituals were at once performed
in an attempt to stave off fate.

In July 1949 the now thoroughly suspicious Tibetan
government instructed the Chinese mission in Lhasa to close
its doors and pack its bags, considering that the devious
activities of its staff were only fuelling the local tensions; there
had been evidence of its interference in Reting Rimpoche's
failed conspiracy, and his pro-Chinese sympathies were
common knowledge. But the decision also expressed another
concern, which was official apprehension about Beijing's
behaviour in the matter of the Panchen Lama.

About ten potential candidates to succeed the late ecclesi-
arch had been identified since 1942, but the final choice, which
was up to the Dalai Lama, or in his absence to the regent and
the National Assembly, had not yet been made, as it had not
been possible to complete the customary tests and examin-

ations. The Chinese Nationalists took full advantage of this
hiatus by making much of a small boy born in the border
region of Ch'ing Hai and arranging to have him proclaimed
the new reincarnation of the master of Tashi Lumpo by a
cooperative member of the late Panchen Lama's retinue. What
particularly upset the Tibetans about this act of blatant
interference was that the man who made the pronouncement
was a member of the Chinese Central Executive Committee,
and that his proclamation was a complete departure from
tradition. So in 1947, shortly before the affair of the regent
came to light, they refused to receive the boy under a Chinese
escort. The Nationalists gave little sign of taking offence, and
waited until 1949 before recognising their Panchen Lama
nominee. That was only just before the seizure of power by
Mao and his comrades, and in the view of Beijing young
Chökyi Gyaltsen Tinley Lhundup, seventh of his line, was an
ideal instrument for the performance of its chosen policy on
the Roof of the World. Although he has not always come up
to his protectors' expectations, and his present existence
makes him more like a hostage or puppet than a free man
responsible for his own actions, this second most exalted
dignitary of Tibetan Buddhism provided his own very special
symbol of the fate of Tibet, compelled to dance to a tune
imposed by foreign masters.

As soon as the Communists had control of mainland China,
in October 1949, Beijing Radio announced that Tibet was part
of China and that the People's Liberation Army had been
ordered to 'liberate Tibet from foreign imperialism'. Lhasa's
rejection of the Chinese claim was immediate and unequivocal, but in vain; nobody heard it, or paid it attention. In
January 1950 India recognised the new Chinese regime,
justifying that action later by claiming that it hoped to be able
to exert influence on the Chinese attitude towards Tibet.

The truth of that suggestion is open to argument. As for the
'foreign imperialists' invented by Chinese propaganda in a
fanfare of lies to justify the unjustifiable, the claim is easily
exploded. There was a handful of British nationals then in
Lhasa; Hugh Richardson, now officer in charge of the Indian

mission, two employees of the Tibetan government, dealing with telecommunications, and a temporary visitor studying the plans for a possible hydroelectric power station. And there were three Americans staying there; a journalist, Lowell Thomas, and his son, and a student of linguistics, based in Sinkiang, who had fled before the Communist advance.

Some weeks later the Tibetan illusions faded, and the fears increased, when the battling General Ma Pu-feng, the same governor who had demanded a ransom to allow the presumptive new Dalai Lama to leave his province, took to his heels in the face of the Red peril and even stooped to asking for transit rights for his routed troops. In Lhasa they gave out ancient weapons – muskets, blunderbusses and suchlike – to civil servants and even to monks, soldiers were trained, and the government sent messengers to India, Nepal, England and the United States to ask for help, while a mission left for China in the hope of reaching some sort of agreement.

Then, as if to turn the screw tighter, on 15 August 1950 a very violent earthquake cost many lives and caused great damage in eastern Tibet, close to the Chinese frontier. Not long afterwards the news came that some hundreds of hamlets no longer existed, valleys and mountains had moved, and the Brahmaputra river itself had altered its course. For hours the sky had blazed blood-red with heavy sulphurous fumes. Robert Ford, a British radio technician then stationed in Chamdo, and working for the Tibetan government, noted: 'It was no ordinary earthquake. It was as if the end of the world had come.' The shock-wave was felt as far as Lhasa, and of course the earthquake was interpreted as a sinister omen.

Pressed by the Tibetans, for form's sake India protested to Beijing against the aggressive statements being made by the new masters of China, but was relieved by the assurance given in late August that the use of force was out of the question. Negotiations were still under way in New Delhi between the Chinese Communist ambassador and the representatives of the Tibetan government when the forces of Mao Zedong launched their attack upon the Roof of the World on 7 October 1950.

The whole of Tibet now turned towards the young man who embodied the nation – its Precious Protector, the Dalai Lama. On the advice of the oracles, and with the support of the grand lamas, the kashag begged the Lord of the Lotus to take charge of the country, even though he had not yet reached his legal majority. The studious adolescent, who in his spare time used to take a telescope to some hidden recess in the Potala and look down at the routine activities of a forbidden profane world, was to find himself suddenly propelled into the very heart of a hitherto unknown reality. 'That request filled me with anxiety', he would later acknowledge.

> I was only sixteen years old and I had nowhere near completed my religious education. I knew nothing of the outside world and had no political experience. Yet I was mature enough to realise my ignorance, and everything I still had to learn .... In my capacity as Dalai Lama I was the only one whom everybody in the country would be ready to follow with no argument.
>
> All the same, I hesitated. But the National Assembly now met and supported the cabinet's request. So, seeing the gravity of the situation, I could no longer refuse to take up my responsibilities. It was my duty to assume them, to leave my adolescence behind me and prepare myself without delay to lead my country as well as I was able, faced with the enormous power of Communist China. Not without a certain apprehension, I therefore accepted. And in the course of a traditional ceremony I was given full powers.[9]

But sometimes it can be very hard to work miracles, even in the city of the gods. Nevertheless, on that eleventh day of the tenth month of the year of the Fire Tiger (17 November 1950) extraordinary rejoicings broke out, amid lavish ceremonial. It was as if that date had to be engraved for ever in the hearts of all who recalled it, with all the symbolism it implied for a people whose deepest essence was now personified by a young sovereign who was both a spiritual and a temporal guide. A general amnesty was declared, and for a few days the impending dangers faded while the god incarnate was restored to his people. But the world of men is ruled by very different laws, as the Tibetans were soon to learn by bitter experience.

Early in November official letters were sent to the United Nations and to several governments, drawing attention to the Chinese aggression. They were a waste of time. There were various sporadic and disorganised efforts of resistance in the affected territories of Amdo and Kham, but Tibet had been isolated, not to say isolationist, for too long. In order to protect the person of the new head of state the civil authorities decided to send him to Yatung, in the Chumbi valley, a stone's throw from the Indian border, in the hope that some sort of negotiation with Beijing might still enable something to be saved. Yet the Dalai Lama had already had personal experience of what Chinese expansionism would mean; his own elder brother, the reincarnated lama of Kum Bum, Thubten Jigme Norbu, had been compelled by the Chinese provincial authorities to bring him a message enjoining him to accept the Chinese seizure of Tibet. Thubten Norbu had had the opportunity to observe at first hand the extortionate behaviour and arbitrary brutality of the invaders, who had also had the effrontery to offer him a handsome reward if he managed to convince his brother.

Before leaving Lhasa the Dalai Lama appointed two prime ministers, one monk and one layman, according to custom, and vested them with plenipotentiary powers to negotiate with China. A long caravan with hundreds of pack animals then set out to carry the sovereign and his retinue to a safe temporary refuge, escorted by forty young noblemen and his personal guard of 200 soldiers, brave beyond question but with a motley assortment of obsolescent weapons. Suspecting, with justification, that worse was yet to come, Tentzin Gyatso took advantage of his semi-flight to forward a portion of the treasures accumulated for centuries in the Potala to a place of safety in Sikkim, in the belief that one day those jewels and bags of gold-dust might prove useful to the Tibetan cause. Subsequent events were to confirm that intuition.

For the time being the young man thought, prayed and

considered a number of different scenarios for the future. By nature he was inclined to lean as far as he could towards a non-violent solution; as a convinced Buddhist he could not in conscience preach violence, even if he understood, and sometimes reluctantly accepted, it when all else failed.

> As long as the path is easy, all goes well . . . . But the day you have to face up to any problems, then you feel depressed. And yet it is largely through difficulties that one learns. Experience enables a person to acquire inner strength, courage and determination. Your enemy brings you that opportunity. That does not in the slightest mean that you have to obey him, or knuckle under to him. It may even happen, depending on his attitude, that you have to undertake a violent action. That may be necessary, but within yourself you do not abandon either calm or compassion.[10]

To make a choice, and the right choice, in those conditions was no easy task. When he was urged to cross the frontier and go into exile for a time – time enough, some suggested, for a friendly agreement to be reached with the Chinese – the Dalai Lama refused and preferred to stay where he was; at least he would have done all he could to alleviate the situation, and in his solitude – the ruler's solitude as much as the monk's – he would be in harmony with his conscience and with his perception of the world. Here, too, he was already emerging as a true master.

Virtually the hostage of the Chinese Communist authorities, there was nothing the Tibetan delegation could do except sign the notorious '17-point agreement', against its will, in May 1951. To this day there are witnesses who claim that the seals used for the occasion were forgeries made in Beijing. In Yatung the Dalai Lama kept a close watch on the developing situation, and was informed about the Panchen Lama's messages of support for the invading armies. Already Beijing had announced that its troops were occupying Lhasa, although the historical record, which is rather better known today, postpones that 'triumphal' entry into the Tibetan capital for another year. But apart from the platonic protestations and bluster of the Indian government, followed by various circuitous statements from the British, the whole world stood and watched as the Land of Snows fell under the Chinese heel.

In the teeth of these events, it took the Dalai Lama himself to maintain even the most tenuous hope of arresting the course of history – although in retrospect he occasionally muses that this was the collective karma of his people. That did not prevent him from fighting a stubborn rearguard action against the successive and systematic infringements and erosions of his power. At the request of the new Chinese governor of Tibet, now declared to be an 'autonomous province incorporated into China', General Chang Ching-wu, who came to visit him in Yatung, the Dalai Lama left his refuge on 24 July 1951 and arrived back in Lhasa on 17 August. Three weeks later some 25,000 Chinese troops took up quarters in the Tibetan capital, whose population was barely 50,000 at the time. With the impact of their arrival history took a harder turn, and the delicate balance of Tibetan society broke, eventually leading to the inevitable explosion.

Frictions quickly grew and worsened. First, like any occupying power, the Chinese required to be fed and lodged on the backs of their hosts. There were immediate repercussions on the Tibetan economy, simply because the arid nature of the high plateau was incapable of feeding so many new mouths without suffering damage. For the first time in Tibetan history famine made its appearance and threatened the native population. The two first ministers, Lukhangwa and Lozang Tashi, stood together to denounce the Chinese seizure and oppose the arbitrary rule of the invaders. They were compelled to resign, and the Dalai Lama chose to back their departure rather than to let them fall into Chinese hands.

In their atavistic need to 'save face', the Chinese authorities tried to keep up appearances and to respect a minimum of proprieties. Thus at first they strove to preserve the veneer of the traditional administrative structures, but by putting their own nominees alongside the Tibetan public officials. It goes without saying that it was the former who took the decisions, and that it was also their job to see them carried out.

In order to counter the paramount and undisputed influence

of the Dalai Lama, the Chinese made up their minds to magnify that of the Panchen Lama, having insisted on his recognition when the seventeen-point agreement was signed in Beijing. Symbolically, but perhaps also deliberately, the Panchen Lama returned to Tibet after the suspension of the two first ministers of the kashag, escorted by an impressive number of Chinese soldiers; he swept like a whirlwind through Lhasa, taking just time enough to send a brief message to the Potala, and made straight for his Tashi Lumpo stronghold. In order to build up a reservoir of reliable collaborators, the Chinese also handed out generous student grants and dispatched hundreds of picked young people to study in their famous 'minority institutes' for two or three years.

Rather for worse than for better, a precarious cohabitation process evolved, with each community living for itself amid a dangerous numerical disadvantage for the Tibetans; for in order to hasten the achievement of its plans, Beijing sent thousands if not millions of prisoners and detainees serving sentences of hard labour to build roads, airfields and communication routes linking the high plateaux of Tibet with the plains below. Tibetans were automatically conscripted to join in. The new roads – one from Sichuan through Kham, and the other from Lanchow through Sining – were at once put into use by the military. It was an intrusion bitterly resented by the people of Tibet, especially when, for the good of the cause, the Chinese presented it to the outside world as a step towards liberation.

When it came to their much-heralded reforms – the pretext for their incursion – the Chinese were taken unawares by the response, and most of all by the Dalai Lama, who had been pondering the question for some time and who put forward some concrete proposals on his return from Yatung. With obvious embarrassment the Han regime pulled a long face, and then waved these suggestions away. Paradoxically they were backed by the Tibetan landowners, who were not at all happy about their god-king's 'revolutionary' views, but that did not prevent him from going ahead and setting up his own

social services office. Among other things he abolished the
statutory provision of free transport for officials, cancelled
peasant debts, and promoted further modernisation by supporting the spread of western medicine and the opening of
more new schools. He also welcomed the improvements in
agriculture and explained to his fellow countrymen the need
for development, kept in tune with local realities of course,
but essential if Tibet was to keep up with the times. In other
words he threw himself quite frankly into the new power
game, and played it with remarkable skill, making no major
concessions and anxious to avoid a violent break. As well as
that, the naturally distrustful peasants were not taken in by
high-flown Chinese speeches, and instead paid heed to the
reforms put forward by the Dalai Lama.

The breach continued to widen, and the Tibetans to be
undeceived, and when the Chinese began to harass the
monasteries and victimise the monks the situation quickly
deteriorated. Although the people of Tibet are inquisitive by
nature, and always open to something new, although they
like to judge experiments according to the evidence, above all
they love to choose for themselves, with no one to dictate the
line to follow. And for them, to meddle with their ancestral
institutions amounted to subjecting them to laws imposed
from the outside.

By their shameless inroads into the country's food reserves
and prodigal use of its gold and silver reserves, disguised as
'loans', the Chinese turned the common run of people against
them. In addition, the monks had not taken long to realise that
the gap between the guarantees provided in the model constitution and the concrete realities which they now observed was
so wide that it was rapidly becoming unbridgeable. So it is not
surprising that there was a rumble of general revolt, that the
testament of the Great Thirteenth Dalai Lama went into secret
circulation all over the country, and that without showing any
outright signs of opposition the people of Tibet went over to a
kind of passive resistance by publicly boycotting the meetings
and other indoctrination procedures so beloved of Chinese
officialdom.

Once set in motion, the machinery was difficult to stop, and this became apparent in 1954 when the Dalai Lama and the Panchen Lama were invited to Beijing to take part in the labours of the National People's Congress. There was alarm in Lhasa, for, even if no one ventured to say so in public, there was a general fear that the Chinese would prevent the sovereign from returning to his country. In other words the Chinese were not trusted, and when the Dalai Lama set out on 11 July the whole town turned out to wish him the protection of the gods and a speedy return. He was lavishly received in Beijing, and Mao Zedong in person attended a reception organised on the occasion of the Tibetan New Year, and feigned an interest in the problems of Tibet. At another reception for the Chinese national day, the Dalai Lama briefly met Chu Teh and Chou En-lai, Nikita Khrushchev and Nikolai Bulganin, as well as Jawaharlal Nehru. A curiously awkward atmosphere prevailed at this meeting between the god-king and the prime minister of independent India; it was as if there was some failure of communication between the spiritual guide of Tibet and the westernised leader of an ancient civilisation. Or perhaps Nehru had already begun to wonder about the commitments entered into by Beijing in April 1954 in the so-called Pancha Shila Accord, a joint statement of the 'Five Principles of Peaceful Coexistence' issued by the two giants of Asia.

In any case, the longer the Dalai Lama remained in China, the greater the anxiety in Lhasa, particularly when the young religious leader found himself paraded in some purely Chinese regions before going on to his native province, and when the consequent shortage of time was used as the pretext to prevent him from making his intended visits to a number of monasteries such as Lithang and Chating in Kham province, Derge, and the district of Nyarong, where he was expected and had to be represented instead by lamas of high rank. Even so, the Tibetans held their peace, for fear that a flare-up might give the Chinese an excuse to keep the Dalai Lama as a hostage. But that did not prevent them from writing, and thousands of letters poured into Beijing begging the sovereign to return home as soon as possible. When he was preparing to leave Beijing, in March 1955 – he had been absent for almost a year – he was informed that the Chinese government was proposing the creation of a 'preparatory committee for the Autonomous Region of Tibet'.

In Lhasa the Dalai Lama's return lowered the temperature a little, but the lull was short-lived, for more and more disturbing news began to arrive from eastern Tibet, where the Chinese had at first been successful in exploiting the traditional animosity towards the capital among the people of Kham and Amdo. This early success had quickly evaporated, especially when the Chinese started to make open criticisms of the people's religious beliefs. These criticisms soon turned to physical attacks and public humiliation, and finally to the summary execution of certain highly venerated lamas. That was too much, but it was not all. Women were raped, goods confiscated, and weapons commandeered, particularly among the Khampas, who were reputed for their bravery and their pride as gentlemen brigands. They at once turned into guerrilla partisans who proceeded to make life very hard for the occupying power.

By way of reprisals, the lamaseries of Chating, Lithang and Batang, identified by the Chinese as centres of resistance, were attacked by rockets or bombed from the air. Villagers were brutally driven out of their hamlets and replaced by Chinese colonists. In short, the Communists behaved like any other invader, except that their total control of the press and information enabled them to cloak their activities under the general heading of 'liberating the serfs' . . . and a few good souls believed the story.

Despite these multiple concerns, and the time he was forced to spend trying to smooth over the various tensions in order at least to postpone, if not finally to avoid, more violent clashes, the Dalai Lama continued his religious studies and his personal education. He was preparing for the philosophical debates which would pit him against the finest scholars in all the monasteries, doctors of Buddhist law and accomplished masters of metaphysics. His teachers and private tutors were unanimous in recognising his exceptional qualities of intelligence, thought and application.

At this juncture, late in 1955, the Dalai Lama received an invitation to make a visit to India to take part in ceremonies which were to celebrate the twenty-fifth centenary of the birth of the Buddha. Beijing said no. The following spring, the Maharajah of Sikkim came to Lhasa in person to reiterate the invitation and to bring the sovereign a personal message from the Mahabodhi Society, the organiser of these festivities. The Dalai Lama accepted, but Beijing claimed that it would be better if he were to remain in Tibet. Were the Chinese authorities tacitly admitting that the situation on the high plateau was not as calm as they had been saying, or were they hoping to send a signal to India and the rest of the world that the Tibetan affair was now settled? The fact remains that in July 1956 a delegation specially mandated by the Dalai Lama and made up of a minister approved by the Chinese and a grand lama hailing from Kham attempted to quell the troubles in eastern Tibet, but utterly failed. Rebellion continued to smoulder on the Chinese border.

Beijing persisted in its refusal to allow the spiritual leader of Tibet to leave the country, but his people were angered by the decision, and they showed it. There was fury in the great monasteries and around Lhasa, for everybody felt that the Dalai Lama ought to take part in these exceptional ceremonies. Even Nehru added his voice to the 'suggestions' from abroad, so much so that the Chinese ultimately had to bow to the prevailing wind, though they did so with the worst possible grace. But their protégé, the Panchen Lama, was also to make the journey, as were the god-king's two tutors, and three ministers. The Dalai Lama also took with him precise instructions from the Chinese about what to say and what not to say, and they were even naive enough to give him the speech he was supposed to deliver. A rattletrap of a car took him to the frontier, then came a horseback journey over the Nathu-la pass, a car to Siliguri, and a special plane from Bagdogra to New Delhi, where he landed on 25 November 1956. The whole trip came at an opportune moment, for he was later to admit that the rising tensions inside his country had put his back against the wall.

> The post of Dalai Lama which had ruled Tibet in happiness for centuries was becoming almost unbearable. In my dual capacity as spiritual and temporal guide, I was keen to oppose any sign of violence among the population. I knew that the Chinese would try to weaken my political authority. In rejecting the reflex towards violence among my people, I was helping the Chinese to destroy the trust they had in me. Yet if they no longer believed in their political leader, they must not lose faith in their spiritual guide, and that was what mattered more. I could delegate my political power, or even abdicate, but the Dalai Lama could never give up his spiritual authority, and I never considered doing so.
>
> So I was beginning to believe that it would be in the country's interest for me to withdraw from political activities, so as to keep my religious authority intact. But at the same time, as long as I was living in Tibet I could not escape from politics. To do that, I was going to have to leave my country, no matter how cruel and desperate an idea that seemed to me. It was just at that point of deep despair that an invitation reached me to visit India.[11]

The religious character of the journey was paramount for the Dalai Lama. He visited the places most sacred to the Buddhist faith, whose memory was to bring him strength through the trials to come. But politics, the inescapable prevented him from confining himself to the pilgrimage he had dreamt of ever since his solitary childhood in the Potala, and he opened his heart to Nehru on the subject. He also met Chou En-lai several times, informed him frankly about his people's grievances, and made four requests: the Chinese troops should leave; Tibet should revert to its status at the death of the Great Thirteenth Dalai Lama; the prime ministers dismissed by order of China should be reinstated; and the Communist programme of reforms abandoned.

Obviously Chou En-lai made no commitment on the basic issues, but he solemnly reiterated the guarantees of scrupulous respect for the 'seventeen-point agreement', and in particular pledged that nothing would be done by force. Armed with these assurances, and comforted by Nehru's possibly misconceived advice, the Dalai Lama decided to return to Tibet, in spite of the contrary advice of several personalities who would rather have seen him remain in India for the time being. But during his absence the situation had continued to deteriorate, and the Chinese authorities urged him to return to Lhasa without delay. He chose to go by way of Kalimpong, in response to an invitation there, and Tibetan officials who came to meet him briefed him on the uncertain, if not menacing, development of the situation on the high plateau.

> I had made up my mind to give the Chinese another chance to keep their government's promises, and to make another gesture, in the hope of recovering our freedom by peaceful means. I was tired of all this politics. All those meetings and discussions had occupied the greater part of my time in Delhi, and I had had to cut short my pilgrimage. I had come to loathe this talking, to the point that I would have considered withdrawing from all public affairs had it not been for my duty towards the Tibetan people. So I was happy to note that in Kalimpong as well as in Gangtok I nevertheless managed to find enough time to meditate and to give religious instruction to the people who came to see me there.[12]

It took barely two years to complete the story. In February 1957, Mao himself publicly admitted that Tibet was not ready to accept the Chinese reforms and decided on a six-year stay of grace. Some 'political cadres' were recalled from the high plateau, and troops left the capital in their wake. This came in apparent response to the wishes of the Tibetans. But the inhabitants of the eastern regions were not deceived, for they found themselves under the full lash of Han oppression; resistance fighters, refugees and monks from Kham and Amdo came flooding towards Lhasa, and the atmosphere grew thick with their stories of horror and violence. Their presence also increased the local food shortages, and hence the more and more palpable popular resentment of the occupying power. A number of guerrilla attacks angered the Chinese, who took a hard line in response. The outlook was threatening, and the Dalai Lama tried once again to slow down the momentum, even if he could not reverse it. Nehru was supposed to pay a visit to Lhasa at that time, but Beijing judged the situation to be too explosive to let the journey go ahead. The Chinese tried to change their tactics, wanting to force the Tibetan government itself to take action to suppress the sporadic outbreaks of rebellion. The government refused; already some missions of conciliation had failed to return, when the emissaries of peace decided to throw in their hands with the resistance.

The year 1958 was a series of outbursts of violence and immediate repressive retaliation, which boded nothing but harm for the future. Communications with Lhasa were being increasingly hampered by repeated attacks from guerrilla bands posted along the roads, too secure in their mountain retreats for the Chinese forces to dare to pursue them. On Tibet's eastern frontier the Chinese had established a kind of *cordon sanitaire* on their side, with heavy reinforcements both in troops and armaments. On the high plateau the temperature was rising, stoked by popular anger and discontent. As the pressures intensified on the Dalai Lama and the Tibetan administration, anxieties increased about the safety of the young ruler. An invitation to go to Beijing early in 1959 for a pan-Chinese conference further heightened these anxieties, but since the god-king was due to take certain religious examinations in January, the offer was politely declined on a plausible pretext.

Once these first tests had been completed, however, Beijing returned to the charge and were vehement in their insistence that the journey was an urgent necessity. This badgering only added to the vexation of the Tibetans, who suspected that the Chinese meant to lay hands on the Dalai Lama and hold him as a hostage, now that they might have begun to realise that he was the very foundation of his country's special character. In spite of repeated warnings from the few foreign nationals resident in Lhasa and Gyantse, and in towns close to the frontier such as Darjeeling and Kalimpong, New Delhi refused to pay attention to the disturbing rumours that trickled through from beyond the Himalayas. Early in March the curtain was ready to rise on the next act in the drama, which was played out in exactly eighteen days, until the Dalai Lama's escape into exile under cover of darkness.

On 1 March 1959 the Jokhang, the holy of holies, buzzed with the presence of thousands of monks and pilgrims. The occasion was the annual celebration of the Mönlam Chenmo, the Great Prayer for the welfare of all beings, and the final high point of the New Year festival. But it was also a vital moment for the Dalai Lama. In front of that great audience of lamas and monks he faced the prospect of sustaining a long didactic debate with contenders of the highest calibre, in order to achieve the title of doctor of metaphysics, the highest title bestowed by Mahayana Buddhism, and one which the very brightest and most learned of lamas may gain after 20 years of constant study. All his attention, strength and thought were focused on this goal, which was of cardinal importance both for himself and for his country's future; the stake was his badge of rank as the undisputed spiritual guide of a nation. And into these preparations, unannounced, walked two Chinese officers of low rank who wanted to speak to the Dalai Lama without delay. He listened most politely to their request, which was to set an exact date for his attendance at a theatrical performance organised by the general commanding the Chinese garrison, and then ushered them tactfully out, explaining that just now he had other considerations on his mind and that he would settle a date in ten days' time, once the ceremonies were over. Disgruntled but helpless, the two officers withdrew and went off to report to their chief.

The odd nature and crass timing of this incident, which bordered on outright provocation, set the Tibetan officials thinking and aroused their suspicions. On 5 March, the day of the traditional procession from the Potala to the Norbulingka, the winter to the summer palace, the Chinese were conspicuous for their absence, although in previous years they had always insisted on attending these solemn yet colourful rejoicings.

Two days later a call from the Chinese interpreter to the abbot representing the Dalai Lama in the kashag, and whose task it was to arrange his public appearances, set the date of 10 March for this famous invitation, which was now looking more and more suspect to the sovereign's entourage. Still no one breathed a word. The usual practice called for more protocol on such occasions, but apprehensions grew again when on the day before the visit the commander of the Dalai Lama's personal guard was summoned by the Chinese garrison commander to be informed that His Holiness should attend upon the general alone, and without his usual escort. If need be, two or three bodyguards would be tolerated, but on the express condition that they went unarmed.

It is hardly surprising that nobody thought well of these Chinese demands, which were all the more alarming in view of the fact that the Dalai Lama's visit was supposed to remain a secret. For lack of a better solution, and because he still had hopes of some notional understanding, the god-king told himself that after all it would be better not to make a fuss and to take whatever was coming. But he was reckoning without the Tibetans themselves. Thousands of pilgrims in Lhasa for the New Year festival had not yet left, and the refugees from the eastern provinces had nowhere to go in any case, so that there were probably about 100,000 people, an unprecedented number, in and around the capital.

So as not to arouse pointless fears, the Tibetan police gave out that on 10 March certain traffic restrictions would be applied on the other side of the Stone Bridge which marked the unofficial boundary between the Tibetan area and the Chinese camp. That was more than enough to set the rumour machine in motion and to raise the temperature by several degrees; everybody knew that the People's Assembly was due to meet in Beijing and that the Chinese authorities had been pressing the Dalai Lama to go there. It was a short and quickly-taken step from there to imagining that they intended to abduct the god-king. So at sunrise on 9 March the streets of

Lhasa were thronged with the presence of a nation on a verge of eruption, straining at the leash in its determination to protect what the people saw as their most precious possession. What they meant to do, at any cost, was to prevent the Dalai Lama from entering the Chinese camp.

To add to the general unease, it was not until late in the night of 9–10 March that two soldiers brought official invitations to the Norbu-lingka for a handful of senior Tibetan officials, together with a request that each of them should take only a single attendant. All these demands were completely at odds with normal practice, which the Chinese had more or less respected until now. Never before had the Dalai Lama been required to forgo the most basic courtesies due to his rank, or to travel without his entourage. The arguments and conjectures went on late into the night, in fact until the small hours of the morning of 10 March, when the Dalai Lama was supposed to report at the gate of the Chinese camp at noon, and enter it alone.

When I woke up that morning, I did not have the slightest idea of what the day was going to bring. I slept badly because of all those preoccupations. At five o'clock I got up as usual and went to the prayer room. Everything was perfectly harmonious, perfectly peaceful and familiar. The butter lamps burned in front of the altars, the little gold and silver bowls were filled with perfumed saffron water, like liquid gold, and the smell of incense floated in the air. I offered up prayers and meditated, then I went down and walked out into the garden, where I used to like to stroll in the early hours of dawn.

Absorbed at first in my concerns, I very soon forgot them in the beauty of that spring morning. The sky was cloudless and the rays of the sun were just touching the peak of the mountain beyond the monastery of Drepung in the distance, and were soon shining on the palace and chapels of the Jewel Park. With spring, everything was fresh and glad: the tufts of new grass, the fragile buds on the poplars and the willows. In the lake the lotus leaves were growing towards the surface to spread out in the sun . . . .

But here ended the last moment of peace that I was to know: suddenly shouts rang out over the wall of the park . . . . My colleagues told me that the inhabitants of Lhasa seemed to be

leaving the town and marching on the Norbu-lingka, shouting
that they were coming to protect me and to prevent the Chinese
from taking me off to their camp.[13]

What with the commotion, incidents, couriers, messengers
and comings and goings between the Chinese garrison and the
summer palace, the morning grew explosive. And towards
midday, under increasing pressure from the streets, the Dalai
Lama made it known that he had declined the Chinese
invitation.

> The tension of the general mood that morning had reached a level
> that I had never previously known during the brief duration of
> my rule over Tibetan affairs. I had the impression of finding
> myself between two volcanoes ready to erupt at any moment. On
> the one hand, and with one voice, my people protesting clearly
> and forcefully against the Chinese regime: on the other, the army
> of a strong and aggressive occupying power. In the event of a
> clash between the two, the outcome was a foregone conclusion;
> the inhabitants of Lhasa would be massacred in their thousands,
> and then the rest of the country would be subjected to total
> martial law, with all the persecution and the tyranny that it
> implied.
>   The primary cause of this situation revolved around the
> question of deciding whether or not I should go to visit the
> Chinese camp. But at the same time I was the only possible
> mediator, and I knew that for the good of my own people I must
> try at all costs to quell the people's anger and to placate the
> Chinese, whose mood must certainly be growing blacker still.[14]

An afternoon of bargaining ensued, while the unrest became
agitation in the streets of Lhasa, and then turned to open
rebellion. Whether through clumsiness or by deliberate intention, the attitude of the Chinese authorities only inflamed the
situation during the days that followed, with a series of more
and more rude and threatening messages. Ngawang Jigme
Ngabo was a Tibetan nobleman who seemed practically to
have gone over to the Chinese in the course of the previous
months, but he removed any remaining doubts about his
ambiguous role when he wrote to the Dalai Lama on 16

March: 'If Your Holiness, together with a few loyal officers of the guard, can hold a position in the interior enclosure and make it accurately known to the General, the Chinese will undoubtedly do all they can to see that the building is not damaged.' This was as good as admitting that the occupying power had well and truly decided to bring the rising rebellion to a bloody end.

In fact some considerable Chinese reinforcements were arriving in Lhasa – mountain artillery, heavy machine-guns, and dozens and dozens of trucks crammed with soldiers and weapons. Conspicuous preparations were being made, as if to intimidate the Tibetans by demonstrating that the very first target would be nothing less than the Norbu-lingka, which was surrounded by a crowd which, although poorly armed, was determined not to let the enemy pass. A feverish exchange of letters went on, with growing difficulty, between the summer palace and the Chinese camp, through the devious medium of Ngabo. On the afternoon of 17 March two mortar shells landed in a pond inside the grounds, close to the northern gate of the Norbu-lingka. The time for doubts was over, the warning was clear, and for the Dalai Lama it was the hour of truth.

Inside the palace, everybody felt that the end was coming and that something had to be done at once, but no one knew what. It was up to me to find the answer and then to take a decision. But in view of my lack of experience of worldly affairs, it was no easy matter.

I am not afraid of death. I did not fear being one of the victims of the Chinese attack. I sincerely believe that my very thorough religious training gave me strength enough to confront the idea of leaving my present body without any apprehension. I felt then, as I still do today, that I am only a mortal being and the instrument of my Master's immortal spirit, and that the end of one mortal envelope is of no great consequence. On the other hand I knew that my people and the officials in my government could not share these feelings, for in their eyes the person of the Dalai Lama remained a most precious thing. They considered that the Dalai Lama represents Tibet and its way of life – some-

thing more dear to their heart than anything else. If my body
should happen to perish in the hands of the Chinese, the life of
Tibet too would reach its end . . . .

Everything was in the realm of the uncertain, except the
concern of a whole nation for me to leave before the destructive
orgy of the Chinese should begin. And that was the sole positive indication that I had in my possession, to make up my
mind. By staying I would further increase the distress of my
people and my closest friends. So I took the decision to leave. I
need not say that I prayed to be given inspiration. And that I
received it.[15]

In the space of a few hours an escape plan was devised, set in
motion in the utmost secrecy, and brilliantly carried out.
The departure time was set for 10 o'clock at night.

When everything was ready I went to the Mahakala chapel, as
was customary before embarking on a long journey. Monks
were praying there; they did not cease their prayers, and had no
idea what was happening. Before the altar, I laid a scarf by way
of saying farewell . . . .

A soldier's uniform and a fur hat had been found for me,
and about 9.30 that night I took off my monk's habit and put
them on. Then, wearing those unusual clothes, I went to my
prayer room for the last time. I sat on the throne and opened
the book of Buddha's teachings which lay in front of me. I
read it until I came to a passage where Buddha advises his
disciples to be brave. Then I shut the book, blessed the room
and put out the lights. As I went out, my mind was empty
of all emotion; I was aware of the sound of my footsteps on
the beaten earth and the tick of the clock in the silence. A
single guard was waiting for me at the inside door of my
residence, and another at the outer door. One of them gave
me a gun which I slung over my shoulder, so completing my
disguise . . . .

Only once before in my life had I passed through the gates of
the Norbu-lingka without ceremony, and that was nine years
previously, when I had been taken to Yatung. In the darkness I
could vaguely make out groups of Tibetans who were watching
all the exits, but no one noticed a simple soldier, or stood in his
way. So I set out along the darkness of the path.[16]

A wary escort of Khampa resistance fighters accompanied
the Dalai Lama on a long and arduous forced march, often
travelling by night and in particularly tough conditions. In
spite of fears of possible pursuit, and aware of the bad news,
picked up on a small field radio and then confirmed by
courier, of the bombardment of Lhasa and the massacre of
thousands of the population, with occasional alarms and in the
teeth of an implacable climate, on 30 March the caravan
reached Indian territory by way of Chuthangmo, on the
Assamese frontier. The exodus of thousands of Tibetans
began soon afterwards.

From that moment on, two Tibets have coexisted in space
and have communicated by means of a capillary system so
subtle that it is often unseen. In the beauty of its magnificent
geographical setting, the physical Tibet has withdrawn into
itself, nursing its deep wounds and prepared to wait out a
fraction of the infinity of time. The other Tibet, the world of
the refugees and exiles, is smaller and tragically deprived,
clinging on, at first simply to survive, and then to live again. It
has closed ranks around its unshakeable faith, cohered around
its masters, adapted to a hard existence in frequently adverse
circumstances, and finds itself reconstituted in the mirror of
the Buddhist monk Tentzin Gyatso, the supreme guarantee of
the everlasting nature of the land of Tibet. When he left the
Norbu-lingka in the deep of night, disguised by utmost irony
as a soldier, the Precious Protector in his new incarnation was
only 24 years old.

4

Next Year in Lhasa

> The finest feeling in the world is the sense of mystery. He who
> has never known this feeling, his eyes are closed.
>
> (*Einstein*)

The highway runs towards Lhasa. Once again the Sheg-la
Pass spreads the spell of its far blue mountains and their
sparkling, eternally snow-capped peaks. The stony fields are
dotted with sheepfolds, tents display the invisible presence of
nomads, and flocks graze peacefully. In the silence and beauty
of the scene there is a sense of flow and lightness, of complicity regained with a familiar world. When the road becomes
asphalt-covered the traveller has only sixty miles to go to
Lhasa, and the mind teems with sensations and impressions.
Why this return to the city of the gods?

It was Bodh Gaya that gave me the answer – another place,
another mirror, another encounter. Nine thousand Tibetan
monks had gathered there from all the monasteries dotted
around India and Nepal, haphazardly rebuilt according to the
circumstances of a long-continuing exile. Down from the
high valleys of Himachal Pradesh with their evocative names
– Spiti, Kulu, Manili – from Zanskar and Mustang, Manang
and Dolpo in Nepal, but also from the distant slopes of
Arunachal Pradesh, still closed to foreigners, and from the
wooded hills and mountains of Bhutan, truckloads of pilgrims converging. Dharamsala, the little hill town where the
Dalai Lama usually resides, had migrated en masse to the

torrid, sacred plain – men, women and children, young and old, lamas and laypeople, tradesmen and beggars.

The most moving sight was certainly the strapping figures clad in grimy sheepskins and dusty boots, with their thick, tangled hair, running with sweat – the Tibetans who had made their way down from the vast and wind-swept trans-Himalayan plateau in the hope of receiving the blessing of their spiritual leader. In their amazement at the unknown world they found, they could hardly believe their own eyes, and kept laughing out loud as if to express their palpable joy at being there, after crossing so many barriers in their crazy venture. And among all those thousands of pilgrims was one friend last seen not long before in Lhasa, who had kept his appointment despite the obstacles in between, in the midst of that teeming crowd, and on the day agreed; it was as if a magic thread was tied, as if that further material proof had come to confirm this extraordinary meeting in front of the squat bulk and powerful presence of the little monastery of Nechung on the outskirts of the sacred town.

Lhasa once again. An unexpected return to the Land of Snows by the caravan route, leaving Katmandu to travel through legendary passes, above all crossing the once hermetically-sealed frontier from Kodari to Khasa, on either side of the Bhotekosi, the forbidden line of demarcation. It was the same line which, years before, had remained closed to our unfulfilled longing at least to set foot on Tibetan soil. On that day, plunged in their thoughts, three lamas contemplated that incongruous but still impenetrable divide, and the silent weight of their nostalgia turned to stone at our feet.

Long gone are the days of the caravans that once strung out along the traditional paths, to the measured tread of ponies, yaks and kiangs, and yet still there is a taste of adventure about travelling to the holy city from the capital of Nepal. For crossing those massive mountain ramparts to discover the indomitable solitude of the high Tibetan plateau somehow comes close to the unacknowledged and perhaps impossible dream of going beyond the horizon. There is a fascination about that obverse side of the scenery, the northern slope of Everest – a touch of unreality. Crossing the Himalayas by road may feel, from time to time, like going through the looking glass if only in the climb towards the Thong-la and over the pass at an altitude of 5,500 metres. The wind catches the mass of prayer flags covering the sacred cairn, and sets them dancing; the air is blue and sharp; the ring of high peaks challenges sky and space. In the resounding silence a string of fifteen yaks comes wading through the snow and the cara-vaneers stare at us in a bewilderment which is equalled only by our own. There is a physical, irrefutable, intoxicating sense of having arrived, of truly standing on the Roof of the World.

In this mineral wasteland painted in sumptuous colours, encounters are surprising for their rarity. Somewhere in the distance a lone horseman appears out of nowhere and rides on towards an unidentifiable goal. Two dark red shapes wander across our field of vision – two monks, one young, one old, returning from a pious pilgrimage to Mount Kailas and the sacred lake of Manasarowar. They will keep on walking for months, first to Shigatse, stopping at Tashi Lumpo, then on to Lhasa and its great monasteries, before setting out along the long road that leads to their own lamasery in distant Amdo. Shepherds muffled in their full-length greatcoats lead seething flocks of sheep and goats towards folds sheltered from the wind by breaks and niches in the ground, while little caravans of yaks link invisible villages along their path. Now and then, whirlwinds of dust hurry past, making shadows quiver over the bare rocks – the legends say that these are spirits and divinities, still riding into battle for the conquest of souls, men and the world. Visions play among the gusts of wind. In these seemingly endless expanses of a silence woven in eternity, the mind has room to take flight and stretch towards its own infinity.

Through having dreamt of it so often, and travelled it so often in search of the small white pebbles sown by the chosen few who have reached Lhasa and by those who never gave up the struggle to arrive, this trail of dreams, silence and adventure quietly unwound before us, at once familiar and astonishing to both sight and mind. Above all there was the light, a constant wonder, its brilliant transparency launching mountains and glaciers vividly into the vastness of the sky. Near the sun that flashes off millions of fractured surfaces on the naked rocks, the power of the world seems to gather and concentrate like a gigantic flux of purifying energy.

Here, at these empty altitudes, this wasteland bleak for men and beasts alike, the ascetic comes as an essential fact of life; the challenge requires that kind of stature, that stone or diamond hardness. Walk on without a halt, or petrify; the choices are either, somehow, to call oneself in question, or to dissolve. Keep walking, for winter, snow and wind will finally catch the wanderer, and many are the stories which tell about the luckless merchant and his yaks caught in the tempest and turned into statues of ice before the wind comes to scatter their bones. But no such spectres haunt our sunlit path. Only a red fox lopes above the scree, and the bells of a cheerful herd of long-haired goats announce the presence of a nearby hamlet.

It is cold in Shegar, more than 4,000 metres above sea level, in spite of a sun that scatters so many shimmering colours that a peacock might almost be ashamed to spread its tail. Board and lodging are equally sparse, and only the amused curiosity of the Tibetans effaces the carping sullenness of the Chinese watchdog-hosts. Rhythmic songs rise from the small courtyards where people are hard at work binding the newly harvested straw, prayer flags decorate the roofs, and children in warm clothes open at the chest trail after us laughing and offer to guide us to the half-reconstructed *gompa*. On the highest hill, on a steep and rocky slope, stand the ruined remains of the former monastic fortress. Crumbling footpaths wind among the debris of the cells, and broken rocks mark the site of devastated, violated emplacements. Ganden rises again in the memory of the previous year, Ganden the mutilated vision of a vanished picture. Here, too, the invader has respected nothing, and the old lama who welcomes us into his tiny, meticulously rebuilt sanctuary smiles with that immemorial and comforting indestructibility which seals the enduring quality of Buddhism. His eyes gleam with mischief, and he is perfectly well able to make himself understood as he keeps repeating 'Gyalwa Rimpoche' in a tone that brooks no denial, the tone of all Tibetans as they ask a passing foreigner for a photograph of the ever-present exile of the high country, the Dalai Lama.

It is the very same gently imperative demand that recurs in the eyes that met mine in Bodh Gaya late in December 1985, when images and sensations were telescoped together for me – or was it in me? The old man with a faltering tread, telling his beads and devotedly exerting himself to perform the ritual walk around the great stupa – could I have seen him elsewhere, high above, the other time? The dusty barrenness of the Indian village made me all the more thirsty for the memory of that blue transparency of the high plateau, and watchful for that halted time that dazzles me with light. Dissimilar as they are, the landscapes overlap and connect; they melt into the whirl of colours; and it is as if a laugh rings out, or bursts out, as if all at once I knew with certainty that it is possible to be both here and there. The magic of words, or the infinity of the quest.

The next day, as always, is another day, a stony road that branches off to thread into a valley that widens before it runs into the massive pearl-grey and wine-coloured silhouette, edged with black and white, of the strange monastery of Sakya. Strange because it has been rebuilt in front of the village, whereas ruins, piles of rocks, the vivid white of a reconstructed *chorten* and a long section of crenellated wall testify to its powerful presence formerly displayed at the foot of the nearby mountain. Strange, too, because of the unaccustomed commotion created this morning by the hundreds of pilgrims arriving out of nowhere to greet the brief visit of a teenage boy, the reincarnation of a dead great master, usually to be found studying at a monastic school in Sikkim, across the Indian border. How did they know he would be there? It was astounding to see that eager yet silent crowd clustered around the young monk duly escorted by his lama and jostling each other to touch him and receive his blessing. On the day before our departure from Katmandu, we too had been blessed by the venerated master Sakya Trizin Rimpoche, likewise exiled in India and passing through Bodnath to consecrate a new monastery.

Now we rejoin the main highway that winds its dusty, unassuming way towards Shigatse, aiming for the gilded rooftops of Tashi Lumpo, that faraway landmark gleaming like a handful of gold nuggets among the mountains. The small city is barely changed since last year, but today it has been invaded by pilgrims, and the shrines are crammed with humble offerings and thick with clouds of incense. Here, too, longing hands reach out with the same familiar murmur, 'Gyalwa Rimpoche', the open sesame that calls to people's hearts and brings out smiles on unknown but suddenly friendly faces. Tens and hundreds of rugged tents have sprung up around the city. Occasional lorries are parked by the side of makeshift encampments, and at dusk the braziers glow and the smell of *tsampa* – the roasted barley which is the staple food of most Tibetans – wafts through the town. There is great excitement at the monastery, besieged by successive waves of visitors, whole families, even villages. They are guided by lamas and novices who have accompanied them from the distant reaches of a vast country that still hovers between legend and reality.

But daily life returns at a gallop, particularly at the summer palace of the Panchen Lama, the second highest dignitary in the hierarchy of Tibetan Buddhism, whose present existence resembles a cruel précis of his people's tribulations. Alternately the puppet and the Trojan horse of the Chinese state, he has failed to satisfy its expectations, and has therefore suffered the worst kind of treatment reserved by the Beijing authorities for those whom they label renegades or traitors. A long absence in a 're-education camp' has caused him to break, but not to bend. When it has suited them, the masters of the Forbidden City have thrust him on to centre stage – as a hostage, to be sure, but perhaps not altogether taken in. As a forced resident of Beijing, kept under constant surveillance, he cannot come or go as he pleases in his own country, and has even found himself obliged to make a visit to Australia as an ordinary member of a Chinese delegation. In the absence of the Dalai Lama he nevertheless retains an appreciable status on the high plateau, and he happened to be visiting his town for several days late that autumn, while we had come there eager to pick up the threads of our previous journey.

The palace courtyard was crowded – young and old, men and women, wearing *khatas*, white ceremonial scarves, stood about in small groups while the endless queue for the audience room kept growing. Quite obviously not everybody was being allowed to go in, and suddenly a commotion broke out. Orders were given, the crowd was broken up, and a big jeep screeched to a halt in a cloud of dust beside a jibdoor, then shot away again, giving just time enough to glimpse the shaven head of the Panchen Lama, dressed in dark red and framed on all sides by half a dozen little men in green with red stars on their caps. In the hazy radiance of the setting sun a wave of silent disappointment ran through the throng, and a shiver stiffened my back.

The landmarks along the way from Shigatse to Lhasa restored the enchantment of the first journey. This time it was not discovery, but the proof that I had not dreamed Tibet. The clarity of light sculpted the mountains and the ferry still wheezed to and fro across the Tsang-po, except that this time there was not a single army lorry on the opposite bank, only yaks, a horde of yaks, a drove or caravan, looking from a distance like a swarm of big black insects lying across the dusty road. As the ferry approached they took on the appearance of a restless woollen carpet. Countless bundles were piled along the verge, and a few bolder animals ventured on to the bank of the river to quench their thirst. Now it was becoming possible to make out the faces of the drovers. Children sprang up from behind the bundles, and burst into uncontrollable gusts of laughter at the sight of us. Slightly above this moving jumble of men and beasts, outlined against the stone, was a figure dressed in a thick high-waisted jacket, with a green and red scarf tucked in around the neck, superb felt boots and a hat of bright red fox fur. With a sword stuck into his belt at a jaunty angle, and his eyes trained on the far horizon, he waited. He seemed to have arrived from a bygone country, the land of the gentleman-brigands.

In the space of a year, Lhasa had changed, or rather 'they' had changed Lhasa. In preparation for the twentieth anniversary of the official proclamation of the so-called Autonomous Region of Tibet, the Chinese authorities had gone all-out to 'clean up' the town and to give it a presentable face – in other words to Sinicise the place as much as possible and to obliterate its one true face, the only one that Tibetans would acknowledge. From the very outskirts of the suburbs, the immediate view of the Potala was marred by the incongruous metal mast of a television station stuck on to the side of Chokpuri Hill, where once the famous monastery and school of medicine had stood. Mere gratuitous insolence at first sight, yet how revealing.

A broad avenue had been cut in front of the Jokhang, the holy of holies of the sacred city, which was now flanked by an open square bordered by 'friendship shops'. Outside the temple stand two great whitewashed incense-burners, taller than a man, with smoke continually rising. Here pilgrims, customers and tradesmen rubbed shoulders, relaxed and peacefully conversed. Last year it was still a gaping building site, and today, behind this new *trompe-l'oeil* exterior, in winding, pot-holed alleyways and lop-sided inner court-yards, the heart of the old Lhasa goes on beating. And the hearts of Tibetans beat hard, they quicken, in the Jokhang.

More than the first time, the crowd here is multifarious, innumerable and contemplative; the queue winds in tight rings from the outer square to the threshold smoking with the acrid smell of yak's butter laid in front of the statues as an offering. To my surprise a new effigy of Chenrezig with his eleven heads and a thousand arms, the protector of Tibet, has resumed its place between Padma, the master magician, and Sakyamuni, the king's son who became the historical

Buddha. A year ago his place was empty – the original statue, hundreds of years old, had been destroyed by the rage of the Red Guards. A constant stream of pilgrims files past in the hushed murmur of the revived traditional litany and bows low before all shapes and sizes of photographs of their exiled spiritual leader. His ubiquitous smiling presence is still more visible and more tranquilly sovereign and protective than it was last year. No matter how you approach Tibet, whether by straight or roundabout paths, the outline of this monk among monks weaves itself into the fabric of the encounter, and eventually becomes an inseparable companion.

Another round of this strange game of snakes and ladders in the city of the gods takes me from a shop crammed with tinkling jewellery and soft textiles to a steep and flowery stairway leading to the Anzi-gompa, the only women's convent still open in Lhasa. Wrinkled as an apple stored in the attic and forgotten, the abbess in her grey robe and thick shoes could not get over the sight of our sudden appearance in her little courtyard. She abandoned her flock of young novices – about a dozen of them had been given permission a few months previously to try out this hard convent life – gathered around the cooking pot bubbling in the fireplace, and opened the worm-eaten door to the shrine. Stripped of its former riches, it was modestly lit by butter lamps at the foot of the altar where sat a statue of the Buddha meditating. In his cupped hands a yellowing, dog-eared photograph had the place of honour; again, as always, the absent leader.

And it was the same story at Palalumpo-gompa. Since the previous year his image had multiplied over the central altar and sculpted walls; it stood out in the light, and hid in the darkness of recesses in the rocky walls. He had won, for now he gave the 'V' for victory in the teeth of every visitor, including the Chinese. He is also in Nechung, watching with a mocking eye over the reliquary which enshrines the effigy of the oracle in full divinatory dress. But the chosen interme-diary has now shed his temporary envelope of flesh, and the link is perhaps hard to re-establish so far away, beyond the

Himalayas. Yet he floats in the bare and ravaged meditation cell, like a watchful presence, and the monk beside me peers into one dark corner with a puzzled expression. A bell rings three times.

A little higher up, standing with its back to the strong wall of tortured rock, Drepung hums with strolling knots of pilgrims, clinks with the noise of coins dropped gladly into offering bowls, and echoes with the litany chanted by the queuing faithful, with the laughter of wide-eyed children, the yapping of a dog roused from its afternoon nap, and the sound of water boiling to make the monks' tea. Tirelessly, the Tibetans are walking the footpaths of their regained ancestral devotion, with a contagious reverence. At the four corners of the town they have pitched their tents, and tethered their yaks and ponies, alongside the open lorries and the braziers kept constantly lit for those moments of rest and continued conversation.

They walk about, as if to revive a lost habit, in search of a memory which the occupying power has attempted to erase, keen to heal the wounded stones and scarred frescoes saved from being soiled by the strident revolutionary graffiti which had disfigured them for a while. In the chapels and caves converted into altar places, the statues practically disappear under the heap of ceremonial scarves, the butter dishes are full to overflowing with offerings, the candles exhale waves of their acrid, heady odour, and hundreds of little dancing flames keep flickering. Quietly and patiently, with slow steps and infinite determination, the pilgrims walk on. Children's heads protrude from the inside pockets of the adults' sheepskin coats, and already their lips murmur the haunting prayer of time out of mind, the litany of yesterday, today and tomorrow ... the eternal new beginning.

In this game of hide-and-seek, Tentzin Gyatso is the winner on every count. He inhabits Tibet as no Dalai Lama before him could have succeeded in doing. As he himself has said, by their ruthless oppression of the Tibetan people the Chinese have made him the most popular of Dalai Lamas. Through being absent from his land for so many years, by the continuance of the long exile that began in 1959, he has become an indefinable presence, at once everywhere and nowhere, a furtive recognition signal and a pledge of victory, a password and a seal of lasting continuity. Up there on the high trans-Himalayan plateau, saturated in space, on the dizzy edge of the unfathomable, he paces through its length and breadth, and his bright laugh rings in every shrine and hamlet. In reply to what some call memory or longing, sometimes perhaps we should simply say fidelity.

'One night I reached Gyantse at last', Alexandra David-Neel noted laconically, at the end of her stay in Lhasa and her hazardous wanderings across the high country. Would that traveller in a different age recognise 'the third town in Tibet, by order of importance, situated on the main highway from India to Lhasa'? Nothing could be less certain, considering how that industrious city has come to seem no more than the shadow of its own memory. Turned in upon itself, as if isolated or forgotten by the rest of the world, it is like a sleeping castle waiting in secret, within even knowing it, to be released from a binding spell.

Of the monastic buildings that once were the central axis of the town's existence, nothing remains but two temples next to the imposing mass of the stupa that rises in tiers at the foot of the hill. Pilgrims who have just climbed out of the back of an old truck head straight towards it, telling their beads as they go, while a lama sets about refreshing the faded colours of a fresco. A faint light, kept going by the meagre flames of butter lamps, makes it just possible, in the gloom of the shrines, to distinguish religious paintings once famous for their mastery.

It would be good to stay and compare my notes with the present reality, to seek out the shadowy corners of the old monastery, climb up through the ruins and look out across the plain that stretches out of sight; but once again we are compelled to stick to the itinerary, which only allows for a stop in Shigatse. Might this be a way of learning to resolve antagonisms and establish the conjuncture of opposites?

Inscrutably sitting on the threshold of a cell, a cat keeps its eyes closed on its inner dream.

Time and space fly here, they twine and untwine on this roof of the world – the place where so many hopes and longings converge that in the end they take substance and materialise, to become a tangible reality elsewhere, under a different sky. The thousand and one pathways of the quest all lead to Bodh Gaya, at the hour of the Kalachakra, the tantric initiation of the Wheel of Time. From Amdo and from Kham, from the unknown limits of the Tibetan world, from secret valleys and grassy steppes, from Koko Nor to Manasarowar, and from sacred lakes to revered mountain peaks, invisible paths signposted by their immemorial use have etched themselves into the needs of men, as constantly as those needs are renewed. Thus, almost by instinct, they follow a dream the colour of eternity, at the moving confluence of an ancient wisdom and a new knowledge.

Land of Snows, land of the gods – at these altitudes, wise men have opened footpaths around the borders of the invisible, and at the far reaches of the territories of gods and men. Some have crossed the awesome frontier – and have returned to show their fellow men that the journey could be done. Through study, personal discipline, research, self-command and knowledge, they perpetuate the unbroken tradition of the lineages of masters of wisdom. As holders of the keys of knowledge, they make no mystery of it, and no display, and to anyone who will listen they offer the password to the beginning of the journey. But the feet still have to walk. There is no secret; the source has not dried up for those who can see it, sense it and set out to discover it, even though many obstacles lie in between. Sentinels stand here and there along the path that every wayfarer has to travel alone.

As the home of the gods and refuge of visionaries, perhaps when all is said and done the Land of Snows is no more than a facet of that myriad of infinities, worlds and dreams that all human beings carry inside themselves. In crossing the threshold of legend, and in walking straight through the looking glass, sometimes the horizon thus glimpsed assumes the indefinable overtones of a homecoming after a long, protracted absence, accompanied by a peal of laughter for liberty regained. It is also the meeting with a peerless figure. Buddhist monk or god-king. With and around and through him, all roads lead to Lhasa.

5

A Day in the Life of the Dalai Lama

To think is easy, to act is hard, but to act according to one's thinking is the hardest thing in the world.

(*Leonardo da Vinci*)

A day in the life of the Dalai Lama? According to Tentzin Gyatso, nothing could be simpler or more commonplace. A day in the life of a monk, like thousands of others in the lives of other monks, like those which have preceded it and identical to all those that will follow it. A daily discipline which nevertheless is not routine, because freely accepted it is the foundation of a way of being.

Usually the Dalai Lama gets up early, at about 4.30 am. He often rises sooner than the sun, which is slower to appear when winter holds the Himalayan mountains in its cold and silence. Sometimes Dharamsala wakes in a fog of snow, or else in the glorious autumn bloom of a cold sun. But high on the spur where the Dalai Lama, the Wise Man, lives, the day has already dawned.

With the passage of the years Dharamsala has become the rallying point of Tibetans abroad, and of adventurers risking every hazard too, and Tibet is there, close by, on the other side of the mountain – the other slope, which is also suddenly another world. And it is not for nothing that in the great new temple the new statue of Chenrezig, the All-Powerful Protector, has its eyes turned in that direction too. Since the Dalai

Lama has taken up residence there, the little town which had been slowly dying, once a favourite resort of the servants of the British Raj for the coolness of its climate after the heat of the sun-drenched plains, has taken on a new, unhoped-for life. It lives again, after its years of neglect; in the quarter of a century since part of it was put at the disposal of refugees from Tibet in 1960, it has been transformed and now wears a pleasantly Tibetan air. A year spent at Mussoorie early in his exile decided the Dalai Lama and his close collaborators to find a more spacious location, where settlement would be less awkward both for the local population and the newcomers. It was essential to avoid unnecessary friction, particularly when problems of survival of an altogether more urgent kind had to take precedence over everything else.

Lying in the far north of what was then the Punjab, Dharamsala first made its appearance on the scene of the British Raj in the middle of the last century; in those days the British made it the summer cantonment of a division of the Indian Army. Helped by a certain amount of snobbery, by the turn of the century the garrison had attracted a composite micro-society made up of a subtle blend of ingredients known only to the British. Around Mun Peak, the central axis of that existence, the little town of McLeod Ganj had spread leisurely outwards over the neighbouring slopes.

Contemporary descriptions conjure up a half wild scene which must have had its charms; the forests teemed with leopards, panthers, jackals, foxes, porcupines and various monkeys, and sometimes it happened that black or brown bears driven down from the Himalayas in periods of extreme cold would venture into the district. The changing seasons and the summer fillip of the monsoon transmuted the land-scape into a painter's palette, with a wonderful variety of wild flowers. But in 1905 the whole scene was spoiled by an earthquake which panicked the official worthies from Delhi and Lahore into a disorderly retreat that took them first to Lower Dharamsala, a little further down, and eventually south-eastward to new quarters in Simla, gradually deserting their old summer haunt.

Indian independence almost finished off the place, which had turned into a ghost-village in the midst of rustling woodlands, much to the despair of a Parsee family, the Nowrojees, which had lived there for several generations and had been trying, without much success, to revive the locality. When he heard about the government search for a place of refuge for the Tibetan exiles, the good Parsee, tethered to his general store, sent a missive to New Delhi. He was surprised when he saw a commission of inquiry arrive, and astonished to learn that his suggestion had been accepted. There was no castle, but the Sleeping Beauty must have lain somewhere in the vicinity.

After a careful examination of the possibilities the Tibetans agreed to Nehru's proposal, though they did ponder on the distance from the Indian capital and the isolation of the site. In heading for that refuge, perhaps the Dalai Lama recalled a Chinese proverb, which he himself puts into the mouth of a close colleague of Chou En-lai, and which was directed at himself: 'As long as it stays among the mountains, the snow leopard keeps all of its dignity, but if it descends towards the plains, it is treated like a dog.'

The fact is that there was little rejoicing when the move was made in April 1960, despite the touchingly friendly and considerate welcome given to the Tibetan refugees, both by the inhabitants and by the local authorities. The Tibetans had done their best; impoverished as they were, what more could they do? Above all they suffered from having to see the sovereign for whom nothing had been too fine, stripped of his former splendours. On the other hand, he himself seems to have taken to the changed order of things with the greatest ease, and he took every opportunity to comfort his people.

And yet. The choice of Dharamsala does awake some curious echoes, and give rise to occasionally surprising coincidences. The valley of Kangra is known in Himachal Pradesh and throughout the whole of India as the valley of the gods. Ever since the earliest times recorded in the long memory of India, legends and myths have linked and intertwined there to the point of weaving a filmy but sturdy

fabric, negligently draped over the appearances of ordinary
reality.

   In the immediate area of Thekchen Chöling, where the
Fourteenth Dalai Lama lives today, there are many caves
whose atmosphere is charged with vibrations from the past;
great yogis lived inside them for years, sunk in deepest
meditation, before their practices of wisdom were taken up
and faithfully transmitted from one disciple to another, on to
the high plains of the Land of Snows. To this day there are
adepts of the mysteries of the Way who spend months here,
deep in the pursuit of high achievements, just next door to the
world of men. In Dharamsala these meditators are held in the
highest esteem, and many are the pilgrims who quietly walk
these groves and shady footpaths hoping for the merest
glimpse of them. For these sages are said to be gifted with
powers, and man is always receptive or curious about the
strangeness that lurks outside his gates. It is true that the
beneficent calm of these wooded hills brings absorbing states
of reverie and seems to engender contemplation.

   About ninety miles away from Dharamsala, though more
than eight hours' drive along a winding bumpy road, at
Rewalsar, is a beautiful lake that Tibetans call the Lotus Lake –
Tso Pema – sacred in their eyes, and equally revered by the
Sikhs and Hindus. Buddhists venerate it because according to
tradition it has a link with the Precious Master, Padmasambh-
hava, who once lent his wisdom to strengthening the Teaching in the high country. The legend tells how the king of
Mandi, the nearby city, was displeased by the sight of his
beloved daughter paying attention to the wise man's teachings, and so gave orders for him to be taken and burned alive.
The moment the pyre was lit, instead of flames it was a lake
that sprang out, and there in the middle sat the Precious
Master, smiling, on a lotus flower. So it is not surprising that
the lake has become a place of pilgrimage, with little Buddhist
monasteries nestling around it. In the courtyard of one of
these shrines a notice on a tree with delicate flowers bears the
inscription: 'Commemoration of Buddha in Rewalsar 1957.
Planted on 5 of January 1957 by the Dalai Lama of Tibet, at

the request of Rajah Bajrang-Bhadur Sing Bhadri, Vice-Governor of Himachal Pradesh'. That was at the time of the celebrations for the twenty-fifth century of the Buddha. Did the young sovereign of the Land of Snows know then that a few years later he would return to the region to embark upon years of exile?

At all events, in 1960 the former bungalow of the district commissioner, buried in the encroaching forest and grandly renamed 'Swarg Ashram', or 'Heavenly Retreat' was repaired and renovated by the rather makeshift means available to receive the Dalai Lama and his immediate retinue. It was there that everything began again, at the mercy of circumstance and at the price of constant effort and a fierce determination to conquer adversity. For the exiled sovereign there was no question of any outcome but to survive and live again, and to win the harsh, unsparing battle for the perpetuity of the land of Tibet.

Some still remember an impression of deep sadness, and of helplessness tinged with the kind of rage that makes a tightness in the throat when there is no other solution in prospect but to clench one's teeth and make a stand. Then, as now, Dharamsala was far from the Land of Snows, and equally far from New Delhi and the centres of decision and communication, from the facilities of the modern world – even under the regained sovereignty of a country which had itself suffered centuries of foreign rule. It was these same precarious and sometimes almost unendurable conditions that enabled the family to find itself again, to restore the links strained by protocol and the demands of court ceremonial, and to lay the basis of the close collaboration essential for the future.

Those difficult years were the time of a hard-fought game which was vital to the very development and evolution of Tibet and its people, when the Dalai Lama was only a political refugee and a young man with no great experience of affairs of state. At the same time, those who had followed him represented a cheap labour force, even by the standards of a developing country. They were employed to open paths through the high mountains, build roads into remote valleys, cut lifelines towards villages lost in oblivion, to do the work that others refused to do. They died in their thousands, struck down by illnesses they did not know; thus tuberculosis wreaked havoc, and to this day it continues to afflict the escapees from the high plateau, guided solely by their wish for freedom and to find their spiritual leader once again.

By way of living space they were put up in hurried camps, temporary accommodation that tended to become permanent. The residence of the exiled spiritual leader was surrounded by barbed wire, and anyone approaching it had to produce official credentials, properly signed and sealed, and pass several checkpoints. But in those days, who really cared about the young monk, so rich with the wealth of his culture and so deprived of any concrete, real support?

The level of the living conditions in the 'Heavenly Retreat' verged on destitution, the extreme austerity of the place expressing both the newcomers' lack of means and the stated determination of Jawaharlal Nehru to tolerate no gesture which might provide the pretext for a Sino-Indian war. Those were still the days of Nehru's belief, or feigned belief, in the goodwill of People's China, when he was trying to persuade the Dalai Lama that with the proper negotiations it would be possible to arrive at a friendly understanding with Beijing. In the meantime, it was essential not to make waves.

The frontier quarrel and the brief war that resulted in 1962 between the two great Asiatic powers were to open the Indian prime minister's eyes, but his humbled pride never allowed Nehru to admit to his blunder, although that did not prevent his peers from publicly accusing him of cowardice and indecision. The situation was all the more embarrassing because, while it certainly poisoned the relations between India and China, it also had an unforeseen effect on public opinion, which saw the Dalai Lama as an avatar, the incarnation of a god of the Himalayas, the chosen abode of the divinities of Indian mythology. And not even Nehru could afford to ignore or dismiss that argument.

The fact remains that in the final analysis India has been

practically the only country to have shown real generosity towards these people driven out of hearth and home; given its own genuine difficulties, the Indian government could hardly have done more, as the Tibetans themselves, and most of all the Dalai Lama, are the first to acknowledge. At the same time, they had to act fast to recruit their strength and start again from scratch, in an unknown and sometimes even hostile environment, but with the will to succeed and remain in the adamantine brilliance of their enduring otherness.

Today Dharamsala is considered as the 'little Lhasa' of India. It may not be outwardly comparable with the city of the gods, but Tibetans will smile as they assure the willing listener that where the Dalai Lama lives, there is the Potala too. In this rebuilt but not reconstituted setting, the buildings that house the spiritual leader and his immediate retinue are perched on the crest of the mountain. The air is bracing there, and if the splendours of the Potala are no more than a memory, the atmosphere is warm and good-natured, and it welcomes passing strangers.

From this balcony seat above the Indian plain the spectator looks down on terraced paddy fields in the valley below and, when the morning mists scatter, patches of bright colour reflect a tropical exuberance. But in Dharamsala, at a height of almost 2,000 metres, the nearby peaks are dusted with snow in the early morning, the flowers bloom in shades of pastel, and in the crystal air the birdsong is overlaid by the deep summons of gongs, and the woodland paths fill with the purple outlines of the files of monks who chant the litany of dawn.

Traditional Tibet has serenely taken root in McLeod Ganj. At the centre of the community the Namgyalma stupa, built and consecrated in the traditional way, forms the link between past and present, in memory of the freedom-fighters who fell during the resistance against the invading Chinese and, further into the past, to the memory of Asoka, the great enlightened king of India who did so much for the propagation of the Buddhist Law.

Facing the Dalai Lama's residence, the temple of Tsuglag

Khang looks rather modest compared with the remembered magnificence of Lhasa. But, as in the city of the gods, it accommodates three statues – the Buddha Sakyamuni, Padmasambhava and Avalokitesvara. The new effigy of the Lord of Infinite Compassion contains two angry faces and one peaceful aspect from the original statue destroyed by the fury of the Red Guards, surreptitiously removed by the faithful from where they lay in a street in Lhasa, and smuggled out through Nepal to Dharamsala.

A little further down, at Gangchen Kyishong, a small square where meetings and public ceremonies are often held is framed by the main building of the government-in-exile's administrative services and by the Library of Tibetan Works and Archives. The latter displays the proud elegance of traditional Tibetan architecture, and its work of research, translation and publication is essential to the survival of the country's intellectual heritage. As for the Medical Institute, it serves several purposes; it is a clinic, a workshop for pounding and drying plants and minerals, a dispensary for preparing traditional medicaments, and a practical school and lecture room for students. Add to that an astrology room, because for Tibetan doctors the patient cannot be dissociated either from his earthly environment or from the influence of the stars.

Tibetan hospitality does not appear to have suffered any great harm by being transplanted from one side to another of the mountain barrier. And the locality seems to have been affected by the presence of this hard-working community which, despite its misfortunes, is borne up by a faith as solid as a rock. And once again it is the Dalai Lama who stands at the heart of this reaffirmed existence that grows stronger with every passing year.

Ten, hundreds, sometimes – for the great festivals – thousands of pilgrims and visitors climb the surrounding hills and fill the peaceful township with the colourful bustle of their comings and goings. The Lingkor, the long path of sacred pilgrimage that once encircled Lhasa, has been redrawn here and is followed with redoubled fervour by the faithful who pace it tirelessly, with their prayer-wheels in their hands, or who even drag themselves full-length along the ground, as they used to do around the city of the gods. Both monks and lay people offer the picture of a life of orderly calm, now that they have left behind the terrible sacrifices of the early years, when sickness and death decimated the refugees. It is a life illuminated by the tranquil assurance of Tentzin Gyatso. Here, perhaps more than anywhere else, his presence is incontestable and comforting, beneficial to all, and paramount in its discretion and simplicity.

The ordinary day at Dharamsala – for there are days which are out of the ordinary, on the occasion of great ceremonies or festivals, departure days for more or less distant journeys, special meetings, or prolonged religious retreats – begins with prayer. The ritual is observed with the utmost care, for at the moment when a new day begins it is essential to be ready to welcome or face up to it. Like any other Buddhist monk, the Dalai Lama devotes most of his early morning time to prayers offered to the divinities, or else to meditation – analytical, or concentrated on a single point, except when it is a contemplation of emptiness, which consists in a sense of making a space inside oneself and listening for what emerges. But other themes – death, for example – are just as important.

Tentzin Gyatso himself says that it is from these early moments of the day that he draws his strength, consolidates his ideas and glimpses the solutions to the many problems that beset him. Beyond doubt, these are also the rare and precious moments of real tranquillity, so necessary to the examination of his own actions and to the study of evolving plans. The Dalai Lama is inured to the process, and makes sure that the time is not wasted and that it is put to the best advantage every day.

Then comes a very important moment in the morning, breakfast time, which usually comes an hour or an hour and a half after rising. His diet is frugal. He himself says that the ideal answer would be to eat what the faithful give as offerings, alluding to what used to be the widespread custom in Tibet and is still the practice among the monks of South-East Asia and Korea, where they leave their monasteries individually or in Indian file early in the morning, bowl in hand, to beg for their food. But the Dalai Lama laughs as he admits that, given his position, the custom is a hard one to follow.

The sovereign makes do with very little – black tea prepared Tibetan style with shavings from compressed blocks of tea, with pancakes, toast or *tsampa*, the Tibetan staple food, made of barley flour either taken plain or mixed with a liquid. These meals are always light, alike in the morning, noon and evening. In any case the rule of the monastic code which the Dalai Lama respects to the best of his ability, requires monks to take nothing after midday except tea or clear soup. Like all Tibetans, in his early years the Dalai Lama was not a vegetarian – it is hardly a practical option on the high Himalayan plateau, when fruit and vegetables grow so sparsely during a brief cultivation season. In the early 1960s he nevertheless became a vegetarian out of personal choice, but found himself restricted in his diet by the fact that he could take neither milk nor dairy products, which Indians use in abundance to supplement their food when they give up meat. It took nothing less than an attack of severe hepatitis, the intervention of his personal doctor, the urgent insistence of his two tutors and the repeated advice of his close relations to persuade the Dalai Lama to vary his meals more, convinced as he was that he was better in tune with himself when he abstained from animal products.

Breakfast is also the most convenient time to make contact with the world of human affairs, which means listening to news reports, first on the BBC, and then supplemented by broadcasts from All India Radio and the Voice of America. For the temporal leader of the Tibetan people the radio is a practical and welcome invention which keeps him in touch with the world's political developments. If for some reason he is unable to listen, he misses the radio. Why the BBC?

For the concision and quality of the information. A daily survey detailed enough to give food for thought and to keep abreast of the main developments. That is essential when one is involved in studying political dossiers and weighing the pros and cons of decisions. And then, much as I would wish to do so, I have no time to read the newspapers with attention – there are so many! So I make do with the main headlines and a few comments in the international press, and occasionally spend some time on review articles pointed out by my colleagues. But you know, I have other things to do, so that I strive to keep to essentials.[17]

For all that, one thing is certain, that for a man who lives in relative isolation and who sometimes admits to being annoyed by the inanity of endless debates with too little practical outcome, the Dalai Lama could teach lessons of his own in political knowledge. He has the gift and technique of picking out the main issues at a glance, grasping their immediate relevance and discerning their possible lines of development, as well as of decoding the real meaning of words under their freight of rhetoric. To one woman journalist who asked him what, in his view, was the best way of winning an election, he gave the very deadpan answer: 'Think of a good slogan, make plenty of promises, then once in power, there can always be excuses for self-justification.' This sharpness of vision enables him to declare in all serenity:

> Sometimes one can look down on politics from above, and accuse it of being dirty. Yet on closer inspection, politics as such is not at fault. It is a tool in the service of human society. Well motivated, by sincerity and honesty, it becomes an instrument in the service of humanity. Yet motivated by selfishness and driven by hatred, envy and jealousy, it becomes dirty. And this applies equally to religion, by the way . . . . Everything depends upon our personal motivation. Money and power do not suffice to solve all problems. What lies inside the human heart is the first thing that has to be resolved; the rest, created by man, will then find their own solution quite naturally.[18]

The morning is mainly devoted to Tibetan affairs. The Dalai Lama always tries to glean as much time as possible for his own studies and his personal self-perfection and for his religious education with other masters. Nevertheless he is aware of the importance of his role as political leader, and keeps a very sharp eye on developments in the everyday secular life of his fellow countrymen. The social structures are forged in such a way in the Tibetan community, in spite of the upheavals caused by exile and enforced adaptation to the realities of the modern world, that no matter what happens the Dalai Lama remains the central focus and final recourse. In the most precise and noble sense of the words, he remains the ultimate Protector and the All-Knowing, and this is what partially accounts for the astonishing interdependence between the Tibetan people and their sovereign, joined in a collusion that goes far beyond the realm of words and fashions.

For a man not short on paradox – are not the true spiritual masters said to transcend all the antagonisms that catch other mortals in two minds? – it is quite natural that he himself should have proposed and executed reforms intended to modernise Tibetan society. Not only had he perceived their urgent necessity in the days when he still occupied the Potala, and put forward practical proposals which cut the ground from under the feet of the Chinese invaders, but one of his first aims in exile was to work out a new constitution for Tibet, which was approved as early as 1963. There is something comic, as well as revealing, about the fact that he had to convince his own supporters of the need to reduce the prerogatives of the Dalai Lama and grant greater freedom of choice and decision to the democratically elected representatives of the Tibetan people. Thus it was under his initiative that the right of suffrage was granted at 18 and the right to stand for election at 25 years of age, while a legislative assembly has met twice a year since 2 September 1960. Made up of elected members representing the three great provinces of Tibet, the four great schools of Tibetan Buddhism, and the native religion of Bon (pre-dating Buddhism, Bon has gradually adopted more and more features from the Teachings, and led an unsung unofficial existence on the high Tibetan plateau until the Han invasion), it has the power of control and supervision over the departments that form a kind of government in exile. A representative of the Dalai Lama attends the meetings.

In the same connection, during the interval between sittings a National Committee acts as liaison between the deputies, the members of the *kashag*, or cabinet, the ministers (called *kalons*) and the departmental secretaries. It falls to the Dalai Lama, who remains the guide of last resort, to appoint the *kalons*. This Committee also deals with the budget of the administration, which is divided into several sectors; the Council of Religious and Cultural Affairs, the Education Council, the Information Office, Security Office and Office of Economic Affairs, and the Departments of Health, Finance and Personnel. A special Council is responsible for the settlement and rehabilitation programmes for Tibetan refugees in India and the neighbouring countries. And a number of offices abroad – in Nepal, the United States, Switzerland, Great Britain and Japan – represent the Dalai Lama and provide the lifelines between distant communities and the heart in Dharamsala.

In order to maintain this modest administration so indispensable to the community, every Tibetan in India pays a tax of one rupee per month. Voluntary contributions are welcome and enable the administrators to extend their fields of action. A liaison officer of the Indian Foreign Ministry lives in permanent residence at Dharamsala, in close proximity to Thekchen Chöling, the home of the most illustrious of the Tibetan refugees, and is the effective channel of communication between New Delhi and the township high in the hills of Himachal Pradesh.

These reforms imposed by circumstances and by his own wish are of vital importance in the Dalai Lama's view, and he himself does not hesitate to observe that 'We can no longer revert to the old Tibet, and even if we could we do not want to, for there were many things wrong in our society. All that had to change. On the day when Tibet becomes free again, with its structures renewed, it will be easier to build again on new foundations.'[19] And for good measure the Dalai Lama has keenly encouraged the creation of parties, and an opposition, so that every Tibetan may express his views with freedom. There was even the beginnings of a Communist Party, but the outcome was not encouraging – too many different tendencies and too few activists. According to one close colleague of the temporal leader, 'the Communist Party members never stopped accusing each other of deviations, and then excommunicating or purging each other'.

This strenuous long-term task has made it possible to mould in exile a community conscious of its traditions, proud of its heritage and individuality, and determined to remain itself and to make its country better known. Once again the mainspring of this continuity has been and will be the Dalai Lama. His constant concern with the education of the younger generation, already in evidence when he himself decided to learn the English language in Lhasa, has led to his giving consistent priority to crêches, children's homes, religious and secular schools, research institutes and the reconstruction of the great monastic universities. Close attention has been and is being devoted not only to this programme of building, and to bringing up the pupils for present-day life, but above all to the quality of education and the painstaking transmission of Tibetan tradition. This is also part of the everyday concerns of the leader of the nation.

For a monk – 'a simple Buddhist monk', as the Dalai Lama likes to define himself – these contingencies lose none of their importance; and there is nothing contradictory about that fact, for in his words 'giving up the world means giving up one's attachment to the world. That does not mean withdrawing from it. The ultimate goal of Buddhism is to serve others. In order to serve others one must remain within society, not be isolated from it.' It is probably this original approach to life that gives him the look of serenity that he directs towards others, and towards the world. Sometimes he will concede 'Essentially, the whole world lives at the very heart of suffering. So it is futile to insult or to mistreat others.'

Might this be at least a part of the secret charm which underlies the curiosity, attraction, devotion, reverence and sometimes fascination that draw other people towards him? It is hard, and possibly unavailing, to find anybody who has come close to him without being struck by his smiling kindliness, his genuinely cordial greeting, and unassuming simplicity. At Dharamsala, as elsewhere, it has been necessary to set a limit on the flood of visitors who would like to meet him. Not because he himself is hostile to visitors – far from it, although protocol imposes certain restrictions – but because his very crowded timetable requires him for other activities.

All the same, most of the time in Dharamsala the afternoons are partly reserved for audiences, public or private. It is often a moving spectacle, and always a privilege, to take part in these. No doubt no one will be surprised that it should be, to say the least, an astonishing experience to come face to face with a figure of such stature, who incarnates at one and the same time an idea, a spirituality, a faith, a country and its people, the suffering of exile and the torch of hope. That is a great deal for a single man, be he a simple monk or the king of a legendary country.

Eyes twinkling with mischief see everything, attention concentrates to so tight a focus that it grows palpable, and a voice of great sweetness plays across a register of tones which occasionally – as during initiation ceremonies – conjure up bewildering depths. In conversation, a gesture now and then intervenes to point the necessary shade of meaning, and out of this harmony of speech and gesture comes the fleeting impression of confident power and iron will, beneath a good-natured and reassuring exterior. Inside this man lurk glimpses of the prowling big cat, the snow leopard, steeped in freedom and solitude, that no cage could possibly hold.

Exchanges of views with visitors are full of teachings. You know, I have seen many, many people – passers-by, pilgrims, curiosity seekers, scientists, freedom fighters, resistance workers, false and faithful Buddhists, fortune tellers and true seekers of the absolute, poor wretches who suffer and others who have lost all hope. One must listen to people. If I can help them, or if they think that I may be able to help them by meeting them, then I readily do so.[20]

In fact these public audiences are rather akin to the traditional *darshan* familiar in Indian society; a kind of individual blessing in a setting open to nearly all who desire it. It is both the price of fame and a tribute paid to spirituality achieved. To approach a master of wisdom or receive his blessing means participating directly, even if only for an instant, in his world where opposites untangle and are transmuted into a tide of purifying energy; it is moving into resonance with the most salutary influences that radiate from his matchless presence. The great sages of India, known and unknown, are past masters of this kind of ceremony whereby the most credulous adulation and an instinctive, imperative drive combine towards the source of a fullness too obvious to ignore.

When, in the months following the move to Dharamsala, the custom of the *darshan* began to grow up around the young exile, there was some alarm among both Indian officials and Tibetan public servants: to the former, it was a kind of disguised publicity that the New Delhi authorities were quite determined to avoid, in order not to offend Beijing; to the latter it meant dissipating an element of the mystery which had always surrounded the lord of the Land of Snows, and which had come, ontologically, to form part of his divine attributes.

Men believe that divinity does not rub shoulders with allcomers, no matter how or where. The gods, who are perhaps aware that they are the creatures of men, pay no attention to this belief and, particularly in India, they appear to have a special predilection for the world of human kind. As for Buddha, to repeat a comparison famous throughout the Buddhist universe, he is like the reflection of the moon; in fine conditions, lakes, seas and rivers reflect the heavenly image, which nevertheless remains in the heavens. And just as the moon can be simultaneously reflected in many places, so a Buddha, Perfect by definition, can be found in many places at once.

Perhaps it is hard to reconcile all these imperatives, but the Dalai Lama succeeds with his customary dexterity. Remembering how, in his great red and white palace, he so regretted being kept away from ordinary life by the ruthless ties of etiquette, he has taken the opportunity to simplify protocol and to circumvent certain barriers erected around his person by considerations which he now deems antiquated or obsolete. It is also this continual, privileged contact with the exiles from the high plateau that gives him the right to speak in their name, and to keep on opposing the twin threats of ignorance and misunderstanding which tend to obscure the Roof of the World.

> It has been very useful to be a refugee. You find yourself much closer to reality. When I was in Tibet I certainly tried to be realistic, but in a way, by force of circumstance, I think that I was slightly removed from the realities. I became a refugee. That was very positive! Thus a possibility arose of accumulating experience and of forging determination and inner steadfastness.
>
> A refugee finds himself in a genuinely desperate and dangerous situation. It is at such moments that one comes to grips with reality. Gone are the days of imagining that everything is fine, and that very realisation is a step forward. One feels a part of the real. In peacetime, everything carries on of its own accord, and even if a problem does occur one makes believe that everything is for the best. It is possible to react like that in times or intervals of calm, but in a dangerous period and during a dramatic change it does no good to harbour illusions any more. One has to accept that what is bad is bad.

And the Dalai Lama goes on to stress:

> If you are wounded by a poisoned arrow, what matters is to pull it out; that is not the moment to wonder where it came from, or who shot it, or what kind of poison it carries. First you must solve the immediate problem, then afterwards you can study it from every angle.[21]

There is a way of being based on the certitude that we all live in the same world and that all of us are mortal, and the Dalai Lama has made this the cornerstone of his attitude towards other people, a sustained openness and tolerance that is expressed in his unfailing patience. Not that this rules out either candour or a heartfelt intelligence. In his hands, this way of grasping the world becomes an effective weapon against indifference or fatalism.

> Even if we are unable to solve certain problems, we must not regret it. We humans have to face up to death, old age and sickness, as well as to natural disasters such as hurricanes, which are beyond our control. We have to face up to them, we cannot avoid them. These sufferings are quite enough for us – why create further problems owing to ideology, to a different way of thinking? It is pointless. And sad. Thousands and thousands of people suffer from it. That kind of situation is truly stupid, especially when we are able to avoid it by adopting a different attitude, and taking account of the basic humanity that ideologies are supposed to serve. [22]

Naturally he pays particular attention to the Tibetans who flock to ask for his advice, both on a personal level and on behalf of their community. Westerners should see these wayfarers from another time, who brave the passes, the weather, the uncertainties and discomforts of the very long road they have to take to cross the Himalayas and avoid the vigilance of the border guards, simply in order to see the Dalai Lama. How many ageing refugees, with their health destroyed by sickness and the brutality of the upheavals they have suffered, have left this life in peace, once they have reached him? But far more numerous are those who know and say that they owe their survival to the tireless protection of this monk whose presence alone impels them to do and to outdo their best, and to keep on, whatever the cost.

So total is this faith, and so deep-rooted in the Tibetan mind, that parents who have slipped through the Chinese net to reach Dharamsala or other places at the time of religious gatherings presided over by their spiritual leader do not hesitate to entrust their children to him. Thus they can feel sure that the child will grow up to be another link in the chain which must be kept unbroken. As for the upkeep of these children who have to be fed, housed, clothed and cared for, they have utter trust in their sovereign; they know that nothing will be spared in the nurture and development of the free Tibet of tomorrow, even if it means appealing to all people of goodwill, banging the drum and blowing on the trumpets to open people's hearts and raise the winds of genuine solidarity.

These responsibilities are bound to be hard to bear on occasions, yet they do not take up all the time available in the day; or rather the Dalai Lama does not allow himself to be taken over by them, and keeps some moments for himself, and in particular for reading. He has the reputation of being an avid reader, and his knowledge of Tibetan texts is unhesitatingly described as encyclopaedic, not to say phenomenal, by everybody who encounters it. Yet this craving for learning does not stop there; and it also embraces spheres as various as astronomy, high-energy physics, neurology, the study of the brain, and modern western psychology. His eyes sparkle with curiosity as he explains:

I love to compare the Buddhist teachings with the scientific discoveries of contemporary research. This game of comparisons is extremely instructive. It is just as fascinating as going deeper into the study of the laws of nature and observing behaviour and responses to the modifications imposed by the rhythm of the seasons. There are so many things to learn, and one must keep perfecting oneself .... The trouble is that my vocabulary is limited and that I am lazy by nature. So, when I ought to be consulting a dictionary to look up the meaning of a word, I don't always have the courage.[23]

At Dharamsala, the exile from the Potala still finds the time not only to accept a few invitations from his neighbouring fellow-countrymen to take part in a school festival, conduct an initiation in a secluded valley or follow the progress of a children's village, but also to do odd jobs and work in his garden. He has even had a small electronics workshop installed in his residence. His passion for mechanics goes back to his earliest years, and he acknowledges that it still gives him real satisfaction to mend something with his own hands.

I started taking things apart when I was very young, because I was curious to find out how certain machines worked. I used to want to know how the motor was made, but now I only repair things that have broken down. As for looking after a garden in Dharamsala, it is almost a hopeless activity. No matter how much work you put into it, the monsoon comes and wipes out everything.[24]

But that doesn't stop him persevering in this ephemeral pastime and from starting all over again with the same enthusiasm. Probably it also gives him a moment of relaxation or contemplation; isn't it the Dalai Lama who says that living a simple life leads to contentment, and that simplicity is extremely important in the quest for happiness?

All the same, if he followed his personal inclination the Dalai Lama would lead a rather more contemplative, meditative life. He shows a marked preference for philosophical studies and reflection: 'These activities have transformed me, they have made a new man of me. I am still making headway, and at any rate I do my best. That gives a solidity and inner courage that makes it easier to face situations.'

Whenever his work leaves him the time, he returns to his studies, and if he can he spends a long moment after audiences or meetings in prayer or meditation. For him, Buddhism is an experimental and intellectual way, not a dogma. That means that there is always something to explore, always something else to discover or to approach from a different angle. This daily training is a discipline, of course, but it brings him a balance or anchoring point rarely achieved to such perfection in western society.

The Dalai Lama is a spiritual guide, and that role does not cease, no matter what other roles he is required to resume in the course of a day's work or a lifetime's living. The teachings he provides, whether or not in connection with some initiation ceremony or specific occasion, are always followed with the utmost attention, not only by Tibetans but by a growing number of westerners, Buddhists or otherwise. In that realm, he is revealed in all the fullness of an accomplished master, and his exceptionally lucid commentaries on the most arduous texts are well worth the most brilliant theories advanced by the philosophers of other civilisations. And this quality of clarity is not displayed solely in the interpretation of traditional works, but is equally present in far more prosaic contexts, as for example when the Dalai Lama confronts the world's press, or one of its representatives, in or out of Dharamsala.

The exiled sovereign is well aware of the key role of the media in modern society, and he agrees to be interviewed with good grace, fielding the most ludicrous questions with perfect affability, and thinking no less of them. He believes that it is his urgent duty to make known the truth about his country, to explain the various influences that play for supremacy around the Roof of the World, and to put his people's ordeal into a broader context of interdependence rather than have it seen as an isolated question on the fringe of world affairs. Although he is not deceived by the fashions that drum up temporary media interests in events whose scope and origins are left obscure to the greater part of public opinion, he also knows how to make the best of the situation; when the media mention him or question him, no matter why, or on what topic, it is Tibet that will emerge. Thus he is also the travelling ambassador of a cause that he refuses to consider as lost.

And like everything he does, he is concerned to do it well, and therefore the Dalai Lama is an impeccable ambassador. He argues a convincing case for the land of Tibet, simply by being himself. And it is another of his special qualities to have an unequalled gift for putting the most shy and timid of conversational partners at their ease. In his presence, tensions are dissolved as if by magic, and he has a gift for smoothing out obstacles, as though merely because he is there; the contradictory forces of the world of appearances are suddenly harmonised into a full counterpoint, as if in a mirror held up to reflect all the wonders and horrors of the world, without ever being soiled or dazzled by them. According to one high official in the Indian diplomatic service who has observed the exiled sovereign and his colleagues for twenty years, he has never seen him upset, 'even in situations which might trouble the most serene and disciplined of persons'.[25]

Now and then, in the hour of the rapid Indian twilight, the Dalai Lama takes a moment's rest, watches a television broadcast – documentaries about natural history or twentieth-century warfare are his favoured viewing – or strolls in the woods around his residence. He takes the opportunity to feed the birds and, after all the words of men and women, to listen to nature. In accordance with the pattern established in his earliest years, he goes to bed early, around 10 o'clock – here the habits of monk and mountain dweller coincide. The day ends much as it began, with a brief prayer or meditation, and the cycle thus completed starts again at dawn next day, punctuated by the inevitable ration of unforeseen events, and by waymarks that vary with the mood of the time.

During his journeys to India or more distant countries, when he visits the Tibetans whose settlement in the south of the subcontinent has been a marked success, or travels even further afield, this genuinely monastic simplicity is harder to maintain. The Dalai Lama's timetable becomes much more crowded, and preparing for religious ceremonies will often take hours. Audiences and interviews are therefore reorganised so as to enable a maximum number of people to meet the Tibetan leader; this is the fate of all the world's leaders, and the sovereign in exile does not escape it. He himself lays emphasis on the spiritual aspect of these travels, and grants particular attention to teaching, initiations and the propagation of the *Dharma*. But at the same time his personality attracts both people and events, and his charisma places him in a more open, if not directly political, perspective, closely linked to the course of contemporary history.

Keeping the necessary balance may sometimes appear an impossible task. It is necessary to pay heed to local circumstances, delicate shifts, the compelling considerations of security, and the capacity for understanding among constantly changing audiences which are inquisitive, of course, but not necessarily on the same wavelength. And receptiveness is not the same, depending on whether he is making a private visit in the west or a pilgrimage in the age-old culture of India, just as the welcome varies from one side of the planet to the other – although wherever the Dalai Lama goes he is involved in responding to the same vague expectation and to a general feeling of a human quest forever renewed.

Yet in all these changing backgrounds and all the diversity of the world, Tentzin Gyatso is himself, above all; a Buddhist monk with a presence so intensely felt that it restores distorted perspectives and gives things their true weight and worth. A day in the life of the Dalai Lama is this, first of all: the manifold, harmoniously balanced, sacred and profane activities of a remarkable person among a multitude of people, ceaselessly and unreservedly devoted to the demanding task of relieving the suffering of all. With, as his only lever, a smile whose light is a beacon shining through the thick of the storm.

6

The Laughter of a Monk

We manipulate signs which are there in order to teach us, and we are blind.

(Rabbi Menachem Mendel of Kotzk)

'My hobby? Laughter!' And the Holder of the Lotus, the Precious Victorious, the Presence, breaks into one of his characteristic roars of laughter. A laugh of friendship and mischief, complicity and encouragement, which expresses so many things at once, and runs through so many shades of meaning that it sums up a state of mind and a character, and amounts to both a way of being and an offering.

On the top storey of the Tibetan monastery at Bodh Gaya the twilight shadow creeping into the soberly decorated audience chamber is suddenly illuminated by that laughter. The day has been long, and it is far from over. It began before dawn, and was punctuated by the morning ritual which accompanies the gradual completion of the sand mandala necessary for the next initiation into the Wheel of Time. This was followed by meetings, then a teaching session, and then discussions, ceremonies, a brief ritual, and still more meetings. The surrounding atmosphere is loaded with solar and human warmth, the density of waiting, and subtle vibrations whose ceaseless waves come and go, ebb and flow, as if to beat in time with the pulse of an immense and timeless heart. A myriad of impressions and sensations fuse in the burst of laughter, then its echo dies away and the twinkling gaze bores into the visitor's. Courteous, friendly, and always relaxed, the conversation resumes and moves on, on to the subject of other kinds of leisure, rare as they are – reading, gardening and making jokes.

The laughter of a monk – an excellent subject for thought or meditation, especially in a world that tends to snigger because it no longer knows how to laugh. On the usefulness of laughter in human relations. On laughter as a means of relaxation or communication. On laughter as a weapon; everybody knows that it can be implacable. The laughter of the master and the smile of the wise man – a laugh of sweetness, a smile of strength. But also a smile of understanding and reassurance, and of serenity too, the reflection of a very particular sense of whimsical humour, as polished as a pebble worn smooth by the years or centuries, through lifetimes of surge and shift. A smile of spume and fever. A laugh like a sword blade – it cuts through ties, whether of ignorance or hypocrisy. A grave, fine laughter, for it reflects an echo of plenitude.

This laughter, which above all means openness to the other, is always sure to enhance relations with the surrounding world. It also seems to be a feature deeply rooted in the Dalai Lama's whole family, a fact his close colleagues confirm. But there is no doubt that it is also a distinctive feature of the people of the high plateau; for the Dalai Lama, the essence of a culture does not lie in its painting or its various artistic expressions, but in its quality of mind.

If it is alive in the people's everyday life, one grasps its usefulness. So that, because of their culture, Tibetans are in general a jovial people. We ourselves had not noticed this, but many foreigners visiting India have remarked upon it and asked us for our 'secret'. Little by little, I have come to think that it derives from our Buddhist culture, which brings out the *bodhisattva*'s ideal of compassion in a thousand and one ways. Whether literate or illiterate, we are all in the habit of hearing and saying about all sentient beings that they are fathers and mothers to us. Even the

man who seems like the worst kind of bandit will have the saying
that 'all sentient beings are close to me' on his lips. I suppose that
that ideal is the cause of our happiness. It is particularly useful in
everyday life, when there are serious problems to be faced.[26]

There is no doubt that the Precious Protector is not mistaken
when he points out something so simple and obvious that it
is, simply, overlooked. In any case, he no longer sees it
either, but puts it into practice; somehow it is etched into his
nature. Yet if the observer's attention is immediately caught
by the ready smile and warm greeting, it is not long before a
different and complementary quality makes its presence felt,
a staggering mastery of the power of concentration and
attention, so much so that it can be perfectly divided.
Without the slightest sign of effort, and not an instant's
pause, it is quite natural to see the Fourteenth Dalai Lama
doing two things at once, and synchronising separate mental
events. Thus, while losing none of his total concentration on
the main issue in hand – a recitation, a ritual, or a detailed
reply, for example – he perceives the slightest change,
perhaps an unexpected presence, your own, and quickly
signals his awareness of it. By way of greeting a smile
appears, contact is re-established, yet without in any way
disturbing the main focus of the moment. It is rather as if a
resonance was found and instantly recognised.

If there is some 'secret' to be discovered to explain this
fluency, the obvious solution is to listen to the suggestions
put forward by the man concerned. If other explanations do
exist, I am unable to locate them, and in any case it is not so
much a matter of explanations – do we have to be forever
explaining everything? – but perhaps of indications or simple
points of reference, like a handful of little mnemonic pebbles,
dropped in a subtle tracking game along the way to a
memory beyond the field of memory. A kind of gamble on
the human being – not a battle against the demon but a race'
against oneself – in order to try to meet one's own challenge
and rise to the level of a personal requirement.

This deep wisdom of the heart simplifies contact to the

utmost degree, and above all it provides a sovereign antidote for tension. You have to have witnessed a few of his meetings with a variety of visitants not only so as to gauge the vast reserves of patience on which the Dalai Lama constantly draws in order to answer the most absurd, if not the most stupid, questions, but also in order to grasp his formidable capacity for unravelling contradictions and defusing aggressive situations. And often a sudden burst of laughter comes to the rescue, as if to re-situate perspectives in the most precise and concrete sense of the term. There is no mockery in this attitude, simply a reminder from the far distance, a statement that transcends words to show that nothing acts more powerfully than kindness in bringing people together.

But the point is that the method works, or at any rate when it is used by the Dalai Lama with the Tibetan people it gives tangible results. It was under the protection of that smile, and carrying no baggage but their courage, endurance and religious faith, that in 1960 the first refugees took possession of the lands granted by the Indian government in Karnataka province, in southern India. It is difficult to imagine a more absolute contrast between their native Tibet, with its mountains, crystal air and barren vastness, and this sprawling tropical jungle, teeming with wild animals, where the land had to be cleared even to make room for the first tents that were the early foundation of the colony of Bykaluppe, and to protect the pioneers against incursions from elephants, tigers and wild boars. The Dalai Lama remembers his first visit:

They had put up a special tent for me, with bamboo walls and a canvas roof, but nothing kept out the dust created by deforestation, which explained the poor morale of the Tibetan people there.

As always, I promised that we would succeed. I did my best, and little by little the situation changed. Then I started to tease people about their faces, which had been so sad and thin not long before, and now looked joyful and prosperous. I admitted that in the past I had only made promises in the air, because I too had nothing to offer them. But the Tibetans always did what I told them, without the least hesitation. And in the end we succeeded.

It was like watering an old flower close to wilting. If you water it with a little hope it becomes fresh again, and full of enthusiasm.[27]

Of course it is easy to object that the privileged relationship between the spiritual sovereign and his people is such that faith explains everything. Maybe. All the same, when other people – western sceptics or orientals of different faiths – readily admit that they feel that stimulating influence, we are forced to conclude that behind that smile lies something else. In answer to this, I recall a remark made by the Precious Master: 'It is so easy to wound with words, and to have a believable air even though not respecting the truth.' Then is it enough to shift the commonly-accepted perspective just a little, in order to view the world like this? For the Dalai Lama, the answer is certainly Yes. But as one of his close relations sometimes remarks, 'for Him, everything is easy. He has resolved all the paradoxes, because He is a bodhisattva. For the rest of us, it is a different story!'

And generally speaking it certainly is a different story. The fact remains that everywhere, and in the most unexpected environments, the sovereign in exile merges into the moment with disconcerting ease and a no less bewildering immediacy, and circumstances and the public – if it is present – are immediately crystallised around that presence. In some way, as if in a kaleidoscope game, he orders the elements and their surroundings into a single beam whose focal point he becomes. It is not that he seeks to claim attention or to stage an appearance; he is in such a way, so fully in his place, that his mere presence makes itself categorically felt.

It is a feeling hard to define with words, devalued as they are by their usage or by the loss of their deeper meaning, but one is almost tempted to say, drawing on the Indian sense of the words and all that it implies, that this monk who stands so close as to be practically familiar is a 'great soul', a mahatma. He has the rare gift of opening possibilities again, simply by being there. It may be in a classroom, a hotel room acting as a temporary audience chamber, or the shrine of a faith that is not his own, in the friendly midst of a rambling conversation,

the hustle of a press conference, the reverence of a religious
ceremony, in an English manor-house-turned-Buddhist
centre, in a château in Normandy, before a handful of the
faithful, a picked audience, or a great auditorium packed with
inquisitive people. At once he is in harmony, calm and at the
same time alert and attentive. There is nothing affected in this
behaviour, which seems to produce an effect even on the most
recalcitrant subjects. Thus at the time of his first visit to the
United States in 1979 it was noticeable that the very same
journalists and reporters who usually didn't give a damn for
anybody's etiquette were finding unsuspected stores of polite-
ness and respect, much to the surprise of the organisers of the
various meetings and debates, who could hardly believe their
eyes.

In certain circumstances, in backgrounds very different
from his own, when it is impossible to overlook the discrep-
ancy between the god-king's ethos and that of the micro-
society which is his temporary host, one furtive question does
arise: Will the imbalance not alter his behaviour, no matter
how imperceptibly? No, not in the slightest, and the phenomenon is all the more disconcerting, because the gap remains,
quite unmistakable, but turned to his advantage. He merely
has to remain himself. Somehow the view changes, as if by
some piece of stage business, from *The Discreet Charm of the
Bourgeoisie* or *The Ghost of Liberty* to *Last Year at Marienbad*,
without knowing exactly if it was last year or if the present is
still to come. But the Presence, the Dalai Lama's, remains.

This respect imposes itself: the Dalai Lama does not impose
it, except by his good grace. For it is a further paradox, among
the many he has in store, that he does not give the impression
of taking himself seriously, although this clearly detracts
nothing from the seriousness he brings to everything he does.
If today he channels the bulk of his energies into working for
the survival of the Tibetan tradition, there was a time when on
occasions he was still a carefree boy in the Potala, when he was
not above fighting cheerful battles with his brother. And
Lobsang Samten used sometimes to say, with an expression
almost as knowing as his famous brother's, that he still carried

the mark of one memorable blow from his younger brother, a blow he had never returned, for how could he fittingly lift a hand against the Dalai Lama?

This tendency towards mischief has not lessened with the years, and some eyewitnesses remember as if it were yesterday certain incidents that occurred during walks in the woods, not long after the move to Dharamsala. As both protocol and security require, the Dalai Lama is seldom quite alone. So he loved to take advantage of the relative peace and quiet of a walk in the forest to give the slip to his escort, dart off up some steep and impossible shortcut – no change here – and wait for his companions further on and higher up, with a smile on his lips, always a step ahead of the game.

In an attempt to penetrate this appearance, go beyond the good nature underlaid by a real and compact strength, and reach what some have called his 'secret', the conversation alights on a theme dear to the Dalai Lama:

> In every meeting, I keep in mind that we are alike, in that you and I are both human beings. To underline the superficial differences, I am an oriental, and furthermore a Tibetan from beyond the Himalayas, born into a different culture and environment. Yet, looking closer, I have the feeling of being myself, and with this feeling I seek happiness and I reject suffering. Anybody, no matter where he comes from, has this same feeling of 'myself' at the conventional level, and in that sense we are all alike.
>
> Granted that as a starting point, when I meet new people in different places there is no barrier or curtain drawn across my mind. I can converse with you as I do with old friends, even if it is a first meeting. In my mind, as human beings, you are my brothers and sisters, my fellows, and in substance that makes no distinction. I can express what I feel without hesitation, as before old friends. Thus we can communicate without difficulty, and establish a link, not just through an exchange of polite commonplaces, but heart to heart. By basing oneself on such a human relationship, it is possible to develop mutual trust and respect.[28]

This way of seeing things has the advantage, at the very least, of not slamming the doors shut straight away and not shutting people away from each other, on the pretext of a thou-

sand and one differences which we tend to cement into
prejudices, if not into distrust or hatred. Hence the smile
flows quite naturally into the fabric of days and events, for it
becomes a kind of open sesame, a pledge of understanding
and openness. It is also a first step towards initiation into
tolerance and equanimity; by mastering oneself, perhaps one
comes – some day, or in another life – to break the shell of
selfishness and to harmonise over a broader range.

The Dalai Lama is well placed for talking about tolerance.
Here too, his laughter sometimes says as much as the words
he uses with surgical precision when he is explaining his
position. For example, when he is asked about his feeling
towards the Chinese:

It is from a man's enemy that he learns true tolerance and patience,
while with a religious master or close kin, your tolerance cannot
be put to the test. From this point of view, even the enemy teaches
inner strength, courage and determination. With an enemy, that
brings you closer to reality and strips away pretensions.

The Chinese .... An old civilisation, very old, highly civi-
lised, very cultured ... and, it seems to me, sometimes a very
strange nation. By 'civilisation' I mean that one can sometimes
have the impression of very friendly, perfectly courteous people,
people of supreme kindness and high calibre. And yet, in that
same country, terrible events are happening. We have suffered a
lot because of them, but that does not prevent us from feeling
compassion for those responsible for these actions. It is sad to see
thousands and thousands of human souls suffering like that. If
one considers the human being as such, one also feels directly
concerned by what happens over there.

Courage is important. There is a saying that where there is a
will there is a way, and it is true. If, in a difficult situation, our
will or our courage fails, if one drifts into the laziness of feeling
inferior, by wondering whether one is perhaps incapable of
achieving such an arduous task, then this depreciation will not
afford the slightest protection from suffering. So it is vital to
build up a courage corresponding to the scale of the difficulties.
The deep root of failure in our lives is to think: 'Oh, how useless
and powerless I am!' It is essential to think strongly and force-
fully: 'I can do it', without boasting or fretting.

Like it or not, we are more and more interdependent. Take for example the thousands and millions of cars that circulate in the West's and the world's great cities. Yet without petrol they cannot move. Although for the moment people are carried by these vehicles, if the petrol runs short, then it will be the people who carry those big cars . . . . Nowadays we can no longer live in total isolation. And to the extent that we have to live together, why not do it with an open mind? What good is it to stare back at each other like china dogs, and so add to the world's disorders?

No doubt you think that I am a gentle dreamer. Yet we humans have a well developed brain and unlimited potential. Since, with patience, even wild animals can gradually be tamed, the human mind can also be trained, step by step. Through embarking on these practices with patience, we come to know by our own experience.[29]

Listening to the Dalai Lama, it is sometimes tempting to say 'Yes, but . . .'. The trouble is that he seems to perceive one's reservations, and answers even before they are spoken:

Teachings are not much use unless they are put into practice in everyday life. Buddha teaches that you are your own master, that everything depends on you. Many problems are created by our own mental flaws. We suffer because we lack something inside ourselves. These problems I describe as unnecessary, for if we adopt a proper attitude these problems created by man do not arise.

To become responsible for oneself, it is not a matter of belief or unbelief, and kindness to others is not the cause but the expression of a religion. Over the centuries there have been many masters who have trodden various paths to achieve the Truth. The Lord Buddha is one of them, and my study of Buddhism has led me to think that in spite of the differences in the names and forms which are used by various religions, the Ultimate Truth towards which they tend is the same.

In the quest for Ultimate Truth, if it is not manifested in us it is because we have not found it. The Ultimate Truth exists. By thinking deeply and reflecting carefully, we will realise that we ourselves exist in Ultimate Truth. In general, we have the impression that there exists a sound of spoken words: but, in Ultimate Truth, if I seek myself, I shall not find myself; and if you seek yourself, you too will not find yourself. One finds neither he who speaks nor he who listens, any more than words or sounds. They are all empty, as empty as is space.

Having said that, they are not completely devoid of existence. They must indeed exist, since we are capable of perceiving them. What I say, you hear, and then you reflect upon it. So my words produce a certain effect, but if we set about looking for it, we find nothing. The mystery is linked to the dual nature of Truth.[30]

And all this for a smile, for a burst of laughter.

The final flourish, not by way of conclusion but to shed a little light on another facet of the man, is a very Tibetan little story that the Fourteenth Dalai Lama likes to put forward for his visitors' consideration. In a way it is part of the heritage of the high country, the immemorial memory of his people.

> Once upon a time, long, long ago, there was a famous lama of great renown, whose name was Drom. One day he saw a man in the middle of making a ritual circuit around a stupa. 'It is good to circle the stupa,' he told him, 'but would it not be better to practise religion?'
>
> 'Without a doubt, I would do better to read a sacred book,' said the man to himself. And laboriously he prepared himself to read.
>
> Another day, Drom meets him again. 'Reading a sacred book is obviously a good thing,' he remarks. 'But wouldn't it be better to practise religion?'
>
> So the man falls to thinking; 'It does seem as if even recitation is not enough. What if I meditate?'
>
> Soon afterwards Drom sees him again, deep in meditation. 'I admit that meditation is a good thing,' he says. 'But wouldn't it really be better if you practised religion?' The man was at his wits' end. 'What do you mean by practising religion?' he asked. 'Tell me what I have to do!'
>
> 'Turn your mind away from the appearances of earthly life', Drom answered. 'And turn towards religion.'[31]

A wink, a warm handshake, a slight nod of the head, hands joined at chest level, the level of the heart. A smile to heal all the ills of the world, and a laugh to give courage for every day.

7

A Royal Solitude

We can do more than we know. Although not everything is
permitted, everything is possible.

(*Roger Bacon*)

In the past, and until quite recently, there were few opportu-
nities for ordinary people to come close to the Dalai Lama; in
every time and place, divinity has always inspired a kind of
awe, difficult to confront without preparation or prior protection. As the reincarnation, not the son, of a supreme principle,
the sovereign of the Land of Snows naturally partakes of its
sacred essence, and he stands, or is placed, far beyond the
narrow sphere of other human beings.

These inherent barriers came to be reinforced by interdicts
decreed by mortal men, both in order to protect and to be
protected from the power of the divinity, so much so that
under the influence of all these obstacles and taboos the man of
divinity lived a life apart from everyday contingencies, if not
above them. The Dalai Lama was no exception – quite the
opposite – and his every appearance was an event in itself.
Court protocol had further increased the distance between
him and the Tibetan faithful; for example etiquette made the
familiar demand that the visitor must never turn his back on
the Illustrious Presence, and had to walk backwards out of the
audience chamber. During public processions, no one could
claim the right to find himself, even for a moment, above the
level of the sovereign's palanquin, so that no one could stand
on a balcony to watch the god-king pass by.

From the very beginning, the invocations, ceremonies, investigations, checks and cross-checks, and strict ritual processes to ensure the authenticity of the discovery, place the chosen child outside the common norms. It is true that other lamas are also recognised by a similar procedure, but no investigation is conducted so rigorously as the search for the Precious Victorious, on which so much depends. The special distinction of the system is also that it preserves a line of descent, and at the same time avoids the position becoming a hereditary privilege, with all the consequences it might entail – the concentration of power into a single entrenched area, a clan or perhaps even a family, the succession going to heirs not fit for the position, or temporal rivalries clashing over candidates. Today it can even happen that the duly recognised reincarnation of a particular grand lama will declare himself incapable of taking on his role and continuing a succession made all the more problematic by a changing world. To adapt to the new circumstances it requires a wealth of energy, willpower and compassion which may prove more than a mortal can provide, even though several times reborn.

As it happens, this situation has occurred inside the Dalai Lama's own family, and three of his brothers, caught in the vice of circumstances, have chosen to renounce the monastic life. The oldest, Thubten Jigme Norbu, was the first reincarnation to be born into the family. As abbot of the Taktser monastery, in Amdo, he was forced to leave his orders with the arrival of the Chinese, and later took the road into exile and settled in the United States. In his view, it was the only way to preserve the line of wisdom which he contained by virtue of the laws of transmission from master to disciple. Having given up his vows – which does not imply any 'sin' in the sight of Tibetan society, for it is much more serious to contravene or break them – he had somehow to put himself in tune with the principles of a new secular life. For some years now he has been teaching at Indiana State University, in the department of Ural-Altaic studies, and continues to be a strenuous defender of the Tibetan cause. He is married to a Tibetan woman, and still feels a profound nostalgia for the high country. Confronted with the Western way of life, he has written: 'I miss the infinite peace that I knew then, and the purity of the scent of the pines and junipers and the wild roses.'[32]

Thubten Jigme Norbu pays particular attention to what is happening in his country, and quite recently he did not hesitate to speak out against an insidious perversion of language which has been spreading on the international scene, the extension of the word 'Chinese' to include 'Tibetan', and the diminishing use of the word 'Tibetan' itself. The mechanism is simple and comparatively well known; official propaganda – in this case Chinese – gradually shifts the meaning of a word towards another signification, and by constant repetition eventually imposes this new meaning, leaving public opinion generally unaware of having been manipulated. Contemporary history abounds with examples of this process, especially in the totalitarian countries. One has only to recall certain reinterpretations of the facts of revolutionary history in Russia and elsewhere, or think of sinister euphemisms such as 'the final solution' or 're-education through labour'.

In the case of Tibet, by a process of semantic subtlety or refined perversity, Beijing nowadays likes to talk about Chinese 'history' and Tibetan 'legend'. And it is with similar motives that the official theory proclaims that, no matter what their origins, all populations living within the present frontiers of People's China are Chinese. The difference is considerable; of course no-one has asked for the opinion of the Uighurs, Mongols, Tibetans or any of the variety of minorities comprised under this arbitrary label. As for those Chinese who are of undeniably Chinese extraction, they are now designated only by the term 'Han'. Until recently the two words were used indiscriminately with a view to glossing over this key ethnic difference.

Thus, while the utter incongruity and patent inexactitude of the new dispensation are glossed over, an ethnic concept conceals and tends to replace a purely political idea, whose purpose emerges on reflection in all its cruelty; by this game of semantic hopscotch, the Chinese mean to erase and totally efface these historic differences of language, in order to obscure and finally obliterate an otherness deeply rooted in the distant past. As Thubten Jigme Norbu has pointed out:

> There is a strange irony for Tibetans when they find themselves suddenly confronted with the prospect of having their identity merged with the Chinese. The irony comes from the fact that, of all the powers which have ruled Tibet, China did so for the shortest time. The Mongols and Manchus never made any such claim, even in their imperial heyday .... This perversion of language is yet another trick to deny our deep identity, and it is more than regrettable that it is beginning to be current in the newspapers. The distortions hitherto used by the Chinese to warp the general perception of our history are now being used to foster the illusion that Tibet has been 'Chinese' for centuries.[33]

In the Dalai Lama's family, the roles appear to have been allotted in advance. Another older brother, Gyalo Thondup, is more like a born politician. Philosophy and religion seem not to matter much to him. His studies at Nanking University brought him into early contact with the Chinese, and his wife herself was born in Taiwan. Nevertheless he has never cut his ties with his own people. A resident of Hong Kong, he seems to have played a not inconsiderable role behind the scenes in the informal contacts established between the sovereign in exile and the authorities in Beijing since the early 1980s, with the winds of change that followed the death of Mao.

Lobsang Samten, the third brother, was two years older than Tentzin Gyatso, and was certainly the closest to him. They both lived in the Potala for a long time, and shared holidays, games and sometimes also theological debates, before the exile. Later, he too discarded the monastic habit, married, and lived in the United States for some time, before taking charge of the Tibetan Medical Centre at Dharamsala, which he ran until his death in 1984. The Dalai Lama's younger brother, the reincarnation of a famous master, gave up his title and duties as Ngari Rimpoche and now bears the name of Tentzin Chogyal. After studying in India, where he also completed his military service in the elite force of the Northern Border Paratroops, he works in close collaboration with the sovereign in exile, attached as he is to his private secretariat.

Since leaving the high country, the Dalai Lama's two sisters have devoted themselves to caring for orphans and the children of refugees. Tsering Dolma, the elder sister, became the founder and driving force of kindergartens that fed, housed, educated and cared for thousands of young Tibetans whom circumstances placed at the hinge, or perhaps breaking point, between two worlds – their own, rooted in an age-old tradition that had to be preserved, and 20th-century society as filtered through the screen of India, which has sometimes acted as a buffer between the olden days and the new way of life.

After the death of Tsering Dolma, twenty-four years ago, the Dalai Lama's young sister, Jetson Pema, took up the torch with a rare selflessness, and although she herself is married, to this day Mrs Gyalpo spares no effort to bring a minimum of comfort and wellbeing to the Tibetan children who are grouped together in several SOS-villages that have become the homes they have lost. Ever since the first massive influx of refugees following the departure of the Dalai Lama, although the orphans of that era have grown up and gone out to make their place in the world, others have continued to pour in.

Knowing at first hand that their culture has been systematically destroyed in the high country, some of the faithful descending from above prefer to leave their children in the care of the Dalai Lama, believing that only this painful decision will enable their civilisation to survive. Then it is up to Mrs Gyalpo and her remarkably efficient team to take up the heavy burden of seeing them housed and fed. Thus, after the great initiation of the Wheel of Time at Bodh Gaya in December 1985, the nursery found itself augmented by several hundred new boarders. (The Great Thirteenth has made it known that in his next incarnation he would have several brothers and sisters to help him in the performance of

his task!) The fact remains that, in spite of innumerable
difficulties, what stands out about these children's villages is
the dynamism and joy that pervade the daily atmosphere of a
community united in adversity, and determined, above all, to
survive.

Now and then, Mrs Gyalpo also acts as an ambassador on
her brother's behalf. Thus she headed the third delegation
from the Dalai Lama to visit Tibet, naturally under the aegis
of the Beijing authorities, with the aim of examining the
alterations of recent years. For three months she scoured the
roads and villages of the high country, and her outspokenness
caused some memorable scenes between her and her hosts,
who were extremely put out by her knowledge and clear
thinking. It is true that when she spoke out she did not mince
her words, and that this cast a chill over the visit, but then
Tibet too has that familiar saying, that the truth can hurt.
Thus, she did not like what she saw in Taktser. In the Dalai
Lama's native village, in Amdo, now partly incorporated by
official order into the Chinese province of Chinghai, the
family house, the one with the famous turquoise tiles, which
appeared in the waters of the sacred lake during the search for
the reincarnation of the Great Thirteenth, no longer exists. It
has been pulled down, except for one grey wall which now
forms part of a newly-built school. And the village, which has
always been peopled by Tibetans, now holds about fifty
families, but only a dozen are of Tibetan blood – the rest are
Chinese colonists, settled in that place more by malice than
goodwill.

Of all the members of his family, Tentzin Gyatso was
undoubtedly the most attached to his mother. Because his
father died when the future sovereign was only 12 years old,
his mother's influence made a deeper mark, even though from
the moment when he was recognised he was separated from
his relations and subjected to the strict discipline of monastic
life. To this day Pema, his younger sister, remembers that in
Lhasa the brothers and sisters gathered once a month in the
Norbu-lingka, the Jewel Park, to spend a little time with the
god-king. The rules of protocol did not permit more frequent

contacts. In those days the young Dalai Lama was very fond of a certain kind of bread which his mother used to bake especially for him. The monks in his entourage were very indulgent with the children, whose boisterous behaviour contrasted sharply with the surrounding austerity. The hours passed quickly, amid bursts of laughter and games of chase, and then life resumed its daily course, punctuated by rituals and ceremonies, studies and initiations. During these years, the children were all growing up in their own way, following their own path, and preparing for a future that none of them could have anticipated. On rare occasions they would find themselves reunited for a few days, and then their roads diverged, until one day in Lhasa ...

As it happens, the family ties drew closer in exile. At first the cramped conditions of the refugee reception centres and the modesty of their resources altered custom and etiquette from top to bottom, brought them together and created better mutual understanding. Differences may sometimes have emerged, but no more often than before did the Dalai Lama seek to impose his point of view; for his close relations, as for his colleagues, each remained responsible for his own actions, and it was for each to judge according to his understanding.

The Dalai Lama's relationship with his mother was no less privileged for all that. She was born with the century, and lived until 1981, and everybody who met her recognised her commanding qualities. Active until the end of her life, she was blessed with that unmistakable intelligence of the heart that enables a person to find the words of comfort that human beings often need. She was known by the name of Gyayum Chenmo, 'Great Mother', and enjoyed boundless prestige and respect among the Tibetans. She had left Lhasa on the same night as her illustrious son, to join his caravan and share the vicissitudes of his flight, and she devoted herself body and soul to the Tibetan community in exile, dividing her time between Dharamsala and Darjeeling, between her other children and the developing man of wisdom. The Dalai Lama said of her:

My mother is a kind and benevolent woman. She cares about each and everybody. She would gladly have given her own meal to whoever was hungry, even if it meant going without herself. Her profound kindness did not prevent her from ruling her family. She adapted easily and was far-sighted; after my enthronement, when new possibilities arose, she was determined that her other children should receive a thorough education.[34]

Even if the notion of renouncing his heritage and no longer assuming his role as spiritual guide might have crossed his mind, the Dalai Lama has never given it any real consideration. 'As long as space lasts, and as long as there are migrators through the cycle of existences, may I remain, to relieve them of their suffering.' This resolve expressed by Shantideva, one of the most revered of Buddhist sages, which the Fourteenth Dalai Lama likes to quote, sums up his position well enough. And he goes on to add: 'For the course of this existence, that is the wish that draws me on, and I know that I have expressed it in the same way in past lives.'[35]

Granted this fact, however, perspectives change, and it is therefore natural to imagine how a life might develop in the light of a different set of values. To feel bound, or rather re-bound, to an uninterrupted chain of exceptional human beings certainly gives confidence, but it is backed by a daily determination and practice which consolidate the underlying reality. Above all, to take on the role of a divinity implies duties, and this can sometimes be felt as a burden. Yet in all honesty and serenity Tentzin Gyatso declares:

In this role I can be a great help to people, and that is why it gladdens me to play it. In any case, I feel at ease with it. If this circumstance enables me to be highly beneficial to others, it also shows that I have the karmic balance necessary to be able to assume it. It is no less certain that I have a special karmic relationship with the people of Tibet. From that, it might be concluded that in view of the circumstances I have had a good deal of luck. Nevertheless, behind the word 'luck' there are genuine causes and reasons: the karmic force of my ability to assume this role, together with the extent of my wish to be able to do it.[36]

There is nothing presumptuous about these words, which in some respects may leave the hearer nonplussed, or at least surprised. The facts simply belong to a different logic, to be handled with extreme care. The Dalai Lama is quite aware of this: 'Many stories are mysterious when the question of rebirth arises.' Questioned about his personal sense of being the incarnation of the Lord of Infinite Compassion, he answers with a tranquil smile:

It is hard for me to give a definite verdict. Without committing myself to the kind of meditative effort that would involve retracing my life breath by breath, it is impossible for me to claim its validity.

We think that there are four types of rebirth. The first, the standard kind, is that of a being incapable of deciding on its own rebirth. It is incarnated solely in accordance with its past actions. At the opposite end of the scale is the example of a fully illuminated Buddha, who simply manifests a physical form with the purpose of helping others. In this precise case, it is clear that the person is a Buddha.

The third category comprises the being who, thanks to his previous spiritual achievements, is in a position to choose, or at least to influence, the place and conditions of rebirth. Finally, the fourth type is called the blessed manifestation. In this case the person receives an influence that gives him the power, surpassing his ordinary capacities, to accomplish beneficial actions such as the teaching of religion. For this latter kind of rebirth, the person must have particularly wanted to help other people in his previous lives. That is why such a transmission of power comes about. Although some of these rebirths appear more likely than others, I cannot say exactly which of them defines me.[37]

While he acknowledges in all honesty that he does not have a very precise and constant awareness of the links that attach him to his predecessors, Tentzin Gyatso nevertheless feels a certainty of being attached to them through mind and spirit, on the grounds of his personal qualities – acquired, developed and cultivated by rigorous and disciplined practice in the course of his present and previous lives. The spiritual leader of Tibet admits to having particular affinities with the Great

Thirteenth, his immediate predecessor, whose open-mindedness, tenacity and political concern for the future of Tibet he is in a good position to appreciate.

> He enormously encouraged the genuine scholars and he made sure, by very much improving the level of studies in the monastic universities, that it became impossible for those who did not hold the proper qualifications to rise in the religious hierarchy. He also ordained tens of thousands of monks. On the other hand he gave few initiations and made few speeches. As for the nation, he thought at length about policy, and was particularly concerned about the problems of the more distant frontier provinces and their administration. He also involved himself in making the machinery of government more efficient.[38]

This resonance with the past does not stop there, and other parallels crop up from time to time in conversation – for on this subject, as on that of his personal accomplishments, the Dalai Lama does not like to dwell; they are too private for display. Nevertheless, he does sometimes acknowledge that he has often dreamt about Atisa, the great Indian scholar who brought about the renaissance of Buddhism in the high country in the 11th century, after the dark age of ruthless repression under the renegade king, Lang Darma.

Himself considered to be a prior reincarnation of Chenrezig, in dreams Atisa has many times brought the Fourteenth Dalai Lama safe and sound through narrow scrapes and walks along the tightrope, to the feet of the glorious image of Avalokitesvara. For Tentzin Gyatso

> the reason for these relationships is simple: when you have a special interest in something, it haunts your mind, and you pay more attention to dreams. And you know, in dreams many things can happen. At the time of these meetings with Atisa I was still in Tibet and making a close study of his texts and commentaries. Later on, this help appeared when I myself was teaching his doctrine and his points of view.
> In the case of the Fifth Dalai Lama it was undoubtedly because he was the first true unifier of Tibet, and also because he was the first to exercise complete control over the spiritual and temporal

powers at the same time. Those dreams were still in Lhasa. And
then, there is also a special teaching that comes from the Fifth
Dalai Lama, and at the time I happened to be studying him,
though not truly following that path. In fact it is a teaching that I
have been practising much more intensively since I have been in
India. I believe that these are some of the reasons that explain
these dreams and conversations.[39]

The present master of the Lion's Throne makes no mystery
about having been in contact with several of his predecessors.
Tsong-kha-pa the reformer, the founder of the Gelukpa
school, has been another rich source of spiritual power and
invincible light; there comes a moment when the element of
mystery fades, to give way to a different apprehension of the
world.

Equipped with such provisions for a new departure into
an existence probably deliberately chosen, solitude is like
a constant faithful companion. Learning its ways is part of
the life of any novice, and all the more so for the Dalai
Lama.

Once he has left his home and family, many limitations govern
the existence and behaviour of a monk. These rules enable him to
be contented with his lot. It is a question of attitude. When you
content yourself with the bare essentials, there is nothing
missing. A monk's life is very gratifying, very happy: if you need
to be convinced you have only to question those who have
discarded the habit. Many of them have told me how hard and
complicated secular life can be.[40]

The Fourteenth Dalai Lama happy? His burst of laughter is
open to all sorts of interpretations, but if happiness does
exist then there is no doubt that he has encountered it, not
necessarily along the winding roads of everyday life, but
perhaps in following those paths, no matter how steep they
are, that change the wayfarer. He has returned from these
with a knowledge of his own limitations, making these the
very basis of his steadfast determination to help other people;
in order to sympathise, one must know everything, and in

order to practise compassion one must have the power to do so. Yet here the Dalai Lama makes one reservation:

> Even an illuminated being gifted with limitless knowledge and power, and with the wish to save all beings from suffering, cannot eliminate the individual's personal karma . . . . To a given extent we are all destined to encounter the consequences of the harmful actions previously caused by our bodies, words and minds. That is the way of things.[41]

Some years ago, Tentzin Gyatso said:

> Although my experience as a Buddhist monk is not necessarily appealing, through my own small experience I am enabled to feel the advantage of these attitudes – love, compassion, and respect for human dignity and human values. At my age I have spent many years striving to develop compassion and kindness in myself. I have the feeling that, thanks to these practices, I am quite happy. In spite of many difficult circumstances, I am happy. If, because of these difficulties, I were always sad, I would not be very effective, because a sad man cannot influence reality. Furthermore, accepting unfortunate events does not mean being discouraged. We try to overcome these difficulties and tragedies, while keeping calm and firm.[42]

As firm as a rock, he might properly have added.

Founded on the light of doctrine and the counsels of the *Dharma*, the Teaching, this approach to existence, which the Dalai Lama calls 'Buddhist realism', enables him to face adversity equably. For, he explains, 'if a solution can be found for a problem, if a situation allows something to be done to improve it, there is no need to worry. If there is no solution in view, then worry is quite pointless. Whatever the reason, worry does not help. There is no need at all to torment oneself, because nothing good comes of an anxious attitude.'[43] While it is easier to preach than to practise in everyday life, this attitude is none the less one of Tentzin Gyatso's major characteristics, and very much the outcome of inner practice.

Here too it is best – and in the Buddhist vein – not to be taken in by appearances, for beneath the sovereign simplicity of the Tibetan spiritual leader lies an iron will, and this will has served and continues to serve as the agent that ceaselessly burnishes an essence purified to match the infinite transparency of the Tibetan sky. Perhaps it requires a series of lives lived in full awareness to reach such a degree of both plainness and intensity – or in any case an existence totally directed towards the spiritual pursuit. The battle against ignorance is fought and won every day, and in the end it opens on to unsuspected prospects.

Mischievous as usual, Tentzin Gyatso asserts:

> When you are feeling ill, it is not enough to read a medical book to pick yourself up again. You have to take some medicine to assist the cure. It is easy to hold forth about doctrine or to hear it spoken of, but much harder to put it into practice. Yet without hard practice of what is taught there is no way to achieve good results. If the cause amounts to a verbal diagnosis, then the effect cannot go any further. When a man is hungry he needs tangible food: the mere description of a tasty meal, be it Chinese or French, is not enough to satisfy our appetite. As Buddha said, 'I show you the way to liberation, but know that liberation itself depends on you.' And he explained in a tantra: 'If you practise what I have said and it yields nothing, then I have told a lie.' Therefore one first has to practise and gain experience: so one comes to understand the truth of the Buddha's teachings.[44]

This does not mean that the Dalai Lama counsels asceticism pure and simple, or preaches that each hearer must renounce his world. He is well aware that there are allowances to be made, and to westerners on the trail of the wisdom of the orient he is liable to remark that material comfort is not to be despised: in every sphere it is excess that leads to error. 'Better to be warm and well fed than cold, ill-clothed and starving', he jokes. In his view, material progress is simply a thing which ought not to blot out spiritual progress, for while it is supposed to bring happiness, the former does not last; all the material goods there are will not be enough to satisfy our desires, and we still seek something more. In this sense, materialism is not everything, and the Dalai Lama contends that 'One of the most important things is compassion, and this is not for sale in any shop or supermarket, and no machine can produce it. Only inner growth is able to create it.' In the confusion of the world we live in, it is therefore essential to overcome ignorance, so as to become fully aware and to take on one's individual responsibility. The task is huge.

Tirelessly, the Dalai Lama stresses how cardinally important it is today to learn patience and tolerance – an attitude which has nothing in common with permissiveness or the convenient lure of helplessness, nor with the easy lapse into discouragement. In order to achieve the grasp of the essence of things, and of the world, Buddhism strongly insists on the need for a conscious training of the mind. The deeper reason for this is quite simple; in order to apprehend the true nature of the cosmic game, wisdom – in the sense of knowledge – is fundamental:

> To create that wisdom, one engages in meditation, because as they are at the moment our minds are not very powerful. At present our mind is dispersed; its energies have to be canalised, like water in a hydroelectric plant, in order to create a strong force. In the mind, this result is achieved by meditation, by channelling it so as to make it very powerful, to the point where it can be used to master wisdom. To the extent that all the seeds of illumination exist inside ourselves, Buddhahood is not to be sought elsewhere. If you stir up the water in a pond, it becomes muddy; yet the proper nature of water in itself is not dirty. As I have often remarked, even when we let through a feeling that torments us, that does not pollute the nature of the mind, whose essence remains altogether transfused with light and knowledge. Hatred is also consciousness, and that is why its nature is light and knowledge, even if it misconceives its object.[45]

Even for the Dalai Lama the learning of wisdom, or knowledge, is a long and patient process, a daily path, and a way of being at every instant; what he is now, what he has become in the course of the years, he certainly owes to a unique conjunction of exceptional people – his tutors, masters and preceptors – around him, but also and perhaps supremely to his own work upon himself. So much so that his presence, ease and charisma simultaneously reflect a personal discipline continually replenished, and the direct perception of a unique-ness with an aura of total liberty tinged with solitude. No doubt that is the price paid for the knowledge that the wise are so hungry to acquire, but also the secret of that unceasing conquest of oneself.

> You yourself can observe that when they find themselves faced with a problem, people gifted with inner strength are more capable of confronting it. In the case of Tibet, and judging by my own experience, limited though it is, I have noticed the truth of this assertion. In my position, in a complex situation and with heavy responsibilities, a man could well develop headaches. Yet a reading of my face would suggest that I was not particularly tormented. Obviously we know that we have grave problems, and that that is a tragedy. Yet we accept them as concrete facts and we do our best. There is no question that an attitude of inner strength can help: it influences the way of grasping and facing problems.[46]

According to the spiritual leader of Tibet, once this inner strength has been acquired and secured, the rest follows of itself, or almost; we only need to persevere, for the essence of Buddhism finally amounts to two basic precepts. The first, 'Help other people', sums up the whole teaching of the Mahayana, or Great Vehicle. The second, 'At least do not harm other people', contains all the teaching of the Hinayana, the Lesser vehicle. These are the complete foundations of the Buddhist ethic.

> The doctrine is not meant for simple knowledge, it is a means of improving our mind. To do that, it must be an integral part of our life. The most important thing is practice. To study Buddhism and then to use it as a weapon for criticising other people's theories or ideologies is wrong. The prime objective is to control ourselves, not to criticise others. It is better to look at oneself with a critical eye, and ask: what about my anger, attachment, jealousy, hate, pride – what am I doing to be rid of them?

First of all, in practice, at the base, one must control oneself, do as much as possible to curb wrongful actions that may harm other people. That is a defensive posture. After that, at the following stage, when one acquires certain qualifications, the goal becomes active – to help others. Sometimes, in the early days, one needs isolation in order to concentrate on one's own inner development. But when one gains a little confidence and strength, one must stay in touch with society, and serve it in any field, no matter what. For it is not enough to single oneself out by wearing different clothing, leading a life apart from other people and isolating oneself from the rest of society. A precept for training the mind states: 'Be transformed from within, and leave the outward appearance be.' That is what counts.

It is characteristic of Buddhism that in practice it requires the brain to be used just as much as the heart. From the ethical point of view it is advisable to practise the qualities of a good warm heart. Yet, since Buddhism is very much wedded to reasoning and logic – the wisdom side – intelligence matters. So heart and mind should work together. Without knowledge and without a fully used intelligence the depths of Buddhist doctrine are unattainable. It is very difficult to achieve concrete wisdom, fully realised. There may be exceptions, of course, but that is the general rule.

Another thing to consider is that at the beginning of good practice, one must not expect too much. We live in a time of computers and automation, and there may be some temptation to believe that inner development is also an automatic procedure, that one has only to push a button and everything changes. But that is not the case. Inner development is not easy, and it takes time. Outward progress – space flight, for example – did not reach its present level in a single leap: it has taken centuries, each generation moving forward from the achievements of the one before. Inner development is much harder, because it is not transferred from one generation to the next. Certainly the experience of past lives exerts great influence on the present life, and this experience will become the basis of growth with the next rebirth, but the transference of inner development from one person to another is impossible. Thus, everything depends upon oneself, and that takes time.[47]

Indeed, it is not easy, when another tradition has laid down different stages of consciousness, to decondition one's mind and learn first to see, then observe, and then to feel and react in a different way. Because for a Buddhist, blind belief will not do, and the aim is to test oneself out and somehow to become one's own laboratory, whose findings are achieved through personal practice.

Although he tends to be thrifty with details and very unforthcoming in the matter of his own accomplishments in this sphere, nevertheless the Dalai Lama is one of the living examples of what a human being can become by exercising his faculties, cultivating his awareness and keeping a careful eye on his own doings. In him, there is no split between what he says, what he does and what he is. No doubt it is a simple fact that, as a pilgrim among pilgrims, he has taken certain shortcuts which have led him faster, further and higher. All he offers is a method, the means to set out along the way and to follow it step by step; his own wisdom and the wealth of his experience offer a guiding beacon whose solitary flame sheds a friendly brightness through the shadows, and opens a breach towards the light.

'If we confine ourselves just to patiently waiting for suffering to fade away and for happiness to fall into our hands, the miracle will never come about', says Tentzin Gyatso. And that leaves no other choice but to pick oneself up, take oneself in hand, and start walking. At first sight, the technique seems fairly accessible. According to the Tibetan form of Buddhism it involves combining the three basic systems so as to venture into a practice that culminates in a transcendence of duality – in fact, to realise the ultimate unity. It is said that, for the outer world, one must suit one's conduct to the discipline of the Lesser Vehicle. Then, on the inner level, the aim is to train and develop the mind with the altruistic intention of achieving illumination, which is rooted in love and compassion. Lastly, in the innermost secret depths of being, by the practice of a deity yoga, one engages in concentration on the channels, the key points and the breathings, in order to encourage progress on the Way.

One of the foundations of this different knowledge lies in a famous yet little-known work, initiatory in the most precise sense of the term, generally referred to under the title of *The Tibetan Book of the Dead*. Now, the *Bardo Thodol* is not the Himalayan version of the Egyptian *Book of the Dead*, or some sort of grimoire for the use of minds inflamed by the prospect of the great departure: it is first and foremost a support for meditation, a guide to making the best possible, most fully-conscious, transition across the bridge between an existence approaching its end and a life ready to begin again. Unless, that is, it should recognise the real and profound significance of the Great Light in the process of the crossing; because in that case the cycle of reincarnation is finally broken, and it is no longer necessary to return. Freed of its chains, and emerging from the mists of ignorance, the being attains direct illumination. The exceptions occur when a person full of the strength of that inexpressible experience deliberately and knowingly decides to re-enlist in the world of forms in order to help other people.

For while it is hard enough to live out every day, dying is no small matter either, and Tibetan society has never neglected what it sees as this crucial aspect of life on earth. A proverb of the high plateau runs: 'The opposite of black is white, the opposite of night is day, and the opposite of life is birth.' Without losing his smile, the Dalai Lama talks about death as a companion in his mind, a familiar presence:

Sooner or later, it will come. If one thinks about it early, and prepares for it, the preparation may prove useful when it comes. If you just believe in this one life, and do not accept that it goes on, it hardly matters whether or not you are conscious of death. The meditation on death and impermanence is based on the theory of the continuity of consciousness at the point of rebirth. If there is another existence it may be useful to be ready to die, for, being prepared, one is less anxious and less frightened by the process of death, and does not complicate the situation with one's own thoughts.

If there are other lives to come, the quality of the next depends upon that of the present existence. If one is capable now of reducing the conception level of permanence, the attachment to existence is weakened. Likewise, by being capable of bearing impermanence in mind – by seeing that the deep nature of things is that they disintegrate – very probably one is less shocked by death when it arrives. By reflecting upon death and impermanence, one generates an attitude of no longer wanting them, and that in turn leads to the quest for the techniques to transcend death.

By leading a life uniquely concerned with the temporary affairs of this existence, without preparing for death, on that inevitable day when it arrives one is incapable of thinking about anything except one's own suffering and fright. That can produce a feeling of regret. Yet if one has often pondered on death and impermanence one knows that it is bound to come, and makes ready with a tranquil heart.

Since the state of mind at the moment of death is a determining cause of the continuity of consciousness in the next life, it is important to keep up the practice of the mind as death approaches. No matter what good or bad things may have happened during this particular existence, what happens just at the moment of death is particularly powerful. That is why it is important to learn what the process of death amounts to, and be ready for it.

During meditation on this specific theme, one becomes familiar with analogies of states that lead to death. In my everyday practice, in meditation, I pass through the stages of death six or seven times .... Certainly it remains to be seen how it will happen at the crucial moment, but at the very least I am working out the basis of success by stimulating the powers of attention and discrimination. For example, before embarking on a war in a particular region, you study a map to identify the hills, the river, the lake and so on, so that when you come to the place you are able to recognise what you see, and you know what has to be done.[48]

For Tentzin Gyatso, is it a matter of such paramount importance to make a successful crossing? 'To meditate on death is a common practice among Buddhists', he replies. It is important to remember that. All the tantric teachings, the practice of the Way and the achievement of the states resulting from meditation are explained on the basis of this ordinary level. Consequently, all higher tantric *sadhana* relies upon the prac-

tice of meditating on death, the intermediate state, and
rebirth. So, like it or not, everybody is called upon, if not
compelled, to meditate on death.

> I believe that, for a Buddhist, the essential reason for this practice
> is that there are two ways to avoid suffering or pain. The first is to
> forget and try to bypass negative things, and strive not to think
> about them. But that is an inefficient method and yields only
> temporary and transient results, becuase the problem remains
> intact.
>
> The other method of avoiding suffering consists in penetrating
> inside it, going to the heart of the problem itself and analysing it.
> In the beginning, the pain or the problem generally seem
> immense – a real mountain of woe. Yet once one has begun to
> reflect on it, seek out its origin, then analyse and study its nature,
> its intensity or gravity crumbles – the phenomenon dwindles
> away. So that this way, one attempts to overcome the obstacle
> and untangle the problem. The Buddhist teaching calls for
> focusing precisely on this deeper nature, and to think in this
> manner about old age, sickness and death: it is a way to get to
> know them, or so I believe.[49]

It must be admitted that in the world of today, this kind of
concern does not stand high on the agenda. And yet . . .

> I have often had the opportunity to discuss this question with
> westerners. It is very interesting. Since I try to keep open a
> dialogue between western philosophy and Buddhism, and also
> with science, on the basis of the relationship between mind and
> matter, the subject is utterly relevant. During my meetings with
> psychologists, neurologists and physicists, for my part I have
> found new ideas, particularly in terms of the latest scientific
> discoveries based on recent experience with caring for the dying.
> For me, as a Buddhist, it is very useful, and it seems to me that
> they too have caught sight of new perspectives thanks to the
> Buddhist explanations.
>
> At first, some research scientists can be noncommittal, and find
> it difficult to broach the subject, but when the discussion is under
> way and their interest is really aroused, then it becomes fasci-
> nating. It is not so much a religious discussion as an exchange of
> academic information. For example, on a recent visit to the Soviet

Union I had my first opportunity to talk to some communist researchers, in Leningrad. Some of them were content to explain everything by means of dialectical materialism, even if it is not entirely convincing. Others are true scientists who try to go further, observe without blinkers, and learn more without a preconceived opinion. But in any case I believe that it is very useful to persevere along this path.[50]

In talking to the Tibetan sovereign in exile, it is tempting to say to oneself that at such a degree life is really worth living. The thought makes him smile; one only has to alter one's vision a little in order to open the horizon and change perspectives.

If I say, 'I am a monk' or, 'I am a Buddhist', compared with my nature as a human being these things are temporary. A human being – that is what is fundamental. Once one has been born in a human form, it cannot change until death. The rest – whether one is educated or uneducated, rich or poor – is secondary. As we have this human physical form, we must safeguard our mental power of judgment. For that, no outside insurance is possible. The insurance company is in ourselves – self-discipline, awakened consciousness and discernment.[51]

It is in fact extremely valuable, in the cycle of births and deaths, to take human form; it is the only form that enables its wearer to shed all burdens, knowingly reject the snares of ignorance and achieve Awakening in a single existence. In Buddhism the best rebirth, offering the widest range of possibilities of fulfilment and plenitude, is resolutely human – thanks to the sharp, patiently-forged and polished perception of the immense potentialities of consciousness.

The faculty of reasoning, the capacity to think and the power of expression single out man as a superior being in relation to his dumb companions. Born human, it is vital to practise kindness and to carry out meritorious actions, for ourselves and others, in this life and in those to come. To be born in human form is a rare experience – so say the Buddhists – and it is best to use this precious opportunity with all possible wisdom and skill. For the gods themselves are mortal.

We all of us want happiness. In great cities, in the heart of the country, in remote villages, everywhere, people hurry to and fro. To what end? Everyone is striving to achieve happiness, and that is proper. Only it is very important to choose the right method in this quest. We must bear in mind that too great an involvement at the superficial level does not resolve the great problems.

Crisis and fears are growing all around us. Through a highly developed science and technology we have reached an advanced degree of material progress, as useful as it is necessary. But compare our inner with our outer progress, and it is obvious that the former falls short. In many countries, crisis – murders, assassinations and terrorism – is chronic. People complain about the decline of morality and the increase of criminal activities. While we are well developed and continue to make progress in the material domain, it would be equally important if at the same time we could make progress in terms of inner development.

In ancient times, when there was war the effects – the amount of destruction – were limited. Today, however, precisely because of our mutual material progress, they beggar the imagination. I have seen Hiroshima. Whatever idea I had of the nuclear explosion that happened there, it was trivial compared with going to the place, seeing with my own eyes and meeting people who had lived through that suffering. It touched me greatly. That is a dreadful weapon. Even if one considers somebody else as one's worst enemy, at a deeper level an enemy is also a human being: he too wants happiness, and he has the right to be happy. By seeing Hiroshima and reflecting on it in that instant, I was even more convinced that anger and hatred definitely cannot solve any problems. Even though the question of violence may also be expressed in different terms.[52]

And why should anyone acquire this perception and change himself? Simply to make the world a bit more livable, less aggressive and more harmonious. Utopia, perhaps, but even if utopias sometimes prove dangerous, a buried dream of a golden age urges us not to dismiss impatiently a step that leads to equilibrium, if not serenity, and to a deeper understanding of the world – provided, that is, that one does not fall into the many pitfalls of illusion and perseveres in the solitude of the path.

When all is said and done, the paradox is only apparent. Each person has to find his own way, according to the sincerity of his wishes, his intelligence and strength of character. The monk is at an advantage, perhaps, since he does not have to concern himself with the lures of social life or the host of obstacles, great and small, that pervade a secular existence. Yet, although bed and board once used to be more or less guaranteed, often in return for a contribution in work or kind, the present situation is no longer quite the same, and what with exile and the growing secularisation of society, religious teaching in the monastic schools is increasingly combined with a practical training.

Things have changed for the Dalai Lama, too. The violent collision between the high country and the reality of China – arms and ideology – has altered the traditional perspective, even if the fundamentals remain unchanged in the long run; as time goes by, the rough surfaces are worn smooth and the essence endures. Another kind of collision – hardly less violent, but equally vital for the future – came with the need to deal with the new demands of organising the community outside Tibet. Here too, the Dalai Lama needed all his abilities, focused upon a single goal, to preserve what had to be preserved at all costs, and win the battle against adversity.

Glancing back over the ground already covered, the most conspicuous development is the growing stature of the young spiritual leader, and the massive scale of a personality which stands out in the light of a solitude accepted, shouldered and transmuted into action.

There are two kinds of solitude. First the feeling of a deliberate search for isolation or retreat. Being alone or isolated is not the same thing as being solitary. Now and then I feel an intense and urgent need to be alone in order to meditate, learn and reflect, and to perform certain rites on my own.

Apart from that, there is another kind of solitude, like it or not, want it or not – the kind that is felt independently of oneself and of one's own will. This is not good, for it creates problems with other people and it leads to disquiet. But in yet another sense, the human being is alone: in the deep sense, each individual is alone. We are born and die alone. It is true that, in the cycle of existences, one is very alone, and always alone. There, no one can help you, and it is up to every person to help himself, and not to abandon himself.[53]

'Solitude, here, is no longer a negation, a lack, it is a positive reality, with a face and a voice.' So said Fosco Maraini in his notes.[54] Might that voice be the Dalai Lama's?

The solitude of the Dalai Lama and the other worldliness of Tibet – there is a strange and formidable interdependence between these two characteristics which ratify the remarkable quality of the kinship between one man and his land and people. Of course, the human being is always the product of an exchange, perhaps an unconscious one, between his environment and his capabilities, but seldom does the symbiosis reach such a degree of balance and subtlety.

The long isolation of the Land of Snows has no doubt contributed to this close relationship, which results from a dual current – one ascending, the other descending – of energy flowing in a closed loop. If the Dalai Lama is somehow first of all himself, together with the veneration of a whole people which surrounds and watches over him, and feeds his image with a beam of convergent vibrations, this focusing of forces shines on to and within him, to radiate outwards again and restore to every individual a fragment of power renewed. It is a curious alchemy. This general refraction phenomenon is manifested in every human gathering, great or small, around a more or less charismatic leader, but in this particular case it acquires an extraordinary dimension – a constant presence, which is both a shield of protection and a pledge of progress.

In exchange, the Dalai Lama continues to be seen as an omniscient figure, and this superhuman trust may sometimes be a heavy burden to bear; it compels its object perpetually to surpass himself, and to walk the highest peaks, alongside the steepest falls, unable to take even one false step. While this is the fate of anyone who holds real power, that kind of solitude does not permit the slightest flaw or weakness. Not that it would damage the standing of the spiritual guide, or tarnish his image – the example of the Sixth Dalai Lama proves the contrary – but in the Tibetan perception, because of the law of causality, there is ineluctably a cause to produce a given effect, and only the general ignorance stands in the way of comprehending such reasons. Nevertheless, there is no question of any divinely inspired infallibility, in the sense understood by the Roman Catholic faith in particular. A highly accomplished lama – and the Dalai Lama is certainly that – can see further into the three times and his actions reflect this knowledge, which takes account of facts whose immediate logic may escape an ordinary mortal.

8

The Lord of the White Lotus on the Lion's Throne

> As the hand in front of one's eyes conceals the highest mountain, so the little earthly life obscures the great lights and mysteries that fill the world, and he who can remove it from his sight as he would remove his hand discovers the great brilliance of other worlds.
>
> (*Rabbi Nahman of Bratislava*)

For lotus and lion to harmonise in such perfect accord, with no apparent dissonance, could happen only in Tibet, that beautiful high country where silence is wedded to solitude and where time finds expression in eternal space. Wild winds, boundless horizons and deep skies bursting into gulfs of light make a perfect blend with the flower-jewel, and provide a fitting background for the mythical big cat.

The lotus has become the paramount symbol of Buddhism because it is born in the mire of drowsy ponds and grows up through the treacherous sweetness of the water to spread and blossom in the air, in a miracle of harmony perpetually renewed. It is present at the heart of legends rooted in the ancient memory of mysterious India, and it faithfully accompanies many stages of the earthly existence of the sage of the Sakyas. Its petals form the base of the throne of the

Awakened, and sometimes it is used to illustrate some parable of wisdom. Whether he is called Avalokitesvara in the Indian style, or Chenrezig in the Tibetan, or the Precious Protector of the Land of Snows, the Buddha of Infinite Compassion often carries a lotus flower in his hand; that is why he is also known as the Lord of the Lotus. His representative on earth, his incarnation or emanation, is the sovereign of the Roof of the World, and as such the title is his by right.

For the Lion's Throne the symbolism is even more transparent, even if it concerns the lion of the snows, the fabulous beast that decorates the Tibetan flag and frolics on its old coinage. There used to be eight of them, carved in wood, gilded and ferocious, their manes streaming in the wind, their combined strength upholding the throne of the spiritual and temporal sovereign, on which no one but he might take their seat. The Fourteenth Dalai Lama solemnly reoccupied it in March 1940, as the apotheosis of the long ride which had brought him from a modest farmhouse in Taktser to the Potala, the residence of the gods. The Lion's Throne is an emblem of majesty and power, and at the same time it is also a sign of its occupant's full suzerainty over the whole of the high country, in both the spiritual and the temporal sphere. A whole elaborate symbolism of colours, proportions, cushions, accessories and details contributes towards making this royal seat the expression of the essence of an approach to the world and to its customs.

Thinly populated for its vast size – which is able to contain the wildest dreams – and travelled by nomads spellbound perhaps by the incessant pursuit of a great vision turned mirage, the land of Tibet has always had a reputation for harbouring unusual characters. As lay people, they had a solid footing in earthly life, and some of them – not many, but they did exist – had succeeded in blending the refined delights of a subtle orient with the comforts of western society, expert in the pursuit of material life. To western travellers, most Tibetans seemed at ease with themselves and contented with their lot.

The knowledgeable photographic eye of Fosco Maraini,

who accompanied Giuseppe Tucci on some of his journeys, encapsulated this salient feature when he observed:

> As far as anyone can be on this miserable earth, the Tibetans seemed to me like a truly happy people. Happiness is not so necessarily dependent on the social structure or system of government as our contemporaries appear to believe; above all it lies in the balance existing between the world around the man and the world he carries in his heart.[55]

That is to say that, tradition aside, the Dalai Lama's sovereignty is also based on an indisputable authority which does not derive solely from social or religious influences. In order to be granted so much trust and veneration, the Lord of the Lotus must himself be a master, in the most precise meaning of a man who passes on wisdom or knowledge. As the heir of countless complementary lineages, the monk who holds this office has always been a true guru, all through the centuries, with the one exception, perhaps more apparent than real, of the Sixth. Since his earliest childhood the Fourteenth Dalai Lama has been seen as belonging quite naturally to this centuries-old pattern.

So much so that in 1957, when resistance groups in the eastern provinces of Kham and Amdo were ruthlessly harassing the occupying power and striving to preserve a few shreds of independence, their leaders decided to ask the Dalai Lama to perform a special ritual, the *Tenshuk Shapten*. It was on the sovereign's return from the ceremonies in India to honour the twenty-fifth centenary of the Lord Buddha, and this rite had a special significance: not only did it express the Tibetan people's allegiance and trust in their spiritual guide; it was also a striking confirmation of his temporal power. To enhance the lustre of the event, custom required many rich gifts to be heaped at the sovereign's feet. And so, it was decided to present the Dalai Lama with a new throne, which could only be made of gold.

As if it was a perfectly straightforward procedure, once decided, emissaries travelled to all four corners of the high plateau collecting money and jewels, so that the offering should be worthy of His Holiness and the celebration. This might very well have been also a pretext for exploring the empty spaces of Tibet and making contacts for some other purposes, but perhaps the most surprising thing about it from the foreign point of view is that it took only a few months to amass a great treasure.

Gompo Tashi Andrugtsang, a brave warrior and one of the outstanding leaders in the underground struggle, tells how merchants and lamas, rich and poor, all joined together to make a gesture. As in the time of Alexandra David-Neel, over half a century ago, women took off their jewels and men their ornaments, and even the beggars gave their mite, to pay for building the giant statue of Maitreya, the Buddha of the Future, in Tashi-Lumpo in Shigatse. And as he went about, Gompo Tashi Andrugtsang admits to having seized the opportunity to assess the meagre forces of resistance and to meet local war chiefs to talk about ways to stand up to the Chinese. Brave as they were, but ill equipped and without the slightest outside help, rich in nothing but an old-fashioned heroism, what could those little groups do to stop the Chinese steamroller?

Once the gold, silver, turquoise and coral, diamonds and pearls and other trinkets had been collected, the work could begin.

> Forty-nine goldsmiths, five jewellers, nineteen engravers, six painters, eight tailors, six carpenters, three blacksmiths and three welders, helped by about thirty assistants, laboured for several weeks to construct that sumptuous throne. Throughout that time, sacred texts were read out and prayers recited, prayers' flags were hoisted and incense burnt. When the throne was finished it weighed 3,164 *tolas* [more than 80 pounds] of pure gold, encrusted with precious stones. The *dorje*, or symbolic thunder-bolt, decorating the front weighed 133 *tolas* [54 ounces] of gold inlaid with diamonds and turquoises in the shape of lions.[56]

To accompany this wonder, by way of presents, there was also a profusion of gold and silver ritual plate for the mon-asteries, lamps engraved with the eight auspicious symbols of

Buddhism, a small table also made of gold, ewers, offering bowls, plates and dishes. These offerings, like the throne, were later to remain in the Potala, to add to the age-old treasure of the Dalai Lamas. Considering that some years later it took the Chinese day after day and truckload after truckload to clear the red palace of its riches, it is easy to understand why.

After a consecration ceremony, held in order to thank the craftsmen for their labours, the throne was presented to the Dalai Lama with great pomp and ceremony on 7 July 1957, under the eyes of thousands of people who flocked to the Norbu-lingka. The young sovereign celebrated the rite and blessed the faithful from high on a balcony. Those who took part in that great day have never forgotten it, and it was undoubtedly one of the last fireworks displays of a way of life under threat of death. Other fires were flickering round about, and ready to break out – those of resistance to the invader, and those of a ruthless repression. But the men who were still free on the high plateau kept their faith in their sovereign, and there were those who hoped against hope to reverse an increasingly precarious situation.

This incidental sidelight on life in Lhasa, while the Chinese were practically occupying the Land of Snows and rumours of their atrocities and extortions were already flooding into the capital, is quoted because it reveals the place of religion in the country's daily life. A not inconsiderable fraction of the male population – about 10 per cent – lived in the monasteries, and everybody's life was led to the rhythm of family worship first, and then of the great festivals and pilgrimages. This does not mean that all Tibetans were mystics, hermits, or ascetics, everlastingly plunged into the contemplation of infinitely far horizons. The great majority of them lived their lives according to social norms defined by custom, which laid down solid but not impassable hierarchic barriers, and left the spiritual wellbeing of society as a whole to the care of its legions of monks. It is a plain fact that among the lamas there has always been a fairly high proportion of masters and gurus. Some have said that the great monasteries were a kind of seedbed, and that the lamas of Tibet were experts in the production of wise men, just as other institutions in other countries turned out doctors or engineers. 'In Tibet,' wrote the Dalai Lama's brother,

> we believe that each of us must do his share by destroying the ignorance which is inside ourselves. It is this conscious recognition of his ignorance and keen desire for liberation that make the Tibetan what he is and which, to my mind, makes life in Tibet so well worth living. Buddhism teaches us that our ignorance is suffering, and we know it. But even this small spark of knowledge brings beauty into our life, helping us to see beauty everywhere and teaching us wisdom.[57]

According to the Dalai Lama himself, there are two possible ways to approach Buddhism: the ways of faith and of reason. The way of faith is good, because it leads to the performance of just actions towards others, and the avoidance of doing harm. However, he goes on to say that in order to avoid the risk of a blind faith it is best first to establish the truth through reasoning, and that is his own unequivocal invitation to that personal contemplation which is the very foundation of Buddhism. He smiles slightly as he adds:

> There is no seal on the mouth of the Dalai Lama, the Buddhist monk Tentzin Gyatso. If there is anything you like in what I say, fine. If not, no problem: all you have to do is reject it. Do not accept anything merely because it was said by someone called 'The Dalai Lama'. Accept it only if it seems reasonable to you and of benefit to you and your spiritual life.[58]

For the way of reason is practically unending. Only that way enables the explorer to deepen his knowledge, to understand each thing and even to reach eventual illumination, or awakening. Certainly, although this way lies open, not everyone can undertake it, for it requires constant effort and much time to devote oneself to it. Nevertheless, those who choose fully to commit themselves to it can go so far in knowledge that their wisdom is gradually transmuted into radiance, and the understanding they gain makes them into torches to light the path for others who are nearing the edge of the way. Such people are all the more precious because they are so rare. Yet their inner light shines far into the distance.

How do you recognise a master, and how do you assess his qualities without being deceived? A spark of mischief lights the Dalai Lama's smile:

> That depends on each person's interests and inclinations, and it is enough to make a careful analysis of things. Before choosing a lama or a guru, it is important to investigate whether that person is genuinely qualified. A passage in the *Vinaya* [discipline] says that, just as it is possible to register the presence of a fish in the water by the ripples observed upon the surface, so the inner qualities of a master can be perceived, with time, in his behaviour. One should also gauge his learning – his ability to explain his themes – and see whether his teachings are in harmony with his attitude and way of living. According to one tantra, this investigation must be particularly scrupulous, even if it has to last twelve years. That is the way to choose a master.[59]

Like an echo, another Tibetan lama, Tara Rimpoche, from the tantric monastery of Gyuto, offers his own explanation: 'The guru must have at least two qualities, compassion and wisdom. If he does not possess the former, there is a danger that he may do harm to the disciple. Without the latter, probably he will only lead him into error.'[60] Masters of this stamp and stature do not seek to draw attention to themselves and are content to be as they are – in the fullness of their accomplishment, which they do not refuse to share.

Listening to their teachings, or hearing their commentaries on the sacred texts, from the best-known to the most obscure – lessons which they do not dispense without prior preparation – the most immediately striking feature is the clarity of thought and conciseness of expression. It is thus with the exegesis of the famous mantra OM MAṆI PADME HŪM, which has become a distinctive emblem of Buddhism in Tibet, being so omnipresent in the high country and so charged with meaning for the Tibetan people. With prayer flags, carved *mani* stones by the roadside, inscriptions perched on mountain slopes, strips of paper flapping in the wind, invocations on the threshold of homes or monasteries, the tireless chant of pilgrims telling their beads or the first halting words of children, the whole of Tibet recognises itself in this age-old litany that accomplishes the country from one century, one age, one life, to the next. The usual translation is the succinct 'Behold the Jewel in the Lotus.' With successive masters and all through the centuries it has given rise to thousands of commentaries and interpretations, scholarly research and modest offerings concerning this symbol of life and of a way of being. The Dalai Lama sums up these accounts with singular perfection.

It is fine to recite the mantra OM MANI PADME HUM, but while reciting it one should also think about its meaning, because the scope of these six syllables is vast and profound. The first, OM, is made up of the three letters, A, U and M. They symbolise the body, word and spirit of the practising Buddhist; but at the same time they symbolise the pure and glorious body, word and spirit of a Buddha.

Can the impure body, word and spirit be transformed into a pure body, word and spirit, or are they entirely separate? All Buddhas are originally beings like ourselves, who in following the Way have become Awakened. Buddhism does not claim that there is anybody who from the very beginning is faultless and possesses all the good qualities. The development of a pure body, word and spirit comes gradually from relinquishing impure states, which are thereby transformed into pure states.

How is this done? The way is shown by the next four syllables. MANI, meaning jewel, symbolises the means of the method – the altruistic intention to be illuminated, compassion and love. Just as the jewel is capable of removing poverty, so the altruistic spirit of awakening is able to dismiss the indigence, or the difficulties, of cyclic existence and solitary peace. Likewise, just as the jewel fulfils the desires of sentient beings, so the altruistic intention to become enlightened accomplishes the wishes of sentient beings.

The two syllables PADME, lotus, symbolise wisdom. Just as a lotus emerges from the silt without being soiled by the mud, so wisdom can place you in a situation of non-contradiction, whereas without possessing wisdom there would be contradiction. There is the wisdom that realises impermanence; the wisdom that realises that people are devoid of substantial existence or of self-sufficient existence; that which realises the emptiness of duality, which is to say the difference of entity between subject and object; and the wisdom that realises the vacuity of inherent existence. Although there are different sorts of wisdom, the principal among them is that which realises vacuity.

Purity must be acquired through the indivisible unity of method and wisdom, symbolised by the final syllable HŪM, which expresses indivisibility. According to the system of the *sūtras*, this indivisibility of method and wisdom refers to method affected by wisdom and to wisdom affected by method. In the mantric or tantric vehicle the reference turns upon the specific consciousness in which the global form, both of wisdom and method, constitutes an identity without differentiation. In terms of seed-syllables of the five conquering Buddhas, HŪM is the seed-syllable of Akṣhobya – the Immutable, the non-fluctuating, that which cannot be shaken.

Thus the six syllables OM MAṆI PADME HŪM signify that in accordance with the practice of a way, which is the indivisible union between a method and a wisdom, you can transform your impure body, word and spirit into the pure and glorious body, word and spirit of a Buddha. It is said that Buddhahood is not to be sought outside oneself; the materials for achieving it lie within. Maitreya said in his 'Sublime Continuum of the Great Vehicle' (*Uttaratantra*) that all beings naturally have the Buddha nature in their own continuum. We have in ourselves the seed of purity, the essence of One Gone Thus [Enlightenment] (*Tathāgatagarbha*), which must be transformed and fully developed into Buddhahood.[61]

For the Buddhist faithful, Buddhism is lived and felt much more as an art of living than as a religion in the strict sense of worship. Certainly ritual, ceremonial, prayers, sacred texts and monastic life contribute to shaping its formally religious outer aspect. The fact remains that it lacks an ingredient essential in other systems of thought, namely the creator god, the supreme and sovereign principle without which there is no salvation. There are still plenty of voices which will

answer that 'these people' are idolaters and that they continue
to bow down and bring offerings to their idols. Indeed. While
it is undeniable that the Buddhist faith as generally practised
among the humblest followers of the Great or Lesser Vehicle,
from the lushness of the tropics to the austerity of the Himalayas, is sometimes very much akin to the blind and simple
faiths of other latitudes, the more we penetrate its mysteries
and its treasure house of philosophy, logic and – why not? –
metaphysics, the brighter shine the wonderful reflections of
its light. As the Dalai Lama explains:

The distinctive feature of Buddhism lies in the fact that it is
essentially humanistic rather than formally religious in its presen-
tation. It sets about defining the problems that arise in life, and
proposing a series of solutions. Unlike most of the world's
religions it does not base itself upon the concept of God. It talks
of man, and how he may attain perfection. Many religions begin
with the idea of God and then use it to settle all the problems of
existence, like creation and evolution. Even if it is an easy
answer, it is not logically provable. That is why Buddha avoided
it and strove to present a doctrine that might be based through
and through upon reason.

By refraining from using the theory of God, Buddha also
avoided various problematic consequences that derive from it.
For example, the danger that people may feel excessively dim-
inished: they may worship God and even sit at His feet some day,
but never be His equal. God is an entity, and we human beings
are presented as His creatures, doomed to be for ever inferior to
Him. We are supposed blindly to accept and put into practice His
word, or suffer the consequences of defying our Creator and
Support. That is very good for fighting egoism, and it is always
good to practise morality, devotion and kindness. But there is a
danger of not appreciating the human potential at its full value.
Besides, the religions based upon a God do not usually allow 'the
word of God' to be rejected, even if it contradicts reason. That
can easily stifle the development of philosophical enquiry.

As well as that, a good number of philosophical problems are
raised straightaway by the theory of God. For example, if God is
all-powerful and if He has created everything, then he also
created suffering and injustice. One might conclude from this

that he is cruel and extremely wicked, like a mother who gave birth to a child with the precise intention of torturing it and making it suffer.

In order to avoid these kinds of problem, Buddha set out to put forward a doctrine founded solely upon reason, and a way expressed solely in terms of human problems and goals. He declared man himself responsible for his present existence, and he provided a series of methods of cultivating and encouraging development away from the state in which we find ourselves at present, and towards perfection. He stressed that it is man who shapes his own destiny: he is responsible for his own growth, or his degeneration. Buddhas are not creators. They are only masters and guides for those who really want to listen. It is up to the individual, whether or not he chooses to take advantage of their advice.

It is up to us to take the direct responsibility for our spiritual life and not to rely on anything or anybody else, for even the Buddhas of the ten Directions and the three Times are unable to help us if we do not help ourselves. If someone else were in a position to help us, surely he would already have done so.[62]

To see what the Dalai Lama means, it is enough to ask him for his answer to a question that must have been put to him hundreds or thousands of times, namely, does he believe in God? 'Believe in God? Hmm . . .' The brown eyes dance with mischief for an instant, then almost disappear behind the catlike lowering of his eyelids, but behind his spectacles the veiled eyes still convey a look of collusive amusement, while one hand offers a small questioning gesture, as if to ask a real question.

That depends on the meaning given to the word, to the term god. If god signifies a higher being, a pure being, I believe that I believe in him, and that we believe in him. We accept the idea of god, not one god but thousands of gods. In the precise sense of divinities, of goddesses and gods – you know, the appeased or angry divinities that one visualises in the course of practice and meditation. In this sense they do exist, these male and female deities, without any doubt. At least, as long as the being is a prisoner of the present world of forms and differentiations, it personifies the divinities under distinct forms. But if you are talking about god as creator, then no, for us, for me, there can be no such being.[63]

No creator god? And yet the Buddhist world is a perfectly coherent structure, which not only stands firm – it is rooted in the depths of humanity itself – but has survived through the centuries, despite its ups and downs, losing none of its brilliance and attraction. So in the beginning was Buddha. But then who was this figure, whose name means 'the Awakened, the Enlightened One'? A man, no more or less.

A human being, though certainly a chosen one, in view of the signs and portents that accompanied the birth of Prince Siddhartha of the Sakya clan. Brought up in the utmost luxury and beauty, eventually he was to discover pain, suffering and death, despite all the precautions taken by the king his father, who had learned from a prophecy that his newborn son would become either a great king and warrior, or a great religious teacher. And when he finally discovered these truths so long concealed, he decided to seek their causes. Years of self-discipline, contemplation, travel and seeking finally led him to a dusty little hamlet in the heart of ancient India, where long meditation as he sat beneath a tree opened his mind's eye at last. This was the Awakening, or Enlightenment. The tree is now known as the Bodhi tree, Tree of Enlightenment, and the little village is called Bodh Gaya. After that time, the sage lived out his earthly life in travel and teaching, tirelessly proclaiming the Four Noble Truths and the Eightfold Path which would enable the wayfarer to be liberated forever from suffering, and to escape the cycle of rebirth.

The powerful tide of lives, generations and centuries has surrounded the Awakened One with a legend, a history, a philosophy, schools of thought – a whole apparatus which at first sight can seem labyrinthine. Questions and answers reveal a guiding thread; Sakyamuni, a man of his time, became Buddha, the historical figure, because his immense will to understand and deep desire to break the chains of reincarnation enabled him, thanks to certain masters and teachings, but mainly through his own efforts, gradually to purify his body, word and mind, and then to reach Awakening. That is why some Buddhist Scriptures say that the Buddha Mind, or Truth Body (*Dharmakaya*), is the Buddha himself, that his word, or inner energy, represents *dharma* – doctrine – and that his physical body may be considered as the *sangha*, or spiritual community, of the disciples. These three elements also form the Three Jewels .... Which is another way of saying that every human being can set out along this path; since there are different levels of mind, the most subtle is the deep Buddha nature, the germ of Buddhahood. All beings contain within themselves this subtle awareness, and through the practice of meditation and right actions it can be transformed into achieved Buddhahood.

And the Dalai Lama comments: 'Our situation is very encouraging, the seed of liberation is within us.' There is no compulsion to believe it, but why not? For Buddhists, there is no such person as a Buddha who has always existed for all eternity and who has been illuminated ever since the dawn of time and for ever more. 'Buddhas', Tentzin Gyatso explains, 'are people who, like ourselves, originally had their minds clouded, and who, step by step, have removed these stains to the point of being transformed into beings having every good quality and without the slightest fault.'

And what is the means of achieving this perfection? 'The simple fact', says the Dalai Lama,

that the nature of the mind is pure light and knowledge allows it. The mind is endowed with the ability to appear under any guise, no matter what, through the power of projection of the object. It is an entity of pure light and cognition, endowed with the nature of experience. Instant after instant, it disintegrates. Yet among its countless causes – classified as substantial causes and cooperative conditions – there must be, as a set of experiences of consciousness, its substantial cause in an immediately preceding cause, which is a prior moment of consciousness. It is impossible for an entity with a character of light and knowledge to be produced by external material elements which are its substantial cause. In the same way, an inner spirit cannot act as the substantial cause of external elements. To the extent that each moment of consciousness requires a previous moment of consciousness as its substantial cause, there is no other way but to assume that the fundamental continuum of the mind has no beginning. Some particular kinds of idea, like the wish to own a car, have a beginning and an end, whereas others, such as ignorance of inherent existence, in terms of their continuum, have no beginning but do have an end. Nevertheless, neither beginning nor end can be ascribed to the spirit of clear light and knowledge. So even if the spirit disintegrates from one instant to the next, its continuum is no less devoid of a beginning.

That being the situation of the mind, how is it transformed? That the mind goes through false states is due to ignorance, to a darkening in relation to the mode of subsistence of phenomena. In order to avoid this ignorance it is necessary to engender the knowledge of this mode of subsistence; and to engender such a consciousness, knowing the nature of the phenomenon, it is necessary to understand the objects which are to be known. On the subject of what ought to be known, there are two kinds of status – the conventional objects which are only simple appearances, and the final mode of being of these objects. The former are objects found by a consciousness discriminating among conventions, while the latter are the objects discovered by a consciousness distinguishing the final mode of subsistence. The former are called conventional truths, and the latter, ultimate truths . . . .

Whatever the phenomenon that appears to us, it seems to exist objectively in itself, by and for itself. If it seems fully to exist in that way, by setting out to analyse it so as to determine whether or not it exists as it seems, we do not manage to find it through analysis. When an object is divided into parts, the whole cannot be found, and there is no means of subjecting it to analysis in its totality.

Furthermore, there is nothing among the objects of knowledge which is devoid of parts. All physical objects have directional parts; for example, even considering the case of quarks, which make up the protons in a nucleus, they occupy a certain surface, and therefore they have directional parts.[64]

Relying on the teachings of the Buddhist schools of the *Yogacara* (Pure Mind) and the *Madyamika* (Middle Way), the Dalai Lama pursues his account with an infectious liveliness:

1 Before the departure for Lhasa, with local dignitaries (1939).

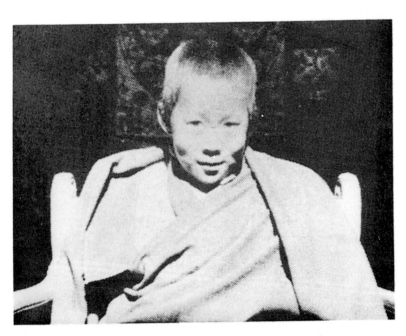

2 The Dalai Lama during an audience at the Potala.

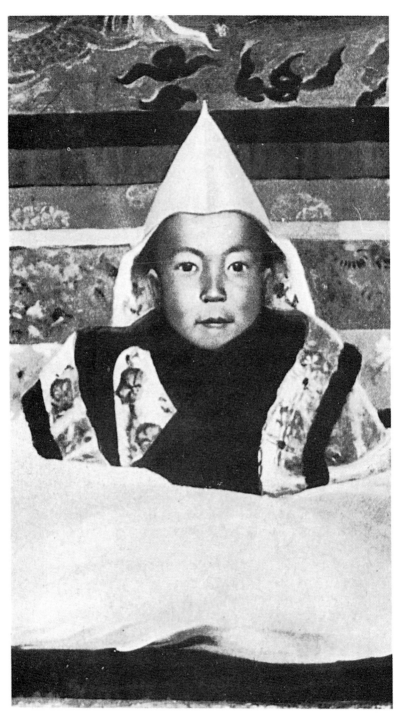

3 The enthronement of the Dalai Lama.

4 Tantric initiation of the Dalai Lama.

5   The Dalai Lama and the Panchen Lama in Beijing (1954).

6   Meeting with Mao in Beijing (1954).

7   The Dalai Lama at a public examination session.

8   Hyderabad House, at New Delhi, in 1956, on the Buddha's 2,500th
birthday, a rare occasion for a family reunion *(from left to right)*: the mother
(1900–81); Tsering Dolma (1919–64); Thoubten Jigme Norbu (1922–); Gyalo
Thondup (1928–); Lobsang Samten (1933–85); the Dalai Lama (1935–); Jetsun
Pema Gyalpo (1941–); Tenzin Choegyal (1946–).

9   The Dalai Lama going into exile (March 1959).

10   Two tutors in the Dharamsala archives.

11 . With Nehru.

12 With Indira Gandhi.

13 'Anything that serves towards peace, it is this that I have come to teach you' (Kâlachakra at Bodh Gaya, December 1985).

14 'You must doubt, because doubt stimulates research, and research is the road that leads to knowledge' (Digne, May 1986).

In fact, our mind instinctively makes a distinction between the whole and its parts, acting so that, when they appear to us, there seems to be a whole which is quite separate from its parts, and parts separate from a whole. Yet this is not in fact the case. For disciples of the Pure Mind school, external objects do not exist. Arguing on the grounds that external objects cannot be found by analysis, they conclude that they do not exist. For adherents of the Middle Way, even if particles without parts do not exist at all, the simple fact that external objects cannot be found by analysis means that these objects are without a genuine basis, not that they do not exist. So not being detected in the last analysis means not existing genuinely, not being non-existent.

Phenomena exist; the fact that they are useful or harmful is an obvious sign that they exist. Nevertheless, they are empty of existence in their way of appearing to us. That a phenomenon cannot in the final analysis, be found indicates that it has no genuine, or inherent, existence. Since phenomena are empty of existence in their concrete manner of appearing, all phenomena exist in the context and nature of an emptiness of inherent existence.

If phenomena really existed in the way they are perceived, subjected to analysis they would be bound to appear more and more clearly to the mind. But that is not the case: that is therefore a sign that they do not exist in the way that they appear to.

Once having accepted the perception that things are not as they seem to appear, this certitude grows stronger, and the sense of grasping the world is modified. It is as in the cinema; images appear before your eye, and you can either simply observe them, or you can tell yourself that in fact they do not exist. By concentrating on this non-existence, after a while the appearance itself begins to blur. It is an approach to appearance which is like an illusion. Or again, take the example of a mirror: the reflection of a face lacks the quality of existence of the real face, but this emptiness of being is not its reality. Its reality is its emptiness of inherent existence.[65]

The further along the way, the more the faculty of reason sharpens and refines, and reaches to more and more subtle levels. According to Tentzin Gyatso, 'by growing used to the state of mind that realises emptiness, and by cultivating it even more deeply both during and out of stabilising meditations, when this mind is transformed into direct perception, then for that consciousness all types of dualist appearance disappear'.

It is a beautiful vision, and makes us marvel at the power of the mind. Yet human beings have travelled this far, and further still. If, from a Buddhist viewpoint, the conventional nature of the mind is clear light, then what obscures it obviously does not derive from its essential nature, and is the product of temporary, fugitive phenomena which can be eliminated. From the ultimate viewpoint the nature of the mind is to be empty of inherent existence. Buddha said that every phenomenon is only nominal, and that this nominality itself is only nominal; even emptiness is empty. In that perspective, how do we situate ourselves, and how do we grasp this reality which may cause the mind to reel?

'The mental attitude is paramount', the Dalai Lama replies.

Thanks to the high development of science and technology we can travel far into space. That's fine. From my childhood I have loved science and technology: they are absolutely necessary for the welfare of humanity. At the same time, when it comes to looking within, even if our head is not very big there is still a lot to explore. So it would be a good thing to direct half of our energy outwards and the other half inwards, and to consider more: Who am I? What is the nature of the mind? What advantage does a good thought bring? What is the advantage of a bad thought? To ask oneself this kind of question, to think, examine and reflect.

Even though it may raise contradictions. What is a person? What is the 'I'? Buddhism affirms altruism, but isn't that another way of saying that the self is non-existent? If Buddhists insist that there is neither a person nor a self, then there should be no person to meditate upon altruism and no person towards whom to cultivate compassion. And yet our own experience establishes that there are persons and there are 'selves'. If the 'I' is established by experience, then what becomes of the theory of altruism? Isn't there a contradiction here? Not at all. Let me explain . . . . The persona, the ego, has many ways of appearing in our minds. On the one hand the 'I' appears permanent, unitary and set firmly in its own authority; in this mode of appearing the ego seems to be an entity separate from the mind and body, the person being the user or beneficiary, while the mind and body are what is used or enjoyed . . . .

On the other hand the 'I' appears as having its own self-sufficient or substantially existent entity, but derived from the same character as the mind and body. In another way again, the ego seems not to exist in the last analysis, but appears to exist by virtue of its own conventional character. In yet another way, the self appears as if it had an inherent existence. Our innate, erroneous, conception of the 'I' is a consciousness that considers the 'I' in this latter manner, as if it had a concrete existence in accord with this appearance.

This false idea exists among all beings, whether or not they have been educated and whether or not they have been affected by a system. Nevertheless, despite all these appearances, none of all this . exists. According to the various Buddhist systems, the non-existence of these respective levels of the self, of reification, constitutes altruism, rising from the crudest to the most subtle.[66]

By meditating each and every day upon these various themes, there are some who succeed in realising the meaning of emptiness, and also of the ultimate unity. Some claim that this kind of ascesis brings to the practitioner 'powers' which in other places are sometimes called magical. The Dalai Lama smiles when he hears this question and answers that this very much depends on the point of view adopted.

Perhaps you are not capable of levitating, flying or displaying similar gifts, but anyway that is secondary, and it plays a part contrary to the one intended if, in that way, you cause trouble in the world. The important thing is to master the mind, and learn to be somebody good. As you practise the teaching, nirvana will gradually come. But if you act under the control of hate or bitterness, it will only move away.[67]

For all that, in Tibet these particular phenomena were not so rare, and were not considered to be so very exceptional; you only have to know how it is done, they say, and better not to use these gifts to do harm. As for Tentzin Gyatso, he feels that this aspect is unimportant; is he himself not credited with uncommon qualities, such as a kind of clairvoyance, or the power to heal? And is he not also called Yeshe Norbu, meaning 'the Wish-fulfilling Gem'?

Here, too, no doubt the Dalai Lama is basically right; Buddhism asserts that the world is an illusion, that it is a product of our perceptions. If the world is decidedly not what it appears to be, then how and why might 'extraordinary' events, in the basic sense of the word, not be quite ordinary at other levels of consciousness, or openness on to other dimensions? An element of mystery is not out of place within the miracle of the world, even, or perhaps above all, when a person is committed body and soul to the spiritual quest at the frontier of the world of men. Thus, what are we to understand by reincarnation?

For the Dalai Lama reincarnation is neither a dogma nor an article of faith, but is explained by the continuity of consciousness which is part of the Buddhist vision of the world. This explanation he considers more logical, and in any case more satisfying to the mind, than any other; it is the ground and deepest cause of that time which has no end and no beginning, that cosmic space which cannot be measured, and that humanity which perpetually evolves at the heart of the cycle of existences. Otherwise – short of accepting the existence of a creator god responsible for all the sorrows and splendours of the world – how are we to explain life, the universe, the human being and all those who have a recollection of previous lives?

Reincarnation is based upon the continuity of the mind, of consciousness. Naturally I am thinking of the continuity of the most subtle consciousness. For many people the crude level of consciousness depends upon the human body, which constitutes its basis. For example, the consciousness of the eye, meaning vision, or of all the organs of the senses, or again certain kinds of emotional imprint. When these bases deteriorate, their functions of consciousness cease.

The subtler consciousness is more independent. What I mean is that from the moment when the brain, or rather the varieties of consciousness induced by the brain, cease to function, when other levels of consciousness come into play. Even though the mechanisms of the brain are very active during the perception of an object or an experience – as it is essential and very important that they should be – the true agent of understanding or knowledge does not lie solely in the particles of the perceiving brain. There is something more. To be sure, it cannot be measured with ordinary instruments, because it lacks a form. But if one does not accept this kind of phenomenon somewhere outside the brain and senses, it seems to me that it is hard to explain our daily activity and life, and our everyday experience.

For example, when people study they learn, they increase their knowledge. But that has nothing to do with increasing the number of brain cells, has it? Our own daily experiences testify that sometimes there are cases when someone goes through a different state of consciousness, or disturbed perception, when an object or phenomenon is perceived in an abnormal manner. If, later on, conditions become ordinary once again, these distorted perceptions may, by normalising themselves, be transformed into valid knowledge, enabling the object to be correctly perceived. The same goes for certain beliefs or presumptions.

If we seek to explain children's or adults' memories of their previous lives at the physical level, it doesn't work, because it is not enough to be confined to saying that we are dealing with transformations happening inside the brain. So much so, that without accepting the existence of a continuity of consciousness one suddenly finds oneself facing a whole series of new questions, and having the utmost difficulty in finding answers to them. It is these reasons that make us consider that there exists a power, or energy, that is aware of these phenomena. Of course there is also dependence with the physical, with the material side. But then one comes back to the question whether matter can or cannot, in certain conditions, produce or develop a consciousness.

We ourselves think that this subtle consciousness does exist. Call it energy, if you wish, or power-that-perceives: that is a matter of terminology. All the same, this consciousness too must have a certain kind of capacity or potential in itself, in order to be capable of perceiving the object. This subtle, or basic, consciousness is manifested in sleep, or again in the course of precise moments of attention, as in meditation. It seems to me that we are dealing here with something that it is very important to realise, and to study scientifically.

In any case, even if this summary explanation does not seem

totally satisfactory, it seems to us to be less contradictory or less inconsistent than other theories. By accepting the existence of a continuous consciousness, or of the continuity of consciousness, Buddhists explain why certain people retain an awareness of their previous lives and can easily look back to the most distant past. Likewise, it is thus possible to explain a universe in constant flux, and with cycles of appearance and disappearance. That is also the fundamental reason for rebirth.

Consciousness *per se* is neither good nor bad. It is and it can be influenced by different thoughts. In the case of negative or violent thoughts, the person who registers them will act under the sway of that influence. On the other hand, a positive thought will exert influence in the opposite direction. And this would tend to show the influence of thought over behaviour as long as consciousness is not fundamentally stabilised.

In other words, we think that it is possible to modify the mind with the help of a certain kind of training, by means based on reason. A mastery of the mind allows a greater control of consciousness, which can lead to tangible practical results. Of course, that requires the proper training, which is also very long. But it is in this way that one may suceed in controlling one's own birth. This is the very basis of reincarnation.

The Buddhist theory of liberation states that through enquiry and contemplation one may succeed in putting an end to negative thinking, and hence to suffering. Some people are simply more gifted, or better prepared, than others. In the same way, in the highest and most precise sense, with extremely strict discipline, one may reach the point of controlling one's own rebirth. Not everybody succeeds, but it is possible.[68]

Although he gives teachings both at Dharamsala and during his travels, not only for Tibetans but for neo-Buddhists from different lands, Tentzin Gyatso himself continues to learn. The Lord of the Lotus devotes part of his time to study and meditation with masters who are the keepers of special traditions of knowledge which, after the appropriate initiation, he is able to practise and then to pass on if he should deem it useful. Nor does he hesitate, sometimes, to curtail all his activities for a more or less long period and go into total solitary retreat in order to take stock.

This does not always go without a hitch. At Dharamsala they still talk in veiled terms about a certain year – 1976 – when things definitely seemed to be taking a dangerous turn. First, the state oracle at Nechung had proffered some dismal predictions and issued several warnings. Then, before the *Kashag*, as he presented his annual report the Dalai Lama had echoed this danger signal and had not played down his criticisms of a kind of general lassitude, and indeed casualness, which he did not relish. Soon after that he withdrew into a rigorously solitary retreat, one of the longest he had ever practised in India. As he was to explain to me ten years later, 'It is a very strict practice, which requires total withdrawal for several weeks, connected with a quite particular teaching of the Fifth Dalai Lama's.'

It took no more than that to throw the entire Tibetan community into a state of alarm. For when people started to think about it, they soon found themselves drawing the comparison between this prolonged retreat and the historical situation in the days of that same Fifth Dalai Lama; Tibetans have not forgotten that it was on the pretext of an indefinite period of meditative withdrawal that the death of the Great Fifth was concealed for years in their country. In order to avert ill fortune and bad omens, throughout the duration of the Dalai Lama's absence, which they took particularly hard, the Tibetans of Dharamsala and of all the communities established in the south of India never stopped praying, organising ceremonies and making offerings at every shrine. A usually cheerful people, now they seemed anxious, and solely concerned with telling their beads, turning their prayer wheels and chanting endless mantras and sacred texts.

In this unaccustomed and oppressive atmosphere, first came a very serious earthquake which took thousands of victims in China, and then Chairman Mao breathed his last. One close Indian friend of the Tibetans was caused to remark 'That's quite enough, stop praying, or else the sky is going to fall on the heads of the Chinese!' For weeks on end a constant stream of offerings and prayers continued throughout the Tibetan community, both in the monasteries and in domestic shrines. The oracles were once again consulted, the gods invoked and their message fervently recorded, ceremonies of long life were conducted on behalf of the recluse, and everybody promised to pay greater respect to the will of the Precious Protector. Three months went by before the Dalai Lama returned to resume his place among his people.

To receive and pass on knowledge and understanding belongs naturally to the responsibilities of a sage who means to help others, all others – or at any rate those who wish to be helped – to open their eyes. That is the aim of the collective or individual initiations that the Dalai Lama gives from time to time; an introduction to the knowledge of things, or explanations, long kept secret, allowing access through personal will and striving to a new level of accomplishment. Thus in 1986 the Dalai Lama devoted the whole month of August to following the teachings of one master of the ancient tradition of the Nyingma line, Grand Lama Dilgo Khentse Rimpoche. Combined with his outstanding personal qualities, the many initiations received by Tentzin Gyatso make the Fourteenth Dalai Lama a master of wisdom among the great masters, and his modesty in no way diminishes the scope of his knowledge. But does the Lord of the Lotus still have something more to learn?

Whatever other people, disciples or not, may think of me, quite apart from the way I am seen, and even if some people consider me as omniscient, from my own point of view I am only a drifter along the Way, and I still have a lot to do. Of course I have the status of dalai lama, I am the Dalai Lama, but as an individual I am only a monk whose foremost wish is to learn and find out more, to receive instruction and use it sensibly.

Besides that, no doubt you know that in Tibetan Buddhism the continuity of the lines of transmission is crucial. That is to say that it is also a good idea to be pragmatic. Even if, in the course of previous lives, you have already received the very same teachings, if you have already carried out the practices required, that doesn't matter: it is in this present life that you are living, so they must be received anew. For if the teaching is transmitted from

one life to the next, and if the various memories and remi-
niscences are there, your knowledge is in vain when you lack the
most important thing, which is the blessing of the master who
passes on the message, to make the practice really fruitful.

It is not enough to say, in a new life: I know, I have already
received this or that teaching in a previous life. In fact, no one says
this, even if it may actually have happened, and many of the teachings I have received stem from this way of seeing. For instance,
recently I studied and received the teaching of a fundamental
Tantric text, *The Essence of the Secret* [*Guhya-Garba*], which we call
'root-text', together with its commentaries. This is a translation of
a text which originally came from India, and which forms part of
the basis of the Nyingma tradition of the Old School. Last year it
was the tutor of Sakya Trizin Rimpoche, of the Sakya tradition,
who passed on the teaching and initiation of one of his school's
root-texts, called Causes of the Effects, to me. It is also vital to
receive the initiation into the particular divinity, under his or her
peaceful and wrathful aspects, in order to practise correctly.

In this case, it is not a question of knowing or of not knowing:
what matters is to receive the continuity of the teaching, otherwise we consider that there is no true transmission of the blessing, the encouragement lavished by the master so as to make the
practice effective. To learn by reading or debate is different. The
blessing has to be granted by a living master for the tradition to
live on, and the guru himself must be qualified and experienced.
That is how it is done.

In my own case, I cannot be content merely with saying that
since I am the Dalai Lama and have already followed these
teachings in other lives, then I may teach anyone, without the
continuity of transmission in the line concerned. I have to have
the authority bestowed by direct transmission, given by another
true master, in order for it to be really valid. Buddha himself
never put all authority into a single hand. In the religious sphere,
no one can say: 'You are the Dalai Lama, so you are superior to
everybody, the greatest of all the grand lamas.' The dalai lama is
a monk, a disciple who also happens to be the Dalai Lama: he too
should bow to the system and respect the general custom. And
anyway, it is good that this is so.[69]

Does this mean that the Lord of the Lotus can be wrong, and
make mistakes, like anybody else?

Of course, undoubtedly, and perhaps even more than anybody else! At the religious level, I believe that the guru is always seen in the full light of day, and his disciples trust him completely, or consider him almost as infallible. Yet individually, as a human being, like all human beings, it is right for him to strive to do his best, and not to be mistaken. Even though, by way of the false, one may arrive at the true. If there is no false, then there is no true either: without the sense of falsehood there could be no sense of truth.[70]

It is this same sense of relativity and deep understanding of the world of human kind that puts Tentzin Gyatso's character on so firm a footing. The humility is not assumed, it is the mark of the wise man, the basis of the master's undisputed sovereignty. So much so that he is able to surprise scholars and scientists who may at first be puzzled by this jovial monk who is not afraid to venture upon far-reaching discussions where the boundaries that usually divide science and philosophy or science and religion are suddenly and revealingly blurred, or perhaps are dissolved into a new and unusual equilibrium of opposites.

Ancient wisdom, modern knowledge – it is one of the most surprising features, though only at first sight, of the insatiable curiosity of the Lord of the Lotus. He himself agrees that his interest in what the west calls science goes far back in time, and into the texts of Buddhism. In all his travels he likes to arrange meetings with scientists in all kinds of different fields, and shows a keen interest in visiting laboratories in the forefront of research.

While he takes a particular interest in high-energy physics and quantum theory, he is just as fascinated by psychology, medicine, biology and neurology; with infinite patience he seeks out the points of convergence between his own ancestral knowledge and the findings of the most advanced contemporary experiments, using the most sophisticated techniques. They are not hard for him to detect and, whereas comparisons are necessarily odious, he does not hide the real pleasure he feels when, in the knowledge of today, he finds a confirmation of the spiritual intuitions of his predecessors.

And anyone who looks at certain *tankas*, the religious paintings executed on cloth, kept preciously rolled up in the monasteries and passed on from generation to generation as knowledge is usually passed on, will find food for thought in their elegant outlines of cosmic visions of the world and the stars; they seem to contain an uncanny premonition of atomic diagrams and of the relationships, as evanescent as they are invisible to the naked eye, of the inner structures of the atom or the cosmos.

On a recent visit to Europe the Dalai Lama paid a visit to the Max Planck Institute, in the German Federal Republic, in order to discuss atomic particles. This is how he sums up his meetings with some of the world's experts in this area:

Obviously the idea of atoms and particles is not new in Buddhism. Our oldest texts have referred to them, and they mention even finer particles. But in comparing these notions with the findings of modern science, we see that the latter have achieved a level of much more refined, precise and detailed explanations. It has produced a definition a great deal more exact that we were able to conceive in our own commentaries.

For a Buddhist, it is therefore extremely important and useful to draw the lessons of these discoveries, particularly in the realm of modern physics. As a result of numerous meetings with different research workers I have realised that when we speak of the subtle impermanence of material phenomena there is an almost total overlap between my own Buddhist point of view and that of the physicists, in terms of constant change and levels of fluctuations.[71]

And he goes on to explain:

As regards impermanence, it is of two kinds: crude impermanence and subtle impermanence. The latter has to do with what those scientists who deal with the very tiniest particles manage to describe because they are not confined by the assumption that the appearance of a solid object – a table, for instance – offers a self-evident account of it, as when it seems today to be the same as it was yesterday; instead they focus on the changes inside the most minute components of an object. The substances that constitute these external objects are disintegrating from one moment to the next. Similarly, the inner consciousness that observes these outer objects is itself disintegrating from one moment to the next. It is precisely this transient disintegration which is the subtle kind of impermanence. The cruder kind is for example the destruction of an object, or in terms of the individual, it is a person's death.

Another point of overlap that interests me derives from quantum physics. There, the theory takes account of the presence of the observer, which is a key question in the scientific explanation of particles and their interrelations. Why is this? Simply because this notion of the observer observing implies consciousness, which is to say that there is a relationship between the person who watches the phenomenon, and who applies a particular technique stemming from a given experience, and the outcome of that action. The person who observes is the one who knows the phenomenon being studied, and that is not possible in the absence of consciousness.

This amounts to saying that, from the angle of quantum science, the observer is somehow a part of the experiment, while Buddhism considers that phenomena exist only as appearance, as possibility, if you like, and that it requires a consciousness in order for them to become what they appear to be. Here too it seems to me that I find a certain convergence between our points of view, even if the words are not exactly alike: they have a different way of conveying similar manifestations of a universe that we apprehend in various ways.[72]

In his own language, Jorge Luis Borges noted 'Words are symbols which postulate a shared memory.' Exactly, a shared memory. For the Dalai Lama, what is memory? According to him,

anybody who is involved in using more and more subtle states of consciousness is endowed with an ever vaster memory the more these subtle states come into play. But in order to go far back in time, one must rid oneself of all impediments to omniscience. By raising oneself to this uncommon level, some people of my acquaintance have become perfectly capable, thanks to this kind of consciousness, to take memory centuries backwards in time.[73]

Following this twist in the conversation, and without stopping when the mind began to spin, the monk continued in a calm voice only slightly tinged with mischief.

You want another meeting point? Then take biology or neurology. You know, in the field of knowledge and consciousness ... Buddhist texts go to some lengths to explain the relationships between the various states of consciousness, and the connections between sensory perceptions and mental perceptions. It is highly instructive to compare them with the modern theories of knowledge, which look into the links that join the brain to the senses, sensations and their reception in the head. So we come back to the question of whether or not phenomena have an objective existence, or if they depend solely on their subjective designation in order to appear as such. Which does not at all mean that we claim that there are no external forms; it is simply that they need a consciousness in order to be reflected, in order to exist.

As well as that, there are also points in common in psychology. Buddhism and modern research come together as regards the development of knowledge and the transformation of methodical doubt into knowledge. Transforming the mind and trying to modify its perceptions so as to eliminate suffering and develop a kind of serenity in dealing with the cares of the world, this too we have in common in this quest for fulfilment. In our view, meditation plays a large part in this perspective, that is to say familiarising the mind with an object of meditation. Of course there are plenty of other ways and means to achieve this understanding, to grasp the essence of things and to consider them with a tranquil mind.

And it is not uninteresting to compare the various cosmogonic views, and to try to bring out the meaning of astronomical accounts, and consider the relation between time and space. Some Buddhist texts talk about particles of space and particles of time .... In recent years I have met quite a few research workers and scientists to discuss this problem. To begin with, it is odd how sceptical they occasionally are, and it seems funny to them to find a monk who ponders on these questions. For some scholars, it is sometimes awkward to break through their own reserve – they are concerned with science, they feel, and not with religion or metaphysics.[74]

Neither time nor space escape examination from the prying eyes of the Buddhist sage. From the outset, the profusion of world hypotheses conveys his resolutely Indian background; just like space, time – that convention that shimmers with its thousands of facets, all of them delusions – has no intrinsic reality. Space and time, too, are empty of inherent existence. Or at least they are – and can it be otherwise? – relative, tied to a given type of consciousness. Do we live in time, or is it time that lives in us? It is no paradox at all, upon examination, so much does it reflect the common experience, for who has never felt a precise instant as having an unbearable duration, or conversely a broad expanse of time leaving the memory of having passed in a trice?

Western science is hardly more advanced than this, and ever since the formulation of the theory of relativity it has seen one long series of quarrels and contradictions among the greatest names in modern physics. From supposition to conjecture, how is science to agree on the objectivity of the notion of space, or perhaps on the passage of time? The quantum minefield is covered with boobytraps, all of them liable to explode under the tread of its explorers. At the distant boundaries of advanced research, as far ahead as the audacity of modern thinking has pressed forward in the effort to remove the final veil, it is as if it encounters a wall of light. Or perhaps a black hole. And when it comes to the lesser game of analogies, it may be that Buddhism is not altogether the loser, even if it is occasionally convenient, and facile, to accuse it of idealism, or else to dismiss it as sheer implausible ravings.

Mind and matter, space and time, high and low – all these pairs of opposites are open to a hundred explanations, a thousand interpretations, and as many variations as there are potentials seeded in a human mind. In a world conceived right away not as a *stasis* but as a perpetual flux, space becomes a kind of visible time. Do Buddhist teachings not refer to the Buddhas of the Three Times, who in their clear-sightedness focus into a single point – the present – both past and future, although the latter belongs explicitly only to the realm of probability, in an enlivening, simultaneous whole?

With that irrepressible thirst for the infinite that underlies Mahayanist thought, in which numbers are taken to hardly conceivable powers which actually aim to express that inexpressible abstraction, the mind tends to reel before the abyss thus revealed, meticulously precise, made of light, though it is. Space and time – those durations of variable curvature – belong to a cosmic vision of indisputable grandeur. But the Lord of the Lotus prefers to evade the issue, as if to say 'Do you truly want to go exploring these furthest limits of reflection?' Not that he refuses to set out upon this path – the gleam in his eye suggests that he himself has walked it and returned, bearing a wealth of knowlege. But perhaps one must first be well trained, and toughened in one's personal battles, before venturing in that direction.

> All those eons, their deep cause and origin, if considered in the texts, are part of a system of worlds within billions of worlds. As if one were describing a galaxy. In terms of matter, it is energy. As for the beings who live inside it, people with the gift of consciousness, the force that engenders them is that of their accumulated actions, which gives rise to their rebirth in a particular form. Matter is physical, while mind is brightness and knowledge . . . . Faced with the growth of science it is important to keep up the balance of man by simultaneously developing the inner knowledge within him.[75]

The Precious Master keeps harping on this theme: with him, all roads lead within, occasionally in an unexpected form – as when he suggests pondering on 'ugliness':

> It is not necessarily a matter of forms deformed. Our own body itself – composed of blood, flesh, bone and so on – may appear very fine, well coloured, solid, and also pleasant to the touch. But when one examines it one realises that its essence is things like bones . . . . If I wore X-ray spectacles I would see only skeletons, and in the same event you too would see walking skeletons. In that fashion, to meditate on 'ugliness' signifies examining the nature of our physical body.[76]

As the heir of numerous traditions of transmitted esoteric

knowledge, the Lord of the Lotus is also a great tantric master, even though his monastic vows do not permit him to practise all its rites. Tantra is one of the ways of yogic mysticism which is based on the mastery and channelling of energy – physical, spiritual or sexual – with a view to attaining Buddhahood. Nevertheless this knowledge, about which all kinds of lunacies have been said and written, is considered one of the most arduous to master, because of the many pitfalls to be avoided or overcome. In return, it is also regarded as being particularly effective, which explains its irresistible attraction for neophytes, especially because it is reputed to confer formidable powers. So the Dalai Lama talks about it with caution and concision, considering that only a proper and painstaking preparation makes it possible really to cross that threshold, and, even then, only under the essential control of a competent guide.

On the whole, the people of this world already have the potentialities which may be developed in the three Bodies of a Buddha. Our five senses and our present physical form constitute the basis of the physical appearance of a Buddha's Emanation Body. The subtle dream body, as the intermediary Body between life and death, is like the Body of Complete Enjoyment. Further, their common root is the Clear Light itself, capable of being developed into a Buddha's true Illumination Body, his Truth Body. The distinctive feature of Tantra is to transform these three ordinary bodies into Buddha bodies.

This is how it happens. The human body is a configuration of energy, made up of 72,000 channels, energy currents that flow through them, and essential drops, or units of consciousness, and energy conjoined, which are found in the channels. By manipulating the essential drops in the channels, by means of the currents, we pass through different levels or states of consciousness. The type of consciousness that we have at this moment, based upon configuration of the moment, is one; that of dreams is another; of sleep yet another. In cases of blackouts, in deep fainting fits or coma, or when the breathing stops, these are so many different states. The final level of consciousness, the Clear Light, becomes manifest at the moment of death. It is the most powerful and the most subtle. Unused, it acts as a basis for the return into the cycle of birth, old age, sickness and death. Yet, once having grasped the nature of cyclic existence, it is possible to be liberated from it. The best of all preparations for this is the understanding, now, of the various types of consciousness through using the channels, drops and inner winds, or energies.

Tantra is dangerous in the extreme. It is not to be accomplished without a competent guide, for it can lead to madness or to death.[77]

These warnings are not to be taken lightly, and they show, in their way, the fragility of the human being faced with the forces that are found inside him, but which it is advisable to master from the moment of embarking upon that way of knowledge. Some people occasionally talk about 'riding the tiger'. For all that, nothing and nobody can do it in anybody else's place.

Buddha once said: 'You are either your own saviour or your own worst enemy.' This applies to each of us. For example, as concerns me, if I strive to cultivate kindness and a positive spirit in myself, then I am my own saviour. If, on the other hand, I allow negativity to take hold of my current of being, then I become my own destroyer.

For the present, we have the privilege of having a human life, with all the possibilities that this implies. Unlike the animals and lower forms of life, we are capable of gathering the fruit of Awakening, an act of supreme goodness for ourselves as for others. Yet death hems us in from all sides, threatening to rob us of this precious opportunity at any moment, and when one dies one takes away nothing but the seeds of our activity and of our spiritual knowledge. A king loses his kingdom, and the beggar leaves his stick behind him.

Illumination has to be seized as long as the chance is there. In much less than a century we shall all be dead. Perhaps someone will then say; 'The Dalai Lama once gave a speech here,' and only that vague echo of the event will remain. We cannot be sure of being alive tomorrow. I want my own life to be as long and as useful as the life of Gedun Truppa, the First Dalai Lama, because right now there are many people who depend on me. But who knows? That is why I practise as intensely as possible, and advise you to do the same. But do not practise blindly, practise by basing yourself upon wisdom and understanding.[78]

Tentzin Gyatso spoke these words in the 1960s, when he was still only a young sovereign in exile, a refugee grappling with difficulties that no one but he could resolve. Since those days, if there have been changes in the Fourteenth Dalai Lama it is because he has never stopped learning and perfecting himself, always setting the example for those who wish to follow. His travels have opened his eyes to other realities, but fundamentally, and more than ever, he is a wise man among the wise. If the Lion's Throne looks less imposing than it used to be in the old days, in the palace of the gods, its legitimate occupant fully deserves his name, Lord of the Lotus.

There is no doubt in asking Tentzin Gyatso whether he believes in the perfectibility of human beings; his whole life is the evidence that he does, and he answers with a smile that in his opinion 'it is the sole worthwhile aim which he keeps striving to achieve, which makes life matter, makes it worth living'. And he adds the teasing question: 'Do you not think so?' When it is the Dalai Lama who speaks, it is difficult to disagree.

In the shifting area between East and West, his figure has grown rather more familiar now that the old stiff etiquette has been relaxed in contact with the new contingencies of the modern secular world, and the Dalai Lama may appear today in any corner of our planet. Wherever he goes, he is first and foremost himself. The eyes behind his spectacles see through appearances, and no doubt see much deeper than he would readily admit. And perhaps he would not disagree with the words of the great British astronomer and physicist Sir Arthur Eddington, as the beginning of this century, when he wrote 'We have found strange footprints on the shores of the unknown. We have devised one profound theory after another to explain their origin. At last we have succeeded in reconstructing the creature who left these footprints . . . and it was ourselves.'

9

On the Highways of the World

> The ultimate truth is always seen as error in the penultimate analysis. The man who is right in the end often appears to be mistaken both in his thoughts and in his actions.
>
> (*Arthur Koestler*)

The Potala. Seat of the gods and dwelling of a king, elegant extension of the hill it stands on, a precious balance of power and serenity, soaring from its white foundations upwards to the sky, the red palace dominates the capital city of Tibet. It too is a symbol, .that of the otherness of the Roof of the World. And yet despite its riches, its deep recesses, its sombre corridors, splendid frescoes, marvellous libraries and mysterious attics, despite its cenotaphs, state rooms, covered walks, studies and eyries, and despite a timetable regulated by custom and the stars, even a Dalai Lama could be bored there.

Tentzin Gyatso acknowledges that life was not always cheerful there. Loneliness, the austerity of study and the rigours of etiquette were not so hard. What sometimes disturbed him was being cut off from the world; not only the outside world beyond the Himalayan horizons, which he sensed and tried to imagine from afar, but also the secular, shifting world that he glimpsed below him, going about its business at the foot of the lofty hill. In order to bring himself closer to the life from which he was kept utterly apart, he took possession of a telescope unearthed from some dusty corner

and spent hours peering down into an existence which was
bound to remain stubbornly closed to him, as he was well
aware. Unless . . . .

The intrusion of Heinrich Harrer into the City of the Sun
offered the young Dalai Lama the longed-for opportunity to
disturb a few of the old habits. Eyebrows were raised among
his entourage, but in vain, for there was no directly opposing
the will of the god-king, even if he was still an adolescent.
Even that long ago, the presence was able to impose itself and
make itself heard. So it was that the Austrian adventurer
taught the Ocean of Wisdom his first smatterings of English,
and some rudiments of geography and contemporary history,
and it was in his company that he first opened various old and
very British maps and found, despite a few white expanses of
terra incognita, whole countries and towns whose names set
him dreaming about an unknown world.

There was India, of course, at the very source of his own
faith. Then, much further afield, lay distant lands like Europe
and America, powerfully attractive in their own way if only
because they held the keys of technology and science. As he
pored over the faded printed sheets, and traced out desti-
nations lying at the end of highways that he longed to travel,
now and then the young sovereign would sigh in his splendid
isolation, and dream about travelling the world. After all, the
tradition of the wandering monk was still embedded in
monastic life, and in those days there were still many pilgrim's ways frequented by travellers undeterred either by the
length of the journey, the rarity of stopping places or even the
possibility of hostile encounters. But these paths were not for
the Dalai Lama: he must follow the signposted roads and bow
to the hierarchical edicts of tradition, for symbol he was, and
symbol he must remain. At least, for as long as China, on the
border, acknowledged the separateness of its incomprehensible neighbour.

After the brutal upheaval of that night in March 1959, the
road of exile was to lead to other caravan routes, and to
encounters with other societies and other people, in search of
new answers to renewed questions. The opening of other

horizons was necessary for the satisfaction of an unfailing curiosity and to appease a craving always hungry for more knowledge. Yet for a refugee, even if he is the Dalai Lama, it is no easy matter to cross frontiers in a world of more and more surveillance and control and more and more suspicion, particularly when at first New Delhi chose to turn a deaf ear to its guest, in its reluctance to exacerbate its already prickly relations with Beijing. Tentzin Gyatso, in his wisdom, bided his time. In any case, with his usual clear-sightedness, he had already set himself some more imperative and urgent priorities: to help the Tibetan people withstand the shock and survive; then to rebuild the nucleus of a viable society on foundations damaged by the arduous conditions of escape and exile; and to take advantage of those conditions to lay the basis of some essential reforms. The travels could come later.

And so they did, numerous and varied, and always as instructive to the traveller as to his hosts of the moment. In the early years of exile, circumstances limited his movements to India, where in the south, in Karnataka, bold pioneers were working to create the conditions for survival. Forced to hire out their labour for building mountain roads in order to earn a living, both monks and laymen quickly paid the price; in tens, hundreds and thousands, they succumbed to the extreme hardship of their conditions, shortage of food, an unfamiliar climate, and the ravages of tuberculosis, as well as of other diseases unknown at their accustomed attitudes, where they had been strong and healthy. Now and then, despair also took a heavy toll; nostalgia for their empty spaces and high winds, the mute rebellion against dying so far from the vastness of the sky, the uncomprehending injustice of the world's indifference, all these made their contribution towards undermining a tottering morale.

The Dalai Lama stood fast for all his people. Tenacious at their side, he insisted, demonstrated, explained, demanded – and in truth no one managed to gainsay him, even though his and his people's resources were and remain derisory. With all its hardships, its generation gap, its battles between the old ways and the new, its rifts and splits, the Tibetan community in exile is well aware of who keeps it going, upholds it and enables it to hold its head high, and knows that it is thanks to him that it has persevered and flowered again.

So visitors should see the excitement when the Dalai Lama arrives among his people. That is the moment when one truly sees what the supreme incarnation of the Lord of Infinite Compassion means to Tibetans, the moment that gives its full range and scope to the nation – no matter how ambiguous and imprecise – of the god-king. In that extraordinary harmony between sovereignty and modesty, power and goodness, perhaps there lies a part of the secret of the Dalai Lama's being. If he arrives somewhere, even when he is not expected, the atmosphere changes at once. It may be the lobby of a big luxury hotel, or one of those symbol-monuments of western societies – the Capital in Washington, the Hôtel de Ville in Paris, or the Vatican in Rome – just as it may also be a tent in a meagre refugee camp somewhere in India; it is difficult not to feel the intense quality of that presence.

Practically every year, after the monsoon, the Dalai Lama goes down from the Himalayan hills towards the south, where he stays in Tibetan communities resettled in regions radically different from the places they once knew. He offers teachings, attends examinations and ordains monks in the great reconstituted monasteries – in particular Sera, Drepung and Ganden. If luxury and wealth are no longer in season, knowledge survives, and is passed on. It was one of the first concerns of the sovereign in exile to create a School of Dialectics in Dharamsala, precisely to preserve the jeopard-ised tradition of long monastic debates. Of course, to this day it is only a humble shack with a tin roof, tacked on to the main temple, which is built just opposite the spiritual leader's residence, but the heart of the matter is preserved, and what does appearance matter?

From the beginning of that new era, the exiled sovereign also took a keen interest in encouraging a new approach to medical studies, in order to keep alive ancestral secrets and techniques essential if his people were to adapt to unforeseen and often adverse conditions. This required collecting bits and pieces of scattered knowledge, and seeking out doctors employed in manual tasks disastrous to the sensitivity of the fingers which were their principal diagnostic instruments in taking the patient's pulses. It also required patiently reconstituting the prescriptions for remedies handed down from generation to generation within families, or from teacher to disciple, and then locating plants, minerals and other ingredients needed for making the pills. Today, on its happily restored foundations, this ancient tradition has seen such a vigorous and effective revival that the fame of Tibetan medicine needs no advertising.

The presence of the Dalai Lama in the Kangra valley has indirectly revitalised the Buddhist roots which may have withered a little in the course of time. Although the whole crescent of the Himalayas maintained its custom of sending monks to serve their apprenticeship and complete their studies in the great monasteries of Tibet, local disciplines had sometimes tended to relax. The settlement of meditator-ascetics in the region has also gradually influenced an atmosphere, which has once again grown conducive to reflection and contemplation. With unfailing attention, the spiritual master responds to the many requests to go here, there and everywhere, to teach, or to consecrate a shrine restored, or another newly built. Wherever he goes he finds a welcome, and it is as if his presence alone prompts each individual, if only in that moment, to give the best he has.

In Ladakh, Bodh Gaya or Varanasi, and in Karnataka too, the Lord of the Lotus adapts his schedule to the requests of his fellow countrymen, but he also allows himself the time for daily study and reflection. There are moments when nothing seems to absorb him more totally than reading some ancient work unearthed in a monastery library, just as sometimes nothing appears to give him more pleasure than to share the offering of a prayer with a handful of monks in a cloister lost in the near-wilderness of its majestic setting.

Yet it is with the same attention and a cheerful candour that the Dalai Lama will take part, in all simplicity, in a school celebration, or stop at the roadside without hesitation for a friendly chat with chance wayfarers. He also displays the keenest interest in following the theological debates of his fellow monks, and does not hesitate to intervene in arguments to explain a point of doctrine when he deems it necessary. The teachings which he gives so freely on his travels are always followed with attention, and his listeners are likely to make a special point of their clarity; beyond question, he has the gift of sharing what he knows, and his words shed light – in the end it hardly matters whether we call it the light of philosophy, metaphysics or plain wisdom.

In India, the Dalai Lama is particularly fond of places associated with the history of Buddhism. There is no lack of these around Dharamsala, but they are even more plentiful in the eastern part of the country, where the opulent kingdom of Magadha (in modern Bihar) once flourished. Sarnath, near Varanasi, where Buddha preached his first sermon in the Deer Park, is one of these favourite spots. The Lord of the Lotus has vivid memories of a certain day, coinciding with the great annual festival, when a solemn procession of the faithful accompanies the public parade of one of the rare relics of Gautama, the historical Buddha. There are very few of these in the world: in Kandy, in central Sri Lanka, a tooth; in the Shwe Dagon, the magnificent gilded pagoda in Rangoon, Burma, three hairs; in Nagarjunakonda and in Sarnath, a fragment of bone. The legends attached to them are beautiful, but even more impressive is the veneration that surrounds them.

It was in Sarnath that the Wheel of the Law, the Dharma, was set in motion, when the Awakened One revealed the Four Noble Truths that bring liberation from the treadmill of suffering. Around the massive and protectively rounded shape of the majestic ancient stupa, near the remains of ancient hermitages, new monasteries are springing up again, where Buddhist monks of every climate and persuasion now work to perpetuate the long tradition of the Law. In the gentle serenity of a quickly falling twilight, a procession of monks in maroon or saffron robes makes its ritual circuit of the stupa which has stood here for over 1,000 years. Some of them sit down on the grass and converse in an undertone, enjoying the welcome cool of the evening after a torrid late afternoon; others doing nothing, lost in dreaming contemplation beneath the trees.

The murmur of the fountain by the shrine continues, and the earth itself exhales a kind of magic atmosphere, tinged by the tender colours of the bougainvillaeas, the delicate rustle of arching branches, the song of the birds among the leaves, the quiet smells of sandalwood and jasmine, and also by the sudden feeling of deep joy. In the peace of the evening an invisible, powerful presence hovers above this privileged place where the earth interrupts its infinitely turning cycle and for the duration of a breath becomes the still axis of a time restored to its eternity, and to the fulfilment of being.

It was probably on just such a day, when the reverent and quietly joyful procession was winding its way around the Mulgandh Kuti Vihara, the shrine at Sarnath, that the feeling grew so intense that the Dalai Lama's eyes brimmed quietly with tears.

That day, when the monks opened the sanctuary, naturally I bowed low, and then I wept. For a long time. Why did I weep? Because I am one of his disciples, and because these few poor relics are all that is left of him. Because it is a reminder of individual responsibility, and of the necessity to practise without a pause, unfailingly, to follow his teachings and continue on the Way, for the human eternity is only for a moment.[79]

Bodh Gaya too holds a special place in his heart. He likes to go there regularly, and is still suffused with the deep impression that he took away from his first pilgrimage to the place of the Awakening in 1956, on the occasion of the festivals celebrating the twenty-fifth centenary of the Buddha. Since then he has often come back to the place that represents 'for every Buddhist the noblest, highest element in his cultural and religious heritage'. During these visits it is the religious aspect of his activities that takes precedence over all the rest; he teaches often, takes part in theological examinations, but above all he takes advantage of the remoteness – a temporal as well as a geographical and spatial condition – of the languid little town, indifferent to the breathing of the everyday worlds, to make retreats. Here he regains a little of that purposeful, reasoning solitude which strips and feeds reflection.

The Dalai Lama's first journey outside India was to two Buddhist countries, Japan and Thailand, in 1967. It was his opportunity to establish more personal links with close but nevertheless distinct traditions. Wherever he goes he is greeted by that warm and admiring deference that the Orient reserves for its spiritual masters.

In Bali, in the north of that island so magically beautiful – all chimes and harmonies – that some have found their personal paradise there, the little village of Banjar stands perched on a hilltop, at the end of a winding path. In this hospitable and tolerant land, a Buddhist monastery does not detract from the tropical luxuriance that welcomes all the gods. The cloister is of recent construction, although the tradition of the Awakened One is rooted deep in the local memory; cheerfully kitsch in the Balinese manner, its tiers of red and grey buildings embrace the contours of the hill and are almost drowned beneath their wealth of vegetation.

The glow of the flowers, the lushness of grasses stealthily making themselves at home and the contorted elegance of the shrubs compete in unbridled imagination to enhance one unexpected detail of the foliage on the horizon. A little way away, a Bodhi tree, grown from a cutting brought from India in the past, spreads its branches above a statue of the Buddha in an attitude of meditation. And each day, a little group of the district's faithful meets here at dusk to share that special instant of meditation with the keeper monk. Dominating the monastic block with its orange and yellow mass, another effigy of the sage gazes into the distance, while at the foot of its plinth a profusion of pink and white lotuses rise up on their tall stalks in their irrepressible aspiration towards the light.

During his visit to Indonesia in 1982 the Dalai Lama spent some hours in Banjar, and his kindly words have not been forgotten. Even though bound to the tradition of the Lesser

Vehicle, the resident monk who is the sole guardian of the place, seeing to its upkeep and performing the necessary rites, recalls with obvious pleasure the offering ceremony which he then conducted side by side with his illustrious Tibetan visitor. With a smile on his lips and a distant look in his eyes, he recalls: 'He is a master, a true master, such as we would wish to see more often in these times.'

Of Borobudur, on the nearby island of Java, no doubt there is little to be said, except that it is one of the wonders of the world – of the Buddhist world, at least. Other sites – Pagan, in Burma, or Angkor-Wat in Cambodia – testify in their now muted grandeur to the irresistible religious drive that once led to their construction. There are some pagodas in Thailand that teach the visitor their smiling lesson of the transient, while in China there are hills considered sacred which offer the wayfarer the restoring shelter of a little wood or a cave propitious to meditation. But no building fashioned by the hand of man expresses such harmonious perfection and sovereign achievement as Borobudur, near Jogyakarta.

The architectural perfection is self-evident at first sight, in the monument's integration into a background of wooded hills with strong and gentle lines, and in the play of balanced volumes between its four-square solid placement on the ground and the curve of the gradually-rising upper terraces. Then comes the perfection of the great stone book which unrolls its episodes of history and legend throughout the length of the ritual progression leading from the lower, earthly milestones upwards to the purified vision, at the borders of the unexpressible, at the very heart of the central axis, passing through the stages of deprivation and of meditation. And lastly there is the perfection of the initiatory mandala that bears the very quintessence of the Buddhist quest – a summary of doctrine, expressing through the sculpted elegance of the one stone gesture the absolute requirement to surpass one's limitations. As the visitor reads these symbols offered for all to see, the cardinal thought of Buddhism is revealed in a radiant light whose meaning is sometimes obscured under the cloud of commentaries that warp its direct apprehension.

When he made this pilgrimage, the Dalai Lama likewise followed the age-old path that runs from the little temple of Mendut, where the Awakened One teaches in the half-light of the crypt under the watchful eye of two *bodhisattvas*, to the entrance to the great mandala, by way of the touching shrine of Pawon, whose bare and empty interior is conducive to the preparatory state of contemplation. And perhaps the gaze of the Tibetan monk lingered for a moment on one external wall where an expert hand has captured the spellbound expression of a being on the threshold of what is to be a fundamental encounter; never, and nowhere else, has stone so powerfully conveyed this ultimate moment, a blend of expectation, hope, and the unknown, when the eye is reeling on the brink of looking from the outward to the inward view. It is that very fleeting halt, that imperceptible instant of hesitation, before the step is taken.

There in the plain of Kedu the sacred mountain has been built by human will, and the unfolding story that it tells from square terraces to rounded platforms is a vibrant tribute, 1,008 times repeated, to the Awakened One. A magic of numbers, a mirage of figures, an enhancement of stone and a spell of beauty; in Borobudur, when he deciphers the not too hidden code of its language, the pilgrim sees with all his body, mind and word the initiatory pathway that goes from the world of men to the creative and liberating vision of ultimate, and obviously Buddhist, reality. At the still point of the turning world, the pivot between break and balance, the world picture that is Borobudur works this miracle of being where the materialisation of spirit and the spiritualisation of matter intersect. It is a rare privilege which hardly has its equal under different skies, and it is not surprising that its extraordinary power should evoke so vivid a totalising image, the mirror of a world in everlasting flux. Nor is it surprising that the symbol-monument is being revived and enlivened today, thanks to the translation of its many facets given by the masters of Tibetan Buddhism.

The Lord of the Lotus centres his travels abroad on the most varied aspects of today's society, usually linking them to a specific theme, but allowing for variations according to circumstance. As a rule, his basic concern remains to see that the Tibetan vision and way of life are better known and understood; meetings are organised in response to invitations from interested groups or circles, and teachings are arranged at the express request of people more or less directly committed to the Buddhist path. As an accomplished master of wisdom, the Dalai Lama is concerned to satisfy the growing curiosity about the Land of Snows which has been evident for some time now, while never bypassing the distinctive features that constitute its special nature and individuality.

Not one prejudice appears to distort his perception of the realities of today's political power games. While he remains undeceived by their rules, he refrains from passing judgment on their concrete application, and when he is questioned on the subject he points out that they are what the players make them. He is well aware that in the course of the various transactions among nations, some may seek to use him, in person, not to mention the Tibetan cause, for purposes which are not his own. So as to avoid this kind of misunderstanding, his sole response is a raw straightforwardness which does not inhibit finer shades of meaning. For whether he likes it or not, Tentzin Gyatso, Dalai Lama by vocation, knows perfectly well that politics lies in wait for him wherever he travels, and that it cannot be held totally separate from the secular aspect of his position.

A visit to the USSR in autumn 1986 may illustrate this proposition. Flying from New Delhi, the Dalai Lama and his small entourage of half-a-dozen first landed in Tashkent, and then flew on to Alma-Ata and Ulan-Ude. From the Buryat capital they went on to Leningrad and Moscow; two full weeks, punctuated by what were sometimes revealing meetings and observations. Of course, the Dalai Lama lent himself with good grace to the ritual of family photographs so loved by officials and civil servants, each one duly standing in the proper row, at the place decided by his status. Of course he

listened valiantly to the routine speeches and to the lyrical
flights of wilted all-in rhetoric. But that did not stop him
thinking, and other and more significant details caught his
attention.

Invited by Soviet Buddhist organisations, at the suggestion of the religious head of the monastery of Ganden
Chökhor Ling, near Ulan-Ude – the largest in the Buryat
Autonomous Soviet Socialist Republic, to the south of Lake
Baikal – the Precious Master knew very well that this initiative could never have proceeded without the agreement of
the Soviet government or the backing of the Communist
authorities. From there to perceiving a possible use of his
journey in the fluctuating game played out between
Moscow and Beijing showed the Dalai Lama a possible step
which he does not mean to take – which does not stop him
admitting that the visit was not necessarily to the liking of
the Chinese, or acknowledging that the start of timid
changes in the relations between the two Communist super-
powers on the continent of Asia might have long-term
repercussions on the situation in Tibet. But he harbours no
illusions; in oriental perceptions, the 'long term' can easily
mean a human lifetime, and exceed one or several generations. Nevertheless, he was struck by certain immediate,
concrete aspects of that visit.

These aspects included a timid liberalisation in the practice
of religious faith; a much greater and less fearful attendance
than during a previous visit to Ulan-Ude, with some
believers coming all the way from Outer Mongolia; a much
more clearly spiritual atmosphere in Zagorsk, where many
young people crowded into the nave of one big church; and a
more open attitude in talks with religious dignitaries. He took
advantage of this relaxation to present the abbot of Ganden
Chökhor Ling with various modest or sumptuous gifts
brought by pilgrims as a pledge of loyalty, so as to open a
school of Buddhist dialectics on behalf of the monks of
Ulan-Ude. At the monastery he met one of his pupils again, a
young Buryat scholar who has been sent to Dharamsala for
some years to serve his religious apprenticeship.

On that occasion I had my fill of various religious contacts, because I was given the opportunity not only to talk to Buddhists from Mongolia but also to meet Muslims, Orthodox believers, Seventh Day Adventists and other Christians. To tell the truth these were often formalities; they tended to be receptions and ceremonies, things of that kind. But after all, it could be argued that each side gained what it wanted: in the USSR they were very fond of talking about peace, and since I claim that the peace of the world arises out of the human being's realisation and practice of inner peace . . . .

For the first time, I was also able to talk to Communist research workers and scientists, in particular at the Institute of Neuro-Psychology and the Institute of Oriental Studies in Leningrad. That was extremely instructive, and there are some very interesting things in the libraries there. And then, in Alma-Ata, it was superb. It rained on the night we arrived, and next morning the mountains round about were sprinkled with a tenuous veil of snow. The mountains are beautiful . . . . Have you ever flown by Aeroflot? [His eyes are hidden beneath lowered lids.] The service has definitely improved since my last visit, a few years ago . . . . Otherwise, you know, Moscow doesn't change very much . . . . All the same, I think that for the Soviet Union Tibet is important, from the political point of view as well as the geographical, as it remains for India and Afghanistan. On Soviet territory, Buddhism is rooted in the Tibetan tradition and, quite apart from the links that go back to my predecessor in any case, they are not unaware of the fact in Moscow.

Travels abroad raise a number of difficulties which are not always easily settled. While financial questions are sometimes an obstacle, they are solved by contributions from Tibetans living in various countries, who are only too happy to welcome their spiritual leader. Some Buddhist organisations join in this effort, as do some private individuals. The New Delhi government also shares the expenses and partly takes care of security, at least on Indian territory. That is undoubtedly one of the major worries of the exiled sovereign's entourage, and though his personal guards are not many, they are always on the alert. Yet even more than these practical details, there are certain decidedly more political considerations that explain, but by no means justify, the attitude of official reserve, not to say ostracism, that continues to surround the Dalai Lama and the cause of Tibet.

It is standard practice in the international community to refrain from all interference in other countries' internal affairs. And the result is that, far more often than it should, that same community overlooks another, supposedly cardinal, rule of social behaviour, which is the moral duty to help any person in danger. It would be pointless to broach the plethora of cases that illustrate this state of affairs; there would certainly be too many to be mentioned in this century, let alone in the general course of history. As for the question of Tibet, it is further complicated by the near total general ignorance about the facts of the high country, which is shrouded in mysteries fed by a host of projected dream fantasies. This Shangri-la, this country of the world's imagination, has paid a high price for the isolation which was both imposed from without and intended from within, and the awakening has been brutal, all the more so because the very fact that it has chosen the Buddhist way of life means that it does not come naturally to the Tibetan mind to respond to injustice with violence. So confronted with adversity and with a motley coalition of more and less reputable interests in which the mercenary goes hand in hand with the ideological, Tibet is left with fewer friends than most. The Dalai Lama makes no complaint about that, and remains convinced that honesty and truth will eventually prevail.

The Tibetan leader strives through direct contact with others to establish bridgeheads, smooth out points of friction and strengthen the areas of agreement, starting with the subject closest to his heart, which is religion, the keystone of human life. Following several meetings with dignitaries such as the Archbishop of Canterbury, Orthodox archimandrites, Muslim leaders from Ladakh or the Soviet Union, and with Roman Catholic Popes, the same outgoing interest in others took the Lord of the Lotus to Assisi in autumn 1986 to participate in the day of prayer for world peace organised by the Bishop of Rome. In joining those representatives of a dozen other great religions, the Dalai Lama sought to reiterate his unquenchable certitude that life can be beautiful and the earth a place of fullness and harmony – once human beings have learned how to behave there.

In the course of events and the passage of time, curious coincidences sometimes arise out of the unforeseen interplay of distant traditions. Ephemeral though they are, these encounters nevertheless throw accidental light on some un-suspected perspectives. Thus, at the time of his visit to the United States in 1980 a small group of Hopi Indians turned up unexpectedly at the house where the Dalai Lama was staying in Los Angeles. These Elders, the keepers of a little-known but still living tradition, and possessors of knowledge too long despised or mocked, calmly declared that they had a message of importance to communicate to the Tibetan spirit-ual leader. Since Tentzin Gyatso is not in the habit of ducking the unexpected, a discussion was arranged.

> It was an odd meeting. They were people of very great courtesy. They wanted to tell me about an ancient prophecy of their people, handed down from generation to generation, which says that one day a man would come from the direction of the rising sun, whose name would be linked with a vast expanse of salt water. [One of the Dalai Lama's names is Ocean of Wisdom.] They thought that this might be me, and they had come to tell me so .... I was very much impressed by their concern with protecting the environment and their respect for nature. That was several years ago now, but this care for everything around us grows more and more important every day, and that is another point in common between them and ourselves.[81]

The Hopi tradition actually says that one day a Brother of the Sun Clan, a true wise man, will appear among them, they who believe that the Axis of the World passes through their territory, just as it passes through the Roof of the World. By another odd coincidence, the Hopi fire ritual bears an extra-ordinary resemblance to a similar Tibetan ceremony, while an ancestral prediction in the high country asserts that 'on the day when the fire bird flies, when horses gallop on wheels, the people of Bod will be scattered through the world like ants, and the Dharma will come to the continent of the red man'. For the time being, the Dalai Lama does not wish to venture into random speculations, and is content to note the analogies, and smile. But his anxiety for the world around us is expressed whenever the opportunity occurs.

> Peace, and life on earth as we know it, are threatened by human activities that take no account of human values .... It is easy to forgive the destructions of the past, the consequence of ignorance, but today we have access to more information, and it is vital to re-examine from an ethical point of view the heritage which is our own responsibility and which we shall bequeath to generations to come .... We have the capability and the responsibility for that, and we must act before it is too late.[82]

One only has to join him in his garden to realise that the Dalai Lama has a relationship with nature which is as organic and as vital as his relationship with his fellow human beings. At the same time it is as if there is an element of detachment, a certain distance between himself and what he is led to do; Tentzin Gyatso is reserved, not to say cautious, if he sees confusion arising between his spiritual role and his temporal activities. In his view, it could prove dangerous to entrust the leader of any religion with political power.

> For example, if somebody like the Pope, who stands at the head of a particular Church, were to become a national political leader, in the long run it could be hard for him to remain objective in his religious as well as his political capacity. To combine Church and State in this way can create problems, without the very greatest flexibility in the two roles. Having to abide by a strict tradition can prove awkward. The role of the Dalai Lama in the religious sphere is not like a Pope's: it is more nebulous and abstract.
> For Tibetans, it is different. When it is said that the Dalai Lama is a spiritual and a temporal leader, that does not lay down any hard-and-fast role in either one of those spheres. The name is a general title which signifies that the Dalai Lama is respected as a master in religion, and that he has a say in Tibetan political affairs. I am free to express my opinion both in religious and in political

matters, and I am not obliged to be the spokesman of any particular institution. So when Tibetans talk about 'combining the religious function with the secular' it does not quite correspond to what westerners mean when they refer to links between Church and State. If I were living in a free Tibet the situation would be different, but as a refugee I am undoubtedly subject to fewer constraints.[83]

This is a fact which westerners do not always grasp at first, and there is no doubt that it gives even greater weight to the Dalai Lama's pronouncements; in a sense, he has total freedom.

However that may be, Tentzin Gyatso's first visit to the United States provides a fair illustration of the west's ambivalence towards the Tibetan problem, its misunderstandings at least, and sometimes its deplorable ignorance. It is a fact that for some years Washington took the line of refusing to recognise the very existence of the Chinese People's Republic, and in particular blocked its admittance to the United Nations for a long time – even invoking, though always behind the scenes, the situation on the Roof of the World. When the *volte face* occurred, and President Nixon's visit to China took place, once again Tibet was quickly relegated to the side-lines, for suddenly opposite but equally futile reasons. National interest must come first. However in 1980, when all the hindrances, serious or not, had at last been removed, the exiled sovereign found a warm welcome on every stage of his American journey – not officially, of course, but unofficially. Here too, his personal charisma worked wonders. But nothing concrete was done, at the political level, to condemn the scandal of the Chinese occupation – no approaches, for instance, to the international authorities. It was not until the Dalai Lama's second visit, seven years later, and the first publicly reported riots in Lhasa, that protesting voices began to be raised in the United States and elsewhere. Not that any nation would go so far as to challenge the very questionable claim of Chinese 'suzerainty' over the Roof of the World: here *realpolitik* goes hand in

hand with commercial interests. Perhaps it was Charles G.
Rose, a member of the Congress, who in 1980 most suc-
cinctly summed up the outstanding feature of the Dalai
Lama when he introduced his guest to his colleagues in
Washington's austere and solemn Constitution Hall: 'The
Dalai Lama encourages people to do more thinking for them-
selves.' As a footnote to history, a few weeks later Pope
John Paul II was to speak on the same platform.

This more or less deliberate blindness to Tibet on the part of
the democracies is not unique to the United States; the
political leaders of Western Europe have nothing to boast of in
this respect. Nor do those intellectuals who usually see
themselves as the conscience of their nation, opinion makers
or spokespeople for the world's oppressed. Admittedly there
is a host of extenuating circumstances in both cases: Tibet is a
long way off and a long way up; it is unknown and mysterious. For some, it is a cross between Tintin and black or white
magic, the sacred mountain and the abominable snowman,
tall tales from impossible pilgrimages and the ramblings of
unhinged minds. And then again, blind or genuine, clear-
sighted or self-interested, China's friendship is well worth a
Mass, even if it means turning a blind eye to the blood of
thousands and thousands of victims.

This selective ignorance has reached such a point that at
present, when for clearly financial reasons Beijing has finally
decided to open the frontiers of a country which does not
belong to it to people who have dreamed of going there, most
of these busy travellers, hot in pursuit of the latest fashion,
seem to prefer not to know that a tragedy has been happening
there, behind an implacable wall of silence, and that it is still
going on, under their own averted gaze. Some even swallow
every scrap of decency, pocket their ignorance and return
with learned explanations of 'why Tibet is not the Chinese
Afghanistan'. At the same time, in Switzerland, France, Italy
and perhaps some other countries, when the Dalai Lama is
permitted to accept an invitation from a sympathetic group,
there is always somebody consigned to remind him bluntly
that his visit is private, while official contacts are carefully

shunned. That is because Beijing clings like a limpet to its own principles, no matter how distorted or unjustified, and does not hesitate to make outright threats in order to have its own way. And in this case having its way means imposing the idea – an utterly false one – that Tibet is synonymous with China.

The Dalai Lama has only modest means at his disposal for wearing down these mountains of prejudice, working both against the sheer mass of China and its mighty propaganda machine. But he considers that having the truth on his side is an inestimable advantage, and it is that reality which he strives to communicate to those who are willing to listen as he travels the highways of the world.

Over and over again during his most recent travels in the west, in the course of his talks in India with people of every shade of opinion, and in impromptu meetings, the question of violence has been put to the Dalai Lama. Among the Tibetans themselves, particularly among the younger generation of those who were born or have grown up in exile, this question has been so keenly felt that for some of them it has been a heart-breaking decision to forswear it. There has been no lack of arguments for violence, and they have been put forward with all the burning eloquence of free young people whose eyes are open to a quickly changing world; theirs is not a deliberate wish to do harm or to destroy, but a rebellion against the conspiracy of silence, a longing to be heard, and exasperation with crying in the wilderness.

No hijacked aircraft, no bombings, no taking of hostages as a means of blackmail, a cheap ticket to publicity and the dubious luxury of contempt. Tibetans would rather starve, because for them it would be demeaning to resort to such methods. Yet there has been, and still is, an underground army of resistance inside Tibet itself. For lack of outside supplies and support its activities are sporadic. In the community in exile there are 10,000 men who have served under the Indian army flag, most of them in crack regiments – parachutists and mountain frontier guards. Tentzin Chögyal, the Dalai Lama's youngest brother, is one of these, and he

sometimes remarks, with a trace of a smile, that never in all
its long history has Tibet had such an army.

But there is one line that none of them would venture to
cross, and that is the one drawn by the exiled sovereign
himself. For as long as he has been confronted with this cruel
dilemma the Dalai Lama has striven to respect his conscience
and his faith. His own experiences under the Chinese invader,
the tragedy of his country, of which he is fully aware, and the
crying injustice inflicted on his people – none of this has
damaged his unshakeable faith in Buddhist non-violence. He
remains philosophically a determined opponent of violence as
a means to achieving an end – for him the former is never
justified by the latter. But that is not to say that he views the
situation without understanding and compassion; ever since
his long and dangerous journey into exile he has expressed his
admiration and deep esteem for the selfless bravery of the
Khampa warriors who protected his escape. But now as then,
he remains unconvinced that violence can in any way further
the Tibetan cause.

In answer to those questioners who sometimes voice their
surprise about what they see as a kind of passiveness or giving
up, in a world where might too often becomes right, the
Dalai Lama serenely replies that he stands by the attitude put
forward by the Good Teaching of the Mahayana: 'Radical
action and violence can be understandable in some circumstances, when the motivation is altruistic, when the motive is
just and there is no other possibility. In that sense, seen in
greater depth, the violence is non-violence, because its aim is
to help others.'[84]

This is no Buddhist version of sophism or casuistry.

> It is both a great shame and a very serious matter that violence is
> assuming such importance in society. All the same, we should
> not forget that there is violence and violence – the kind that no
> one pays attention to, and the kind that everybody sees and talks
> about. In neither case is it a positive method.
>
> From the Buddhist point of view, if violence is considered as a
> bad thing it is because it does harm, because someone or some-
> thing is damaged. But there is more than one way of doing harm.

It does not necessarily mean using brute force. For example by smiling, very politely and pleasantly, when the aim in view is none the less to injure, to do harm. That is also a kind of violence. It can also be much more direct, indeed physical. For example, if a mother smacks her child – it hurts, of course, but she is not acting with the intention of doing harm. The appearance is violent, however, even though the deep meaning is different: it is a way of helping, the motivation is good or just. Poisoned honey is much worse than this apparent violence.

As for violence or non-violence, that is something else. It is a question of method, not of purpose. When there is no other choice it can be explained, if not justified. The just motivation, based on altruism, makes it understandable, but it is right to remain detached, and not to take pleasure in hurting. In order to help other people, when there really is no other way, it is admissible. The angry goddesses and wrathful gods are there to indicate that violence can be resorted to as a method, for these are powerful instruments, but it is never, never, an end.[85]

It was in the same terms that the spiritual guide of Tibet recently addressed his fellow Buddhists in Sri Lanka, once a paradise island but now a battlefield for bloody ethnic hatreds. This intervention gives a perfect illustration of the exiled leader's approach to the antagonisms of the present day:

It is easy to talk about grand principles, but the real test of practice comes only in the heat of a difficult situation. In their affairs, human beings are bound to have differences of opinion and conflicts of interest. Nevertheless, we cannot hope to provide effective and lasting solutions for these problems solely by the use of force . . . .

For some time I have been following the situation in Sri Lanka with sorrow and concern. The present ethnic troubles are all the more distressing if we bear in mind that the two communities are the followers of two ancient religions which are like the waters of a single river. Attempts are being made to work out a solution. I would like to appeal to all my fellow Buddhists of the *sangha* for them to take the lead in the movement for a peaceful settlement of the situation.

Our master showed us the way of non-violence, tolerance and compassion. In spite of the dreadful injustices suffered by my people under the Chinese occupation I have always striven to find a peaceful solution. In the case of Sri Lanka, whatever the differences and the eventual outcome of the present conflict, the fact remains that the two communities have many things in common and that they will have to live together in future. So it is in the long-term interest of the two communities to try to find a peaceful solution through tolerance, goodwill and trust, rather than through hatred and violence.[86]

Even though he often says that it is not necessary to be religious in order to feel responsible and to act justly, together with his colleagues of other religions the Dalai Lama seeks to establish ties between what the various currents of thought have in common – the notions of justice and honesty, truth, altruism and kindness. Contacts with the Jains, for instance, are cordial. In the words of the Precious Protector:

It is because Jainism and Buddhism are almost twins, born in the same distant age and descended from Hinduism. The cardinal concepts of our two world-views are closely akin – perhaps the Jains are even stricter than ourselves on certain principles. For instance they are strict vegetarians, whereas not all Buddhists are. Like us too, they base their attitude on *ahimsa*, non-violence.

I cannot say the same about relations with the Hindus: it is more diffuse and problematic, because they each worship in their own way, and there is no leader who can speak in their name. All the same, it is sometimes possible to make progress in discussions with ascetics or scholars. With the Muslims? It is rather similar: they have no single leader either, so that it is largely dependent on individuals.

Look at the Muslims in Ladakh. At the religious level, they are Muhammadans. But in race, customs and culture, they are Tibetans. The majority of them are Shiites, which means strict observance of the precepts of their law, with the consequence that they have little or no relationship with other religions, and for example they will never share a meal with Buddhists. But in my own case they have sometimes agreed to do so, and I assure you that some of those meals were delicious! All the same, the truth is that these tend to be social contacts, and that other, more emotional reasons account for them. The Ladakhi Muslims feel very close to Tibet in general, and the Dalai Lama in particular.

I remember very few serious theological discussions with Muslims. One or two, perhaps, particularly with Sufis, because oddly enough at first sight, they are very much interested in compassion and in certain methods of Buddhist meditation. But that approach has to do with technical details, attached to a specific training .... What if I were to meet the Ayatollah Khomeini? What would you expect me to discuss with him, if not religion, God and the practice of compassion?[87]

The Tibetan master often makes a point of saying that he is not in the least bit interested in converting other people to Buddhism. What matters to him is that the Buddhists should make their own contribution to society as a whole, in keeping with their own ideas and their own concept of life – that they should play their part in the world, and not remain aloof. When he teaches or gives lectures abroad, his themes always reflect this point of view. Nevertheless, some visits seem more intense than others, if only for sentimental reasons – as the Dalai Lama himself admits.

An unusual experience awaited anybody who stopped at Digne, in the Alps of Haute-Provence, in May 1986 – they would have been taken aback to find it running a Festival of Tibet. Samten Dzong, or the Fortress of Meditation, or more simply the Alexandra David-Neel Foundation, swarmed like a frantic beehive with the tension of waiting to greet the Tibetan master. Yet that was not the first time that Tentzin Gyatso had visited that secluded spot where the explorer spent the final years of her long life, and where if you looked hard you could almost find reflections of the far Himalayan spaces she loved so much. But in 1982 the Dalai Lama had only passed through, staying just long enough to lay the first stone of what was to become the conference centre, museum and library which he came to inaugurate four years later. In addition, the very welcome guest was to give three days' teaching and a public lecture, lend his presence to an exhibition devoted to Tibet, and also receive the title of honorary citizen of the lavender capital, together with the keys to the city. So many activities were bound to keep the security authorities and the faithful little organising group continually on their toes.

As usual when the Dalai Lama travels, he was surrounded by a marathon atmosphere that left him unaffected; the Ocean of Wisdom found the time to grant audiences, meet journalists, talk with friends and to radiate a serenity illuminated by flashes of the joy of living. Once, when she had just been presented with the Légion d'honneur, Alexandra David-Neel sighed: 'Of course the distinction makes me happy, but I would so much rather have received the Fourteenth Dalai Lama here.' When told of this remark, Tentzin Gyatso gave a hint of a smile, raised one eye to heaven in a half-questioning, half-joking manner, and said: 'With her intense Buddhist practice she must have had a very good rebirth. Perhaps up there in her paradise she is watching us talking, and smiling to see her wish come true.'

Two lectures in two days in Paris, several meetings and various contacts – all of them private, of course – a small reception at the Hôtel de Ville, then three days incognito in a country house in Normandy completed that later visit to France. There were very few moments for leisure in such a crowded timetable, but one or two unusual escapades all the same. The first was an impromptu visit to the abbey of Bec-Hellouin, where the Benedictines have still not recovered from the appearance in their midst of this figure at once so mythical and so unexpectedly familiar. The rule of St Benedict caught the attention of the Buddhist monk, who discerned within it some distant echoes of his own practice of meditation and contemplation. And Tentzin Gyatso felt a monk's appreciation of the quiet of cloisters removed from the secular bustle of crowded cities where the mind is so buffeted that the man has no time left to dream.

The other escapade may seem even more unexpected. To the surprise of his entourage, and taking advantage of what was intended to be a rest period, the Dalai Lama expressed the wish to go and see the D-day landing beach at Arromanches. This meant hasty rearrangements, notifying the mayor of the little town, opening the museum and taking the necessary security precautions, just to satisfy the wish of the Precious Protector. But the sudden whim was not so capricious as it may have seemed, as he explained to me a few weeks later:

> I wanted to see, and to feel. I have read a lot about that famous beach, the Normandy landings and the Second World War. I wanted to see the actual, concrete, place where so many people suffered and died, where they sacrificed their lives. I also wanted to see the weapons, those big guns and all those rifles that I had trouble imagining. By coming close to those devices, the weapons and the sand, I felt and shared the feelings of the people who were there at the time . . . .
>
> A great deal of suffering, fear and pain. The anxieties of the men who came from the sea, and the fear in the bellies of people preparing to fight. Hatred too, a lot of it, waves of hatred. Even if it was only for a brief moment, I wanted to share all that with those who went through it and died there. I had to see for myself, so that I too could share the memory of what has been. [88]

The memory of what has been . . . . Long ago, in the Potala, the young Dalai Lama used to run his inquisitive eye across dusty maps, all faded and dog-eared, and so seldom used that they practically fell apart when unfolded. A long long way away, far beyond his immediate reach, he sensed worlds of change and movement, so distant that it was hard for him to imagine them. A serene-eyed monk, inhabited by infinite eternities, how does he see the world of men whose highways he travels today?

> The world today . . . . The West appears to me to be preoccupied essentially by the material side of things, but that in itself is not enough: in spite of its indisputable advances it does not succeed in fulfilling all of mankind's desires. That means that there is something lacking in its understanding of the world.
>
> Without the inner dimension a human being cannot be complete, he can go no further to understand himself and define his own world. We all have a past, and a future. We are here on a visit, tourists seeing the sights – we are only passing through.
>
> The world used to seem much more interesting and desirable to

me before . . . . With experience and the passing years I have had
to bow to the fact that it was not necessarily as pleasant a place as I
might have imagined. Human thought builds structures often so
much more beautiful than the world's reality.[89]

PART III

Of the Three Times and the Ten Directions

10

A Road to Shambhala

Knowing how to speak has always meant knowing how to be
silent, knowing that you do not always have to speak.

(Octavio Paz)

The land of Tibet has engendered so many dreams of light and
beauty that we can only wonder what its own dreams are. In
any case, where does wonder begin when one is living in a
land of dreams? The horizon lies so close at the end of the vast
plain that once across the invisible rampart perhaps there truly
is the land of marvels. Or at least that realm of mystery,
hidden from almost every eye – which does not prevent it
from existing – but visible for the pure in heart, for centuries
the focus of the longings of tireless pilgrims, a land where
great sages are said to have inherited priceless teachings.

Shambhala is to Tibet what in other countries is variously
perceived as the Sacred Mountain, the buried heart of the
world, the crossing from the visible to the invisible, or again
the future golden age. A symbol at the confines of infinity and
eternity, the magical country exists in all the power of the idea
it embodies; as a dimension containing the humblest beliefs
and the boldest thoughts and speculations coming down
through the centuries in the tales of the founding heroes, it has
been constantly enriched by the perceptions of generations of
meditators, ascetics and other travellers along the way to
knowledge, and to the accomplishment and plenitude of the
great sages. How should Tibet, the overlord of mountains,
not have its own still higher country of the mind, made more

appealing and secret because it towers above the shining
heights of Tibet itself? To travel to Shambhala, one has only
to follow the guide, though bearing in mind that both lovable
cranks and true seekers of the absolute have taken the same
path, and lost their way. For even in the land of waking
dreams, the rainbow spires of mirage can conceal real
dangers.

The history of Shambhala alone expresses and epitomises
the paradox of the quest. It is closely connected to the Wheel
of Time, the Kâlachakra, one of the highest tantric initiations
in Tibetan Buddhism and therefore one of the most secret, for
it is extremely complex and presupposes a vast knowledge of
the most various aspects of the tradition. Yet it is the one
initiation in Anuttara-yoga Tantra that is given openly, at
least in its initial stages, to the most assorted audiences;
anyone who shows the slightest interest may take part.
Simply to be present at such a ceremony is considered
beneficial, as it is supposed to ensure a rebirth into the hidden
kingdom that guards the purity of Buddhist teaching and
guarantees the continuity of the Dharma. And when the
ceremony is conducted by the Dalai Lama in person, the
auspices are all the more favourable, for he himself is the
direct heir in an uninterrupted line of descent that reaches back
through the centuries, it is said, to the Buddha's original
teaching.

Is it myth or reality, this mysterious kingdom whose name
signifies 'the source of happiness'? 'That is not an easy
question to answer,' the Dalai Lama concedes, with a smile so
elusive that it is open to all sorts of interpretations.

It will be a clever man who can scan a map of the world and
identify the exact location of that marvellous country. It is said in
the guidebooks that if you set out from Bodh Gaya and head
northward to the Himalayas, you finally come to a tremendous
wall of ice and snow . . .
　　We Buddhists believe that there well and truly is a place, a little
like a heaven or a paradise, or better: a pure Earth, next-door to
our everyday world, that the ordinary man cannot see, where he
cannot go, and which no one can reach if he does not practise a

particular method, through meditation or otherwise, through dreaming for example. But the intentions of whoever sets out along that road must be thoroughly pure, devoid of selfishness and ill will. If not, it is impossible to reach Shambhala, for it is a world very different from our everyday life. Nevertheless it is absolutely not a place in the mind's eye, it exists materially in our universe. If so many basic teachings come to us from Shambhala, how can it be supposed that it is only a legend?[90]

And that leaves the listener puzzled, for if Shambhala exists in that way, then it ought to be known. But does time exist? That is also the question, since the mythical kingdom of the inhabitants of Tibet is unthinkable unless closely bound up with the other dimension of the everyday, which blurs on reflection into a pure convention of the mind. And one should not forget that Buddhist meditation is explicitly aimed at changing the level of consciousness, not at rationally explaining a world which dissolves, in the last resort, under the searching beam of an infinite light.

In dreaming about the dreams of other people, the paths of myth eventually come together, even though they sometimes seem parallel. It is a matter of dimension or comprehension: the journey to the East leads unerringly to the lost horizon of the hidden valleys, shrines of wisdom veiled in patient waiting for the fulfilment of time; the sacred mountain is what harbours the King of the world, he who governs over the senses and over things, and who is also known as the Lord of Justice, or Master of Wisdom. And the book supposed to act as a guide lists so many familiar localities that they are open to interpretation at every conceivable level.

To put it simply, when the teaching becomes perfectly readable and unswervingly follows the scrupulous subtleties of the sand mandala, when the real geography masks, by unveiling it, a parallel reality, then the path of the quest reflects echoes of Agartha, El Dorado or the Grail; the road grows to be a means of initiation, and leads to conjectures in which time and space combine, and where each wayfarer, if he so wishes, can only provide his personal answer. It is the

answer demanded by the sinless state of the warrior ready to
face every danger with an unclouded mind, or contained in
the backward look that enables the poet to perceive what the
ordinary mortal has forgotten, if he ever knew it. Every quest
can only be individual, even if from time to time a sleeping
instinct suddenly launches some random group, clan or horde
into the wild pursuit of a dream half glimpsed or vaguely
sensed.

'The greatest mystery is not that we are thrown on to the
earth by chance,' said André Malraux decisively. 'It is that in
this prison we should make images of ourselves strong
enough to deny our nothingness.' And Borges echoes the
refrain: 'No one can know whether the world is fantastic or
real, or whether there is a difference between dreaming and
living.' Words, nothing but words. But it is with words that
man builds the walls that enclose him, and perhaps it is by
waking out of this kind of collective hallucination that he can
become aware of the power of his own mind.

So say the wise men of the Himalayan spaces, and it is a
means of approaching this legendary Wheel of Time, without
which there may be no land of marvels, or overwhelming
urge to start the journey, or will for knowledge to show the
way. One has to learn freedom, the kind that brings liberation
from all our chains – whether of gold or iron – in the Buddhist
view, in order to reach the primal unity of the three kingdoms
– physical, mental, spiritual – as the Kâlachakra teaches. For
when consciousness is fully awakened, yesterday lives on in
the memory, tomorrow belongs to the imagination and now
will soon be past: only the present matters, and it is eternal.
Grasping the Wheel of Time means becoming the master of
time.

Challenge or gamble, successive wise men of the Tibetan
mountains have taken it up. For century after century they
have sought Shambhala. At times they have found it. With
one and the same gesture they have sent through time a great
dream that comes sometimes in the guise of history, sometimes as reflections of prophecy. Is it surprising to find it
beginning with the wise man of the Sakyas, the historical

Buddha, who in the twilight of his earthly life passed on the teaching of the Kâlachakra to an audience of chosen disciples that happened to include the high king of Shambhala? For the authentic tantric tradition is not accessible to allcomers: it requires great depth of knowledge, and only a minority of adepts is capable of going to the heart of it. So, shortly before he entered into the peace of the highest accomplishment, the Enlightened One donned the appearance of the powerful divinity of the Kâlachakra, in a body of light perceptible to the eyes of knowledge alone, in order to reveal that way of final liberation to the wise men and gods gathered for purpose in Dhanyakataka, in southern India. At the same time the Buddha was teaching the *Prajna Paramita Sutra*, the Book of Supreme Wisdom, on the Peak of Vultures, near Bodh Gaya.

According to the present Lord of the Lotus, these mystical teachings, which are recorded in the sacred texts of the *Kanjur* and form much of the basis of the Tibetan Canon, were communicated in a spiritual dimension invisible to ordinary sight, but which is no less real than our own. Dawa Zangpo, or Suchandra by his Indian name, king of Shambhala, the land of Shiva, returned to his distant kingdom armed with that precious knowledge, which he at once transferred on to tablets. In addition, he had a mandala made in three dimensions, a shining dwelling of divinity, to assist in the visualisation essential to meditation. Not content with having drafted the first commentaries, he initiated all his subjects of the 96 vassal provinces into this wisdom. In the dust of centuries a veil of peace and oblivion settled over the happy realm devoted to the study and practice of this knowledge, under the leadership of a line of great religious monarchs nearly each of whom reigned, it is said, for a hundred years.

Nevertheless, with the eighth royal generation the sovereign Manjushrikirti fell out with a number of followers who considered the teachings too complex and tedious. Deteriorating from a theological argument to a personal quarrel, the disagreement all but turned sour, but in the end the king agreed to work out an abridged version of the Kâlachakra, more satisfying for disciples. From this era dates a second line of twenty-five sovereigns which still endures and which some day – soon, perhaps – will give rise to the Messenger-King destined to conquer misfortune and to overcome the powers of evil. Meanwhile, in the world outside Shambhala, that is on Earth, events take their course, with the spread of Buddhism from India into central Asia and China, while the Wheel of Time continues to turn, concealed from prying eyes, in the kingdom beyond the earthly frontiers. In Tibet, during and after the sixth and seventh century, Buddhism enters into paths of mysticism, and a little later the history of the precious teaching buried in the mists of memory reaches the ears of an ascetic, the great Indian yogi Tsilupa. He now decides to go in search of that lost knowledge and sets out for Shambhala.

And yet the famous sage himself was not to reach the heart of the lotus formed by the legendary land ruled by its all-knowing king; far from the world of men, at the summit of a very high mountain, he met a hermit who asked him about the reasons for his hazardous journey. The anchorite warned him that he still had a long road ahead of him before Shambhala, and many dangers awaited the bold pilgrim before he came to the impregnable wall of knowledge, well-guarded by the snow leopard, fog and mists. Nevertheless, he offered to introduce his temporary guest to the knowledge he sought there and then, so that the pilgrim now recognised Manjusri, the Bodhisattva of Knowledge, bowed down before him and was initiated into the mysteries of the Kalachakra. That is how the lost teaching returned to India. Some years later another master took up his pilgrim's staff in his turn and brought back a fuller version of the secret text from Shambhala.

Whether these journeys are real or imaginary, do they indicate that the source of that knowledge lies somewhere in upper Asia? The theory seems plausible, particularly seeing that it is corroborated by other traditions, such as *The Source of the Peach Blossom River*, from the era of the Chinese T'ang Dynasty, or the legend of the folk hero Ge-sar, the king of Ling. The ancient Taoists located the heavenly palace of the West in this same region, beyond the mountain ranges, on the

Jade Mountain, while Khirghiz legends point to an identical source – beyond the Altay Mountains and the Mongolian steppes in the golden sand desert of the Takla Makan. The collective memory has preserved the recollection of flourishing cities of the past, in the heart of a hardly mythical central Asia, such as Khotan or Uttarakuru. The Scythians believed in a dream place towards the North Pole, beyond a desolate region of gloom and snows impassable to ordinary mortals. The Greeks and Romans had the Hyperboreans, Thule is part of a similar vision, and Gilgamesh, the Babylonian hero, sets out to bring the secret of immortality from the Garden of the Sun. Then again, Arjuna, the glorious prince of the *Mahabharata*, seeks power and knowledge in the north, in the region of Kailas, the sacred mountain, and Lake Manasarowar. Curious echoes, coming from such a range of peoples, cultures and ages of the world, all of them clinging to the image of a promised land.

In this case, the teaching of the Kâlachakra, issuing from Shambhala, flourished in Kashmir and Bengal towards the end of the first millennium AD, and it was not long before it reached the solitudes beyond the ·Himalayas which are so suited to contemplation and to the quest for unfamiliar paths, through the efforts of the master Somantha, who brought it to the monks of the high plateau. Little by little this esoteric wisdom fused with Tibetan doctrine to the point of becoming one of the pillars of the teachings of the Gelukpa school. Tsong-kha-pa, its founder, took a particular interest in this technique of meditation, which he mastered in its fullest implications. In a direct vision of Shambhala, he is said to have been personally initiated by the sovereign of the forbidden kingdom.

From scholar to ascetic, hermit to sage, master to disciple, the line of descent has come down through the centuries in an unbroken sequence. When we consider how much store Tibetans set by this unchanging, direct mode of transmission, it becomes obvious how much they value the initiation bestowed by their present spiritual leader. He himself was introduced to this tradition of knowledge by his tutor Kyabje

Ling Dorje Chang, the ninety-seventh descendant of Tsong-
kha-pa the Reformer on the abbey throne of Ganden, and
chief of the Yellow Hat school.

Why this doctrine rather than another, and why this way to
the quest rather than the more commonly trodden paths
offered for the pilgrim's choice or sagacity? Buddhists aver
that no one can claim that a way is good or bad, except by
having trodden it, and that it can only be judged by the
outcome, in other words by the illumination that the wayfarer
has or has not found. That is to reaffirm that there are as many
paths as there are travellers. However, some learned lamas
also say that the teaching of the Wheel of Time is of prime
importance to the modern world, because there is a very
specific link between Shambhala and the Earth we know and
live in.

Some have identified features in this fundamental Tantra,
the Kâlachakra, features that might connect it to the Indian
tradition, at least in the similarities to be observed between
Kalki, the future redeemer, and Rudra Sakrin, the ruler of
Shambhala, whose role it is to conquer the opponents of
wisdom. When the time comes he will raise a countless army,
equipped with every imagined and imaginable weapon, to
pacify the Earth and to restore the reign of justice on it. But it
may also be that these warriors from another dimension are
only the creation of free and powerful minds, mirages lethal
to the paralysing illusions of mankind. In the depths of the
collective consciousness, what people, what nation, what
civilisation has not dreamed of the perfect king, just and
impartial, whose task it is to oversee the workings of a
harmonious society with justice for all its members? The
image of the Great King is also deeply entrenched in the
human mind, but here again the various degrees of understanding remain dependent on a discriminating reading. He
may even be seen as the watchman, the man who answers the
question, What of the night? There is something of the last
judgment and of the resurrection in this belief, which is
equally open to many interpretations.

At first sight, one is bound to wonder about the exact

meaning indicated by a meticulous chronology, whereas the adversary is clearly designated as a barbarian according to the Buddhist view. For some day the king of the barbarians, drunk with power and blind with self-admiration, having conquered all the world, will hear tell of the fabulous wealth of Shambhala, and will not rest until it belongs to him. So he will hurl his legions into battle against the unknown country that limits – as he thinks – the scope of his own power. Quite obviously, the move will bring his ruin, at least in the earthly sense, for his defeat will also put an end to his ignorance; he will have found the real meaning of life from the Buddhist perspective. According to astronomical reckonings based upon the Tibetan calendar the gigantic decisive battle will take place in three or four centuries' time, in the days of the thirty-second king of Shambhala. At present it is the twenty-eighth who rules that land of peace, and the clash of the two worlds will constitute the awesome prelude to a new golden age.

Of course, every lama, if not every Tibetan, has his personal idea and interpretation of the prophecy, and indeed of the actual teaching. Tentzin Gyatso himself continues to ponder the matter, but when one is the Dalai Lama, variations on these other worlds are part of a different pattern, and dreaming belongs to a distinct level of consciousness and leads to vistas that may cause the mind to reel. Such as Shambhala. Even if Yeshe Norbu, the Wish-fulfilling Gem, hedges and pretends to cast around for just the right summary account, the gentle gleam in his eye conveys deep knowledge as well as a droll complicity; there is no need of witchcraft to detect that the road to Shambhala is no mystery to him.

> You must understand that the Kâlachakra embraces a most enormous range of phenomena, from the human mind and body all the way to the global, cosmic and astrological outer aspect. In this sense, it is one of the fullest of teachings. There is an inner as well as an outer Kâlachakra, both of them linked together, of course, and naturally bound up with the third, the all-embracing, the one that indicates the means of purification, and hence of detachment. Through thorough and assiduous practice of this

high tantric discipline it is possible to achieve illumination and
come to awakening in a single lifetime.

That, in a way, is the significance of the Kâlachakra, and we
firmly believe in its power to reduce tensions. The initiation is
given publicly, because we deem it capable of creating peace, the
peace of the mind, and therefore of advancing peace in the world.
One day, in the centuries to come, the kingdom of Shambhala
could well reappear in the reality that seems to be our own, and
contribute to the general task that remains to be achieved in this
world.

In so far as I myself practise the Kâlachakra and am in direct
relation with that tantric way, it is evident that I take a very close
interest in Shambhala. For me, it is not an ordinary place, but
rather a state of mind or consciousness, which can be lived or
experienced only by virtue of individual karmic links.

Yet, even for me, Shambhala remains an enigmatic and indeed
a paradoxical land. For example, according to the Scriptures, in
three or four hundred years there will be a battle on this planet, in
our world, with the powers of Shambhala. They will come here,
to this world, to bring the Good Teaching. It is in the logic of the
cycle. How is this to be interpreted? What forces are really
involved? In fact, I find that it is rather hard to explain, for if
Shambhala is a kingdom of peace, and it can only be that, why
these terrifying weapons and this dreadful battle? Unless the
reference is to a country of the pure Land, which exists only on
the mental level, as we speak of the pure Land of the Bodhisattva
of Knowledge, Manjusri, or of the *dakinis*, whose present but
unseen divinities who are guardians of the shadows and guides to
the nearby spaces.

Then there is a further possibility, that it could involve another
planet. As yet, we have not developed the potential or the
technological means to travel to other planets. There is still
progress to be made, before we can communicate across space.
Though one hopes that those people are not the evil little green
men in the science fiction stories, pouring in from space to impose
their ruthless domination over humanity .... No, surely not,
because it is said that the lord of Shambhala is very handsome and
intelligent, and that he is gifted with all the qualities of justice and
compassion. Well, we shall see in the end, shan't we?[91]

Another Tibetan tradition, that of Ge-sar of Ling, can also be

connected, if only by association, with the legendary realm.
Like most of the mythical heroes emerging from the depths of
upper Asia, Ge-sar, lord of Ling, is a master. Some say that he
is a reincarnation of Padmasambhava, who consolidated the
hold of Buddhism in Tibet, whereas others consider him as an
incarnation of Avalokitesvara, the Lord of Infinite Compassion. 'Perhaps he will return,' the Dalai Lama comments.

> You know, the idea of liberty, and also of liberation, is firmly
> rooted in the heart of the Tibetan people, whether in the case of
> Shambhala or of Ge-sar. It is possible to see him as the warrior
> liberator, the leader who cuts the ties of physical dependence, but
> also of spiritual ignorance. Once again, it all depends on the level
> of perception, on the chosen way of interpreting. I know very
> little more.[92]

Among the possibilities of apprehending the mysterious
country, as the vision of the path unfolds, there is some
almost initiatory reading to be done. Inevitably, obstacles and
battles, encounters and reverses insistently suggest stages of
the quest for self-knowledge. In any case, the three levels of
understanding of the Wheel of Time indicated by the Dalai
Lama himself point unequivocally to an enquiry which should
lead to the limits of the self, and return bearing a spark of
wisdom about which the masters say that it enables the finder
to live in the light of death.

In this respect, the best-known guide to that sibylline land –
The Way To Shambhala, written in 1775 by the Third Panchen
Lama, Lobsang Palden Yeshe – is quite clear cut. Described in
its outward particulars and by its names, in which imagination and the most concrete detail go together, India is
depicted through the eyes and contemporary knowledge of a
Tibetan scholar inarguably versed in the sacred texts, but
limited by a geography whose practical dimension clearly
escapes him. But his words still display a firmly established
scale of values, while certain complaints about the upheavals
and decadence of the moment have a peculiarly modern ring.

On the one hand an academic discussion, so the guide
reveals; on the other a logical and coherent interpretation of

the spiritual and even metaphysical aspect of the quest: if the author passes very quickly over some means considered as magical, he elaborates rather more on the stages of the meditation, those which are supposed to give 'powers' to the adept. But in the same breath he gives warning that this is not the object of the search, and that one must not let oneself be caught in the trap of illusory achievements. Even the last watch seems longer on the threshold of awakening, for one has to learn to see the world as it is, and not to be satisfied with the image one creates of it. The deeper the precipice appears, the more beautiful the discovery of the infinite vastness that stretches before it.

Moreover there is no use trying to force an entry; the journey to Shambhala is also a schooling in the necessity to give time to time, and the Kâlachakra requires a personal discipline that leaves very little room for other activities. Once again it is a question of choice; every remotely serious spiritual experience demands a total commitment and is based on renunciations. The transcendental dimension of the quest has great difficulty in satisfying rational explanations; the inexpressible joins the inexplicable. Not that this prevents speculation about the ultimate finality of this progression, in so far as a handful of witnesses exist to testify, by their sole presence and individual experience, to the undeniable reality of the outcome of the quest.

In following the footpaths of Tibet, there are encounters which engrave themselves indelibly in the memory and become integral parts of a life; looks or smiles that nothing can ever erase. So it is with Dr Tenṭzin Choedhak. At first sight he is self-effacing and almost meek, his voice so peaceable that it sounds thin, his back slightly bent inside a dark jacket of indeterminate colour, you would walk straight past him in a crowd; he is hardly noticeable, except if you should meet his eye. Seldom does such a degree of vivid understanding make itself so powerfully felt, without a word; his tangible compassion is instantly conveyed. His astounding eyes combine tenderness with power, and the sharpness of one who has seen so much that he is left free of everything but a fierce determination to devote his life to others. After all the suffering endured and all the evil and evils he has witnessed, the man remains anchored in the rock of his faith, which is the source of his strength and the creator of the gift that he never ceases to lavish upon all others, without exception.

Since his early childhood, in a Tibet that no longer exists, Dr Choedhak has been a traditional monk. A strict and sober life of study and concentration took him from his native village to the famous School of Medicine, on the Iron Hill in Lhasa, where he pursued both his religious and his medical training. Appointed personal physician to the Dalai Lama in 1956 – there were four in regular attendance – he was to suffer cruel treatment after the bloody repression of the rebellion against the Chinese in 1959 – interrogation, torture, and forced labour in a camp at the edge of the Gobi Desert. He spent some terrible years in that penal colony, notorious as one of the hardest in People's China, watching his companions in distress die, one after another, but unable to do anything for them. In 1962 he was brought back to the sinister prison of Drapchi, in Lhasa, for 're-education'.

It was the arrival in 1979 of the first delegation sent by the Dalai Lama and led by his brother, Lobsang Samten, to examine the changes in Tibet that finally brought the release of Dr Choedhak. A year later, and quite exceptionally, he was given permission to leave occupied Tibet and went first to Nepal and then straight to Dharamsala to resume his duties on behalf of the exiled sovereign. Today, the only thing that Dr Choedhak consents to say about those appalling years is that he was saved by the regular practice of a particular tantric meditation; day after day, or rather night after night, he drew strength and comfort from that practice in confronting a reality which far surpassed the wildest nightmares of a fevered mind. All the angry gods and demons, the dreadful divinities and frightening genies of the Tibetan pantheon might have seemed like mild fantasies by comparison with the sufferings endured.

No doubt that is why his smile is one of those which, in a

survivor of the house of the dead, contain an unspeakable awareness; Dr Choedhak does not judge – not now, and probably not ever – but he sympathises and he helps. He listens with infinite kindness to the patients who pass through his modest consulting room in the Tibetan Medical Centre which he runs in Dharamsala – listens, not to words but to sounds inaudible to the lay ear; with fingers vibrant with sensitivity, he takes their pulses to 'listen' to the body describing its own troubles, and to interpret its complaints. With people of so high a human quality, and who show such a superhuman attention to others, one is compelled to believe them when they insist that their spiritual practice has been and continues to be their sole protection; at this level, doubt has very little meaning, and the mind simply yields to the facts, even though it also has to accept that it must be a long journey that leads to this degree of mastery. Perhaps it is the paradoxical nature of this accomplishment that temporarily disorients the outside observer; once having achieved the awakening at the end of the path, all perspectives shift, and the world is re-ordered into the structures of a different dimension, both of space and time. Even to catch a glimpse of these unfathomed depths can cause the beholder's mind to reel.

To set out in search of Shambhala essentially demands letting go of all attachments and making for unknown territory strewn with pitfalls and veiled by forebodings of uncertain dangers; it is also a search for total freedom, liberation from the boundaries of everyday existence. The traveller has to be free in order to undertake the journey, and aware of what lies in wait along the way; it is the price of the solitary struggle that lies ahead in order to attain what some call individuation, a complete integration of the personality, achieved at the moment of crossing the threshold of the glittering palace of the king, in the heart of the heart of the lotus. By unleashing the inner energy through the proper means, and making offerings to conciliate the hostile forces that bar the way forward, only to be transformed into allies in good time, the seeker advances slowly, step by step, through unexplored regions of his own consciousness, finally to reach a fundamental reality, the matrix of all riches.

The ultimate significance of the Wheel of Time, its eschato-logical or apocalyptic dimension, can well be summed up as a re-birth; the conquest of wisdom means coming to a new birth into the world, not as a superman but as a fully realised human being who has thoroughly explored his limits and possibilities, in order to come to light. The outer, and inner secret wheels of the tantric teaching come together to shine beyond the shadows of dispersed illusion – a standard image of the process of learning which enables the learner to be his own guiding light, and then, as the depositary of this precious jewel, to remain among men, simply among them, in order to help them to become themselves.

Of course, this is very much an oriental approach, and generally despised by western eyes, which are dubious to the point of anxiety, and supremely distrustful of these unclassi-fied and therefore perilous regions indexed under the unrelia-ble title of 'affairs of the soul', and to be approached with the utmost caution. In fact, the essence of the kingdom, its content and symbol are found in the journey, in that descent towards a deeper consciousness, which radically alters the meaning and indeed perception of the world. This is another way of saying that in order to waken to one's true nature, one must die to one's own illusory image. For some, it is finding, or giving, a meaning to life. Carl Jung once wrote 'Fortu-nately, in its goodness and forbearance, nature has never put into most men's mouths the fatal question of the meaning of their lives. And when no one asks the question, one can only keep silent.' For their part, Tibetan Buddhists seem never to have ceased to ask it. Would they be right to consider that certain teachings ought to remain hidden, as long as the times are not ripe to divulge them?

These parallel worlds, perceived with palpable suspicion by the rationalist western mind, have an indisputable reality for Tibetans, from the humblest to the most accomplished. People do not joke with the spirits on the high Himalayan plateaux, even if they sometimes hesitate to talk about them; they are plain facts of life to be taken account of, as one takes

account, for example, of the snow that falls unexpectedly and
blocks a pass, or the great wild wind that suddenly blows up
to go chasing after an invisible runaway horse. To know that
that reality is as real as any other, one has only to bear in mind
the key role played by oracles in the daily life of Tibet.

To act as an intermediary on behalf of the guardian entities
has never been a minor matter for those chosen to carry the
messages of the gods – what other word is available to convey
this notion? For, like it or not, the choosing of the messenger
comes first, and then the apprenticeship. No important
decision can be taken without their aid, and their warnings
have always been heard, even when their protective presence
has proved to be insufficient when confronted with the brute
power of human beings.

·Nowadays the function of the oracle is hard to carry out in
the conditions imposed by exile, and communication may
seem a delicate task, particularly with Dorje Drakden,
'Renowned Changeless One', supreme protector of the high
country, or again with Palden Lhamo, the divinity who is the
Dalai Lama's special guardian. 'Not at all,' says Tentzin
Gyatso.

> There is not the slightest problem. It is not the medium that
> counts, his absence does not prevent the divinity from being
> there. It is advisable to use other channels to communicate with it,
> links of consciousness more subtle and refined than are normally
> used. Also, there has never been a medium for Palden Lhamo,
> and the need does not make itself felt. Of course, the intermediary
> can make matters easier, but it is not a serious problem when
> there is no physical body fit and prepared temporarily to welcome
> the divinity. There are other means than mediumistic trance to
> receive the necessary messages.[93]

Is Buddhism, particularly in its Tibetan version, a true science
of mind, as it is quite often perceived in western countries? 'I
think that there is an element of truth in that opinion,' the
Precious Master answers.

For me, Buddhism is first a humane religion. In fact it seems to be basically concerned with the development and improvement of the mind.

On the occasion of initiations, rituals or ceremonies, when it is a case of explaining and visualising the divinity and its symbols, there is no doubt that the disciple's techniques, and means of applying and transforming the mind, are called upon. That is to say that this aspect is paramount in order to make progress along the path of Buddhist knowledge.

A science of mind .... Again, it all depends upon what is meant by 'science'. At present, the meaning of the word is confined to what can be measured with precision. From that point of view, obviously it is not possible to measure either mind or consciousness. It is something different, completely distinct. So if science is limited solely to what can be measured, then it is difficult to argue that Buddhism is a science of mind. What is certain is that it is based on actual facts and that it uses them with the aim of refining or sharpening consciousness. But all this does not happen overnight.

It must be realised that our personalities do not transform themselves just like that, suddenly, by the wave of a magic wand. One has to put one's own weight into it and not balk, or shrink from the effort. Our natural frames of mind only change slowly, and it also takes time to become aware of that. To achieve an outcome requires patience and determination; it is not a matter of an outward change, as with a change of nose or hair style, it is a transformation of the mind, a deepening of consciousness.

The highest tantric teachings, like the Kâlachakra for example, aim to sow the seeds of a better understanding of oneself and of the world, to alter perception, the way we look at our surroundings. Knowledge is important, but at the same time more important still is the mind that conveys it. Using the mind alone, while the heart remains on the sidelines, can only increase the troubles in society. The human must be tempered by an open, compassionate heart.[94]

The Lord of the Lotus will go no further in his explanations; according to tradition, the secret teaching ought to remain secret, and the initiates who have full access to it, wise men among the wise, are bound by the vow and commitment not to reveal what ought not to be revealed. Between the risk of

obscuring a knowledge they see as exceptionally valuable, and
that of exposing it to a perilous deterioration should it fall into
unpractised or ill-intentioned hands, its true keepers choose
the greatest circumspection. By the yardstick of time, and a
different scale of memory, they trust in the everlasting
survival of the hidden kingdom and know that those who are
meant to find it will reach it some day, by their own pathways. In these circumstances, perhaps there is no great sense
in taking the prophecy literally, even if for the majority of
Tibetans the journey to Shambhala is understood in its most
immediate, that is to say its most obviously terrestrial,
meaning. But only those who are thoroughly fitted for the
way can set out along it, for it requires perfect coordination of
means, and a good guide.

Yet the Tibetans are a pilgrim nation; they walk tirelessly
on for hours and days, weeks and months, and even for years,
when the idea of pilgrimage takes root in their mind. Then
they set out and they travel, alone or in smaller or larger
groups. Nothing seems able to stop them, neither dubious
portents nor the administrative barriers of the present day.
The former can be remedied by offerings, prayers and the
proper ceremonial. The latter are made to be overcome, all
the more so because they felt to be utterly arbitrary and
meaningless hindrances.

An ancestral nomadic atavism is combined with what
seems at first sight to be a surprising indifference to temporal
possessions; of course one is aware that they make life easier
from day to day, and they are appreciated for that, but the
traditional frugality of customary practice prevents them
from being indispensable. Material wealth is prized, but there
remains a keen awareness that it represents an illusion of
power, and that spiritual values, though harder to attain, are
less ephemeral. This conception, which for centuries has
pervaded the daily life of the high plateaux, so shielded from
outside influence until recently, goes some way towards
explaining the liability of Tibetans suddenly to set off along
the highway as if on the spur of the moment, or by an
impulse springing from the depths of instinct. It also means

that an initiation given by their spiritual guide is a hundred times worth the sacrifices accepted in order to take part in it, and effaces the memory of the countless barriers overcome, to leave nothing but the memory of a radiant presence. It was this feeling that one day drove them in their hundreds and thousands – but they knew the hour and the time – towards Bodh Gaya, for a spectacular ritual of the Kâlachakra.

Treading the thousand and one pathways followed by the generations of all those who had preceded them in the timelessness of the centuries, and trusting unreservedly in the guardianship of Tara the Protector, who was born from a tear shed by the Lord of Compassion, they return to the sacred places of their faith, supported and vitalised by that presence perpetually renewed. It is a little akin to the idea of the eternal return, waiting for the advent of what is written for all eternity; the cycle of life is made in such a way that it must necessarily pass through death, and that all existence is mortal – the lives of men, as well as doctrines. In order to bring about the coming of Maitreya, the Buddha of the Future, the barbarians have their karma to work out, and their destiny is to launch their forces against Shambhala when the moment comes. There will follow a long period of creative wisdom and peace, invaluable for the spiritual progress of humanity.

Even if not all have the time or ability to follow the path to the end, they will at least have tried to take the first steps; that too will be taken into their account. With a steadfastness made all the more remarkable by its smiling friendship, the Dalai Lama continues to point out the requirement for personal improvement, and to appeal to the individual's responsibility for the welfare of all. In the infinite cycle of time, it is rare to meet the dual good fortune of being born among humans and in an era of light, illuminated by the presence of a Buddha.

Certainly, in contemplating the life of the world one may well find oneself asking what an era of shadows might represent, but Tentzin Gyatso's answer to this objection is that it is a matter of perspective.

It does seem to me that the general mood in today's world is not exactly a happy one. Even though there is an overall knowledge of what is good and what is bad, despite that there is a tendency to act in the opposite way: on the pretext of external pressures or hostile circumstances, the wrong path is taken. In my view, that is certainly not beneficial to anybody, but all the same I remain convinced that it is possible to change this attitude. I have great hopes for the new generation. In the quest for the happiness which is everybody's goal, there is a variety of methods: some prefer science and technology, others religious practice, others again a system of government or the banner of an ideology.

Every individual seeks his own way, and in our world which is growing smaller every day, and where we are ever more dependent on each other, it seems to me that it is vital to develop a sense of universal responsibility. I have always been convinced, and now more than ever, that every spiritual value, whatever it is, has a great part to play and a special responsibility to assume in this field, in order to contribute to a genuine world peace. Not forgetting all the same that world peace comes by way of the inner peace of every individual.[95]

In the moving and sometimes disconcerting world of symbols to be deciphered, as if in an initiation into the reading of a paradoxical alphabet, attention focuses on the frontier runner, the one who knows the way through, and can point out the traps to be avoided. That is why those who follow him are bound to put complete trust in him, although the travelling is up to them. It is the fundamental responsibility of the tantric master, who also knows that he must not bow to every wind that blows, and that there are moments of silence which are likewise deeps of contemplation. For the perfect inner light is only for a few to achieve.

That was the meaning of the meeting at Bodh Gaya. Unknown to the organs of what likes to call itself the world press, constantly on the lookout for sensation, whether genuine or sham, the little town in Bihar went through those few days of the initiation living on the borders of the everyday world, in an imperceptibly different dimension, subtly shifted away from the ordinary frame, in a strangely free-floating present time, an essence of being or becoming.

Perhaps the dimension of Shambhala? Others would call it a step through the looking glass, or the rainbow footbridge between emptiness and eternity.

Then the sand of the magic mandala drifted, the colourful and kaleidoscopic gathering broke up, and the pilgrims went their way. The world returned to itself again, and resumed its everyday colours, but those who took part in the initiation ritual now carried a hope – that of being reborn perfectly qualified to achieve awakening, thanks to the practice of the Kâlachakra. When the time comes.

Did the world return to itself – to indifference, selfishness and mundane interests? No doubt it did. And yet . . .

> What you write in ink in small black letters
> May be completely lost
> Through the action of a simple drop of water.
> But what is written in your mind
> Stays there for eternity.

So said the Sixth Dalai Lama.

Call this the poet's intuition, or the wise man's affirmation; the silence restored to Bodh Gaya resounds with the pounding of a heart that goes on beating, unheard by the heedless ear drawn to the thousand other sounds of life. On the obverse side of space, the silence beneath the Bodhi tree is capable of becoming an initiatory force, and Tara the Goddess smiles on the passerby who stares at her before he bows down low. She keeps watch, because she knows that time always fulfils itself. This is the Law of the Wheel, and this can be the symbol of Shambhala; a beautiful story which dissolves into the heart of the lotus, a wonderful vision of love and justice beyond the frozen mountains of the infinite, a formidable litany that beats its everlasting accompaniment to a nation marching towards a rendezvous with itself.

11
To Time's Fulfilment

Truth never triumphs, but its enemies finally die.

(Max Planck)

'The twenty-first century will be religious, or it will not be at all.' André Malraux's remark causes the Lord of the Lotus to stop and ponder for a moment. His eyes meet those of the effigy of the Buddha which occupies the place of honour in the light and friendly audience room in Dharamsala. The large picture windows open on to verandas, and the whole dwelling is surrounded by trees and flowers. The weather is calm in the little mountain town, birdsong trills in the silence, and the ventilators are still. Autumn is scattering the first patches of gold and amber across the foliage, and the blue of the sky is heightened by the proximity of peaks already covered by a veil of silky snow. A monk slips between two doors and placidly disappears. Eyes narrow to become a lynx's gaze behind the spectacles, and the trace of a smile appears, as the unhurried answer weaves itself into the pattern of time.

I do not think so, that is not my opinion. There is always a middle way, a median possibility. Even in the past it is hardly possible to speak of a completely and absolutely religious society, and today, still less . . . . There have always been those who were drawn to religion, others who resisted it, and then the ones who take neither view. It seems to me that things will go on like that. As for the twenty-first century, I do not know . . . .

No doubt there will always be different currents of opinion, extremists on one side or the other, religious fanatics and convinced atheists. Early in the century the anti-religious forces were possibly much stronger. Today it would seem that the neutrals are more numerous, and at the same time, here and there we see a revival of interest in spiritual things, like sprouting seeds. One is also bound to admit that the materialists today are legion – materialists in the sense that money plays an essential part in their conception of life. Not every problem can be settled by money or power, for it is not possible to go on ignoring the inner dimension indefinitely. Perhaps that is what the French writer wished to express?

In that case then, seen through the sharp eyes of the Lord of the Lotus, how will the future look? The great battle for Shambhala, prophesied for some four centuries from now, is still a long way from the human view, and meanwhile the world keeps turning, events keep transforming it, and men keep questioning themselves. Even if, unknown to themselves, the inhabitants of the blue planet have a privileged link with the hidden kingdom, before they discover it they have to confront the dramas of the everyday world – those of Tibet, for example, and the Land of Snows remains at the centre of the Dalai Lama's worries. He is thoroughly aware of the upheavals which have affected the Roof of the World during recent decades, he is well aware that the past is past, and incidentally he makes it clear that in any case it would not be desirable to return to structures now decidedly superseded.

In his view, before making any other assessment, it is vital to define the misunderstanding which underlies the disagreement between Tibet and China. By their history, culture and tradition, the two countries are inevitably neighbours; nature has made it so. Politically, however, they have always represented two distinct entities, even if in centuries of fluctuating interplay links of a specific nature have grown up between them. The kernel of the tragedy is unquestionably to be found in the Chinese wish to impose the image of a factitious similarity, while the Tibetan determination to display its radical otherness has not weakened, and on the contrary has been reinforced, with the passing years. Certainly there is a real danger for the Roof of the World of being submerged by the influx of wave after wave of Chinese colonists in search of living space, but forced assimilation has never been a viable long-term solution in human history, short of accepting the physical disappearance of a community too numerically weak to stand in the way of the invader.

It is in similar terms that the lord temporal and spiritual of the Tibetan people visualises the future, and that future is inevitably tied up with the attitude of China. Drawing the lesson of recent experience, the Dalai Lama does not conceal his anxiety:

Today, Tibet is directly threatened in its national identity: dumping a mass of Chinese colonists on to our territory involves a threat to the native population of assimilation and absorption. At the beginning of the century the Manchus formed a different race, with its own culture and traditions. Today there are no more than 2 or 3 million Manchus living in Manchuria, where 75 million Chinese have settled. In eastern Turkestan, which the Chinese call Xinjiang, the Chinese population has risen from 200,000 in 1947 to 7 million, or over half of the 13 million inhabitants. In the wake of the Chinese colonisation of Inner Mongolia, the Chinese now amount to 8½ million of the population, compared to the 2½ million Mongols. According to official Chinese statistics, the region of Koko Nor in north-eastern Tibet, where I was born, now contains nearly 3 million Chinese for 700,000 Tibetans.

It is not uninstructive to recall that Sun Yat-sen the father of the Chinese republic, considered Tibet, Mongolia and Manchuria as foreign countries. In the 1930s Mao Zedong, who was fighting but not yet in power, upheld the independence of Tibet. Some years later, in 1954, when I paid a visit to China, Mao told me that as long as we were poor and backward China would help us, but that afterwards it would be up to us to come to the aid of China. The Chinese proclaim that they did not go to Tibet as imperialists or colonists, but that they came as 'liberators'. What kind of liberation is it that denies people their rights, and their freedom to determine their own fate?

It is impossible to quantify the enormous material losses suffered by the Tibetan people under Chinese domination: wealth accumulated through the centuries in our 5,000 monasteries has been sacked, plundered or dispatched to China, not to mention the irreplaceable loss of precious manuscripts written in Sanskrit, Pali and Tibetan. And now the Chinese have the impudence to claim that they have spent something like 3 billion dollars on the development of Tibet over the last thirty years. Why do they forget to mention that they keep a minimum of 300,000 troops there, and nearly 1,700,000 state officials?

The time seems well and truly come for them to go. They ought to go home and devote themselves to solving their own country's problems. That would be as worth while a decision for themselves as for Tibetans. We have the right to follow our own way, and to live by the standards of our culture and our own identity. All peoples have that right, and no nation can claim a right to colonise others.

I readily admit that a slight improvement became noticeable in Tibet at the beginning of the 1980s. There is more food, greater economic flexibility and fewer restrictions on movement in certain regions. But to satisfy basic necessities in food, housing and clothing is not enough for human beings. Animals are probably satisfied when they are fed, housed and well treated, even if it is temporary. But in a human society freedom remains the fundamental requirement, an inalienable right that cannot be replaced by temporary improvements in economic conditions or food supplies.

We Tibetans have nothing against the Chinese. All we ask is what belongs to us by right. We consider that the Chinese too have a right to happiness and prosperity, but not at the expense of another nation or another people. China has no right to decide the fate of the Tibetan people. No doubt in the past there were periods when Manchus and Chinese held some sway over Tibet, but what nation in the world can boast that it has never suffered the influence of outside powers, whether military, political, cultural or religious? That does not give anybody the authority to make claims on behalf of the sovereignty of the stronger over the weaker. Such statements lack any real basis.

If the present policy goes on, soon Tibet will no longer be Tibetan. It will be one territory among various others, peopled by Chinese and dominated by Chinese culture. People should be aware of that. That kind of colonialism is anachronistic and uncivilised, and people of goodwill all over the world must condemn these practices. Tibet possesses a unique cultural heritage, and it is a land of great natural beauty. Already the Chinese have ravaged and exploited a large part of our forests, and they have also wiped out most of our wild animals. The preservation of this natural heritage is not the responsibility of Tibetans alone, because our culture is one of the world's oldest traditions and belongs to the patrimony of mankind. Furthermore, many of its aspects are as beautiful as they are useful. If it is destroyed, the loss will not be grave for central Asia alone – it is world culture that will lose.[96]

That is the meaning of the silent war that Tentzin Gyatso has waged without respite ever since he found himself forced into exile after the ruthless suppression of the anti-Chinese uprising in 1959. Without ever resorting to spectacular murderous gestures to draw the world's attention to a cause which is just as dramatic as others that are blazoned over the front pages of the world press by aircraft hijacks, bombings, kidnappings, hostage taking, assassination and blackmail, Tibet's spiritual leader measures his words and simply claims justice for his own.

Some people consider that the Tibetan question is a strictly political matter. I do not think so. We Tibetans have a cultural heritage different from the Chinese. We feel no hatred towards them, we deeply respect the age-old riches of the Chinese culture. That does not prevent us, the 6 million Tibetans, from having the same right as the Chinese to maintain our own culture, as long as we do no harm to anybody. Materially we are backward, but in the spiritual domain, in terms of development of the mind, we are infinitely rich. In the past century we have remained a peaceful nation kept in being by its special culture. Now, unfortunately, in the last 30 years this nation and its culture have been deliberately overthrown. We love our culture and our country, and we have the right to preserve them. Furthermore, the 6 million Tibetans are human beings, whether or not they are materially backward, and they have the right to live as human beings. That is the whole problem.

I have placed myself in the service of this cause in order to serve humanity, not for reasons of any wish for power, or out of hatred. Not only as a Tibetan, but also as a human being, I believe that it is worth while to preserve that culture and that nation, for the sake of their contribution to the world. That is why I persist and insist, and that is why I say that it is not only a political matter. No matter how strong it is, might cannot be right for very long, while the flame of truth keeps burning. I am still convinced of that.[97]

In 1989 the Dalai Lama will have completed thirty years of exile and almost solitary combat, with hardly any outside support except for private international contributions – and these have come from all over the world – for the sake of preserving an ancient and unparalleled variety of human experience. While the Tibetans inside the country have fought with the means at their disposal, without really having the knowledge or the ability to fight against the weapons invented by the ingenuity of modern man, outside their country Tibetans carry on the struggle to perpetuate their own otherness.

These years of suffering, sorrows and countless hardships, the Dalai Lama has taken as they have come, with his unfailing clarity of mind and readiness to stand up to adversity. It is for that reason that he has established a government in exile, which no state has dared to recognise. But that does not prevent it from functioning, or from devoting itself to the tasks it has assumed.

In the present circumstances it hardly matters whether its representation is officially legal or not. Sometimes legality can be a front for illegality, and the reverse is equally possible. What matters is that the majority of Tibetans have set their hopes upon this government. That is why we too bear an enormous responsibility. The period we are passing through is the darkest in all the 2,000 years of Tibetan history. Under these conditions I consider it a great honour and privilege to carry the responsibility that my position involves.[98]

Nevertheless, the ground already covered has contained many encouraging and positive landmarks. There is now a proper Tibetan constitution, suited to the realities of the

modern world and adopted by the elected representatives of
the Tibetan communities in exile. Democracy too is a process
of learning, and one which only the refugees are at present
undergoing; in Chinese-controlled Tibet, although the individual may try to think and consider in his own way, he
nevertheless remains subordinated to the Chinese system of
applying social regulations imposed by a still much resented
foreign domination

The basic charter, inspired and modelled in India on the
initiative of the Dalai Lama, is only provisional, in the sense
that it is ruled by imperatives peculiar to exile. However, an
inspection of its articles shows that it is the most open and
progressive that Tibet has ever seen – yet another paradox,
considering the man who stands behind it, since the exiled
sovereign is both the legitimate heir and the incarnation of an
age-old teaching and way of thinking, and hence a conservative, and at the same time the personification of a modernising urge and the builder of a different kind of future, which
makes him an innovator determined to break the stranglehold
of paralysing traditions. But the Dalai Lama leaves no room
for ambiguity; when the time comes, this constitution will be
submitted to the judgment of all Tibetans who remain inside
the country, and the final decision will be up to them. This
right belongs to them because of the suffering they have
endured, and the future lies in their hands; the political and
economic system of an independent Tibet will be the expression of their wishes.

Tentzin Gyatso is not afraid of casting a critical eye over
the past, and he readily admits that a greater openness to the
outside world might possibly have altered the course of
contemporary history on the Roof of the World. He insists
on the narrow-mindedness of the traditionalists who
opposed the creation of western-inspired schools, in particular in Gyantse and Lhasa, at the time of the Great
Thirteenth, for fear that western habits would corrupt and
even destroy the Buddhist faith of the younger generation.
'My predecessor was a man of stature, and very far-sighted,'
he observes.

But he was dealing with a very conservative society, and it was sometimes hard for him to convince others in authority in Tibet of the soundness of his ideas. No doubt there would have been a few unhappy experiences, but it would not have been the fault of modern education, or of the west. It would have been our own fault, because we would have failed to give young people a deep and firm enough philosophical grounding in their own tradition.[99]

That is also why today, in spite of the material limitations of exile, he continues to be vigilant and demanding about the quality of the studies and education provided for the rising generation. So it is hardly surprising to find him concerned with a field as special as language.

There is the problem that we ourselves have in India; namely, the Tibetan language remains to be developed in such a way as to have a vocabulary for modern western subjects. Unless the Tibetan language becomes adequate in this way, it faces a problem of survival. At the moment it is not sufficiently developed in this direction. We don't have words for many of the concepts of modern science, and thus it becomes impossible for our people to receive a scientific or technical training in our own language. This is not particularly surprising and is not something that we need to feel ashamed of; our culture developed independently without intimate contact with the west, and therefore our language reflects this. This same situation exists in reverse for the west; there are many concepts in the Tibetan philosophical and spiritual sciences for which there are no precise equivalents in English. English simply has not developed sufficiently in these directions to incorporate these concepts.[100]

Yet the Lord of the Lotus does not venture into great theories or scholarly elaborations concerning the future face of Tibetan society; as a good Buddhist monk, he prefers to keep a close eye on a practical evolution on which he willingly admits that he has no concrete leverage. His influence is primarily of a spiritual or intellectual order, and his personal standing enables him to give his opinions, but it is other people who each lead their different lives, and it is up to the Tibetan people as a whole to build their new world.

One thing is certain, however: that it will not be possible to ignore the changes which have arisen, and that it will be necessary to take account of the new deal, to adapt to different social rules and adjust to some partial secularisation of the Tibetan way of life. In any case, for many years, even before the Chinese invasion, undercurrents of renewal had been flowing on the Roof of the World, at least in the urban centres. The tragedy of Tibet will prove to have been the fact that its leaders, often caught up in internal quarrels or group or individual rivalries, did not pay them attention in time, as if hypnotised by the changeless mineral nature that surrounded them.

At the time when he was attempting to practise the difficult balancing act of cohabitation with Communist China, between 1950 and 1959, despite his youth and political inexperience the Dalai Lama was cautiously exploring ways of possible change. Like all his fellow countrymen he was caught unawares by the invader, time and history. The brutality of the succeeding upheaval will have cost his country and people very dear, moulding the shape of a different future; now it is essential to restore those links that may still be restored, and to set about making the best of conditions as they are. Some of the responsibility lies with the community in exile, on the frontier of the two worlds – between a country now only a dim memory, and the society in which they have mostly grown up, the young Tibetans of the new generation are charged with the often thankless role of bringing the two together.

> Until now, since we have formed a little Tibetan community outside Tibet, in the circumstances we have preserved our cultural heritage fairly well. If our younger generation has changed its style, if they dress differently and cut their hair differently, in general the state of mind and way of seeing things have not fundamentally changed. The younger generation remains deeply instilled with our culture, which it respects, and it practises Buddhism. As for the more distant future, it is impossible to tell. We are only refugees, it is true, but we are free, and this freedom is vital for the development of the human individual

and to safeguard the future. At present the genuine Tibetan culture and the true Tibetan Buddhism are to be found outside the geographical frontiers of Tibet.[101]

The analysis is as lucid as ever, considering the circumstances of exile and the results already achieved. The question that now arises is that of time. The young Tibetans are dispersed across the world, not just in India, they are absorbing a culture and social habits quite different from their own, and there is a widening gap between them, the refugees settled at different points in the Indian subcontinent, and those who remain in the Land of Snows. Customs and habits vary, but it is undoubtedly the preservation of the spiritual tradition that poses the most painful questions. The principle of the reincarnation of wise men and grand lamas now arises in totally new terms, even if the lines of descent appear to be continuing for the time being.

It is also true that exile has brought about the birth of many Buddhist centres of all persuasions in western countries, where a certain interest, or at any rate an infatuation, in the Tibetan schools has emerged. The remarkable flexibility of the doctrine enables it to adapt without major conflicts to a variety of conditions, around masters who put down roots elsewhere. If they sometimes find attentive and zealous disciples, and if they try to remain beacons of light in the grain of the age-old tradition, they are often at the mercy of the thousand pitfalls that foreign social norms always harbour deep within themselves, as protection against vaguely defined dangers, resented as threats of aggression.

So in the course of the last few years the proliferation of more or less respectable sects on the fertile soil of a blind quest pursued by a bewildered generation of western youth has sometimes caused Tibetan Buddhism to be pigeon-holed as yet another element in this range of dubious experiments. Ignorance and misunderstanding encourage such confusions, against which the only defence is the power of discernment. On the other hand the fact that some monastic teachers have returned to secular life, having put off the habit either by

choice or by compulsion, is leading Tibetans to consider a
greater openness towards western candidates wishing to be
taught according to the monastic tradition of Tibetan
Buddhism; here both sides venture on to new ground.
Sometimes the exchange proves fruitful, and the men or
women who are not afraid to persevere on this path generally
enjoy the esteem of their masters and their fellow disciples.

> The essence of the Buddhist teaching does not change. Wherever
> they are followed, they hold true. That does not mean that
> superficial aspects like certain rituals or ceremonies are necessarily
> suited to a new environment. These things will change. How
> they will turn out in some given time or place it is hardly possible
> to predict – it depends on the process of time. When Buddhism
> was established in Tibet for the first time, no one had the
> authority to say: 'From now on, Buddhism has come to a new
> country, and it has to be practised like this or like that.' No such
> decision was taken, and with time a unique tradition was grad-
> ually shaped. Perhaps that is what will happen in the west, and
> perhaps some day there will be a Buddhism interbred with
> western culture. Depending on the country, the cultural heritage
> is distinct, and while the essence remains unchanged the practice
> differs from one place to another.[102]

In the precise context of the future of Tibet, it is impossible to
overlook the relations between Buddhism and Marxism.
While some reconciliation is conceivable, in the spirit of the
former's vision of the universe and the latter's theoretical
doctrine, a possible understanding runs foul of the fundamental contradiction between the methods of the religion and
the ideology concerned. One makes tolerance and kindness
the touchstone of its conception of the world, the other has no
scruples about the means it chooses in order to gain its
partisan ends.

> I have thought very long and seriously about this subject, because
> it involves millions of people, from Thailand to Siberia. Among
> Buddhists, the ancestral faith remains very strong and deeply
> rooted to this day, as I have been able to observe during visits, for
> instance to Mongolia. Decades of Communist power have not

been long enough to eliminate religious belief, and Buddhists are not easily convinced to give it up. Even if, officially, the attitude of the authorities continues to be overtly hostile, the only effect is that thousands of people suffer because of it.

Basically, Buddhism as a whole, particularly the Mahayana, and original Marxism have certain things in common, I believe. In Marxism it is the poor and disinherited who take precedence, the least privileged level of society. That is quite right, because attempting to bring about a true equality, particularly in economics, is very good. In Marxism it also seems that everything depends on the individual's own actions. In Buddhism too, because we consider that there is no creator, the essential things depend on oneself, and it is rather like an act of self-creation. So it would be possible to find points on which a dialogue would be possible. But that presupposes real open-mindedness on both sides, and a more realistic attitude . . . .

Yet it should not be forgotten, and history shows plenty of evidence for this, that Marxism does not constitute a total answer for human society, in particular because Marxism is a theory based on materialism alone, on matter, and it utterly ignores consciousness. Now for a Buddhist, there can be no matter without consciousness. Without a knowledge of consciousness it is not possible fully to explain matter, just as without an adequate understanding of matter it is hard to give a full account of consciousness. Leave consciousness out of account, and it is impossible to achieve mental serenity. So by comparison with Marxism, Buddhism can offer something more. And in terms of economics, perhaps Marxist theory can complement Buddhism.[103]

As a determined advocate of non-violence, convinced and convincing in his view that only by being open to others can the real problems of being be resolved, the Dalai Lama exhibits a keen awareness of the threat to the future of mankind which is represented by a generalised indifference to violence. There is not the slightest doubt that a part of today's world is suffused by a climate of violence so widespread that in the end, and almost imperceptibly, it comes to seem commonplace, so universal that it appears to be inevitable. With no ethical grounding, and a façade of generous ideas or

revolutionary longing for the general good, man too often
becomes an enemy to man. The Tibetans have learned that
lesson to their cost, and they warn against the self-inflicted
plague that holds the mirror up to the barbarian in mankind.
Tentzin Gyatso confines himself to reminding us:

> To resign oneself means opening the door to violence: it is
> tolerating the intolerable, folding one's arms instead of taking
> action.
>
>   The present generation lives in a world under pressure, where
> systems keep growing more and more complex, and confusion
> reigns. All and sundry talk and hold forth about peace, justice and
> equality, but in practice it is another story. Not because the
> person or individual is bad, but because of the general environ-
> ment: the compulsions are too strong, and they influence people
> in a negative direction. Perhaps the younger generation will be
> more successful in facing these responsibilities. [104]

Is this an admission of failure? Not at all; it is straight
thinking, or what the smiling Dalai Lama likes to call
Buddhist realism. Because there remains a goal towards
which people turn by instinct – that of liberation or salvation,
the deliverance from negative thinking that Buddhists call
moksha. For the Lord of the Lotus the exact meaning of the
word is

> setting at liberty, liberation. Usually, while a man remains caught
> in the grip of negative thinking, we say that he is a prisoner, that
> he is locked in prison. Once negative thinking ceases, or its
> influence is overcome, one is freed from prison – from that
> prison, at any rate. So that is salvation, or liberation .... But
> beware now, not liberation in the Chinese way, this is an inner
> liberation! [105]

In any case, this manner of conceiving life and inner peace, of
pondering the meaning of existence and being ready to listen
to others, have created a figure, or character, of no ordinary
kind. Looking at the course of his life, it is striking to observe
the extent to which this subtle monk, sensitive to every shade
of difference, draws towards himself so many currents of

sympathy, interest, curiosity and enthusiasm. The same observation reveals his inner strength, and by the same token it reveals the underlying reasons for the Chinese attitude towards him; no promise or half-truth can diminish his certitude of championing the cause of elementary justice for his people. He contains as it were a dimension of eternity that dissolves trivial arguments, unearths pretences and shows fine words for what they are; hot air means nothing to the Dalai Lama.

The Beijing authorities have experienced this quality for themselves. In the wake of the so-called opening of Tibet, after an almost total ban except in the case of a few ironclad supporters of the official Chinese line, advances were made to the sovereign in exile. Ungraciously convinced, but convinced all the same, because facts cannot be wished away, of the basic loyalty of the entire nation to its undisputed leader, even if he has to live abroad, the Chinese authorities came to a decision about a possible visit by the Dalai Lama as early as 1980. They nevertheless waited until November 1984 before they made the decision public, a move which was bound to be interpreted immediately as a laconic blunt rejection of any prospect of genuine negotiation.

For Beijing there can be no question of 'bargaining', and the Chinese government has no intention of going back on its policy of the fait accompli. The Tibetan leader is firmly invited to commit himself to 'working for the unification of China and in favour of national unity', and likewise to give up any idea of independence for Tibet. As well as that, he would have to put a stop to the annual demonstrations by Tibetan refugees on 10 March, recalling the bloody suppression of the rebellion against China in 1959. Lastly, if he wishes to return to the 'mother country', Chinese style, the Dalai Lama 'will enjoy the same political status and the same living conditions as before 1959', except that he will be expected to take up residence in Beijing, and at any rate not on Tibetan soil. To make up for that, he might just possibly find himself appointed to the position of vice-chairman of the Standing Committee of the National People's Congress, the Chinese parliament. Just like the Panchen Lama. These conditions do at least have the merit of clarity, but it is hard to imagine the Lord of the Lotus yielding to them, even if now and then his eye does cloud for a moment with nostalgia for his upland country.

Yet from time to time rumours are heard about a possible visit to Tibet. There are very few meetings and interviews when the idea does not crop up incidentally, if only in a theoretical way, and because there are certain predictions in the scriptures or the oracles which can only be interpreted in accordance with the spiritual sovereign's physical presence in his red and white palace in Lhasa, the Potala. With a disarming smile, Tentzin Gyatso evades a direct answer, hedges diplomatically, or returns the question, according to the mood of the moment. He may also happen to point out that the Jews waited for 2,000 years to go home, that all it takes is sufficient patience, and that a Buddhist like himself is ready to face any eventuality. He explains:

After the visits to Tibet made by my first delegations, early in 1983 I did in fact express the wish to go there in person, perhaps in 1985, so as to see with my own eyes what was happening in Tibet and so get to know the situation at first hand. I thought then that, in so far as there had been certain changes to be seen since 1979, by 1985 it might be an appropriate moment to go there.

Unfortunately, late in 1983 many Tibetans were arrested once again, some public executions took place on the pretext of a campaign against banditry, and some people disappeared without trace – no one knows what became of them. As the Chinese say, two steps forward, one step back, or again, sometimes one step forward and two steps back ... Many things have happened since 1979–1980, particularly when Hu Yaobang came to Lhasa, when he publicly apologised and admitted the errors of the past. He also promised at that time to follow a more moderate, more realistic path. But subsequently the very same events were repeated, which means that nothing is truly certain, nothing can be taken for granted. Afterwards the Chinese publicly reiterated a number of conditions governing my possible visit to Tibet, and the result is that I have no intention of going there.

It is not my own person that concerns me: my constant care is still whatever may be good for the Tibetan people. I myself am only a simple Buddhist monk, I can manage anywhere. The most important thing is my own inner freedom, but that is a different question. I am directly concerned about the fate of 6 million Tibetans. The Chinese try to ignore that, and they pretend to be dealing with the Dalai Lama alone. That is neither fair nor correct.

At the time of those first contacts, they also appeared to believe that in Tibet itself, because of political indoctrination and by other means, people would stop being loyal to the Dalai Lama. That being so, they thought that it was a good idea to invite him, because no one would come to pay him homage, he would no longer be respected, and consequently he would be much easier to manipulate. Well, during our delegations' visits people came from all over the country to express their loyalty and trust in me. That was totally unexpected by the Chinese themselves.

In fact, I have the impression that underneath, the Chinese leadership is not at all anxious to see me back in Tibet. In any case, I do not want to go unless I feel sure that it might do some good to the Tibetans. As well as that, I have received a great many messages since then, saying that their authors would like to see me return as soon as possible, but at the same time warning and urging me not to go back in the present circumstances. Even some Chinese people whom I have met during my travels have told me the same thing, saying that they themselves did not completely trust their own government and that I had to be very wary.

The Chinese sometimes have rather curious attitudes: as soon as I displayed the wish to reply to their invitation, they launched a propaganda campaign against me and laid down their conditions again. On the one hand they proclaim that they are looking for an open dialogue, and on the other, as soon as the answer arrives, they change their tactics and resort to tricks like that. It throws doubt on their sincerity, and that explains why we have suspended all plans for a visit.

Obviously their invitation was nothing but propaganda, and they have no real interest in dialogue. As well as that, there are certain clear grounds for assuming that they meant to use my possible visit as a means to legitimise their claims over Tibet. So we had to put a stop to the plans being considered, especially because I was receiving messages from inside the country, and in particular from various resistance groups, urgently imploring me not to go so far as to put myself into the hands of the Chinese. It was a question of security and trust .... So much so that without a real change in the attitude of the Chinese leadership I strongly doubt that any valid discussions can be resumed on this matter in the near future. Yet in the long term only a generally acceptable solution to the Tibetan problem can bring real and lasting peace to Asia.

You know, the Tibetans love me, perhaps just because I am so far away from them. Altogether, through their rigid, intransigent attitude the Chinese have made me the most popular of all the Dalai Lamas.[106]

Not even the anti-Chinese demonstrations which took place in Lhasa in October 1987 and March 1988 have managed to alter the Dalai Lama's attitude, and he remains as faithful as ever to his principles of non-violence. Without mincing his words, he deplores the consequent repression, while reiterating his admiration for those of his people who did not flinch from laying down their lives for the sake of waking the conscience of the world. After all the sporadic troubles previously hushed up by the Beijing authorities, the protests of October 1987 caused an unprecedented furore in the world media. The policy of greater openness advocated by Deng Xiao-ping and his followers rebounded against them, and what it particularly hurts the Chinese authorities to recognise is that by proclaiming their longing for freedom the Tibetans have inflicted a stinging snub upon their occupiers. For the Han Chinese, there could be no worse offence.

By a coincidence which some observers saw as more than accidental, at the time when the first stirrings of the coming demonstration on 1 October appeared in Lhasa, the Dalai Lama was on a visit to the United States. He had accepted a private invitation to consecrate a stupa at the university of Indiana, and he had been the guest of the US Senate's subcommittee on human rights. The explosion of anger on the Roof of the World did not take him by surprise, but nor did it cause him to change a programme of activities which had been arranged some weeks before. So he arrived as expected in Manali, a small locality set in the Himalayan foothills of the Kulu valley, where a congregation of 3,000 Buddhists from the surrounding region waited to hear his commentaries on one of the best-known texts by the great sage Shantideva.

Beneath a changeable sky, sitting in a rustic bungalow which used to be one of Jawaharlal Nehru's favourite resting places, in the middle of a clearing where the Tibetan flag flapped proudly in the wind, the Dalai Lama was his usual affable self. But his words were more clearly political, although spoken in a serene and lucid tone. Even the brutality of the Chinese reaction, although confronted by nothing but unarmed monks and civilians, did not surprise him.

That is the Chinese way. Sometimes I have the impression that they have a guilty conscience. They have built up their own idea of Tibet, and through repeating and repeating that they came as liberators, they have let themselves be taken in by their own propaganda. So much so that at the moment when any incidents break out they are disconcerted and refuse to recognise the real causes.

Because in spite of certain official changes in recent years, superficially positive, the harm remains serious, and the resentment deep in the people's mind. These demonstrations are only a symptom of a disease which has lasted for over thirty years, ever since 1950, when the tragedy of the invasion took place. So it is understandable that at a certain moment the anger of the people should break out. The Chinese reaction was brutal, but the eyes of the world were witnesses.

That is important, because while I admire the courage of the Tibetans who took to the streets in order to express their true feelings, it is also necessary for the world to know about it. It is necessary for world opinion to realise that Tibet is living under a regime of colonial occupation, and that Tibetans have had enough of being the victims of colonialism. If the situation is as the Chinese describe it, in other words if the majority of Tibetans are so happy, then why do they continue to have faith in me when I say the opposite? Most Chinese think that Tibet was poor, backward, dark and cruel, barbarous. If they have done so much

for Tibet, as they claim, how are we to explain these reactions of
the Tibetan people against them, and why do they go on claiming their independence with such determination?

   If the process of sinicisation is not stopped, and the transfer of
population into the Tibetan highlands halted, the Tibetan people
will soon find themselves a minority in their own country. It is a
grave danger, and we are aware of it. In a way, it is the final
solution to the Tibetan question in the Chinese style. If world
opinion pays no heed, it will be the end, the annihilation of the
Tibetan people and its civilisation.[107]

In his constant concern to seek out the positive elements
which may outweigh the negative, the Dalai Lama has put
forward a five-point plan in an effort to revive the possibility
of dialogue. 'These five points are not new,' he is careful to
emphasise;

   I have raised them at different times before, but taken altogether
   they may possibly provide the beginnings of a discussion. The
   plan consists of transforming the whole of Tibet into a peace
   zone; giving up the Chinese policy of population transfers,
   because it amounts to a threat to the very existence of the Tibetan
   people; respecting the basic rights and democratic liberties of the
   Tibetan people; restoring and protecting the environment of
   Tibet, by having China agree to give up using Tibetan territory
   for the manufacture of nuclear weapons or for storing nuclear
   waste; and starting negotiations on the future status of Tibet, and
   relations between the Tibetan and Chinese peoples.[108]

Looking back, it is obvious that the October riots which
momentarily drew the spotlight of world attention on to Lhasa
caught the Chinese authorities unaware. They broke out at a
moment which was particularly awkward because it only just
preceded the opening of the Thirteenth Congress of the Communist Party, with its internal arguments between reformist
and conservative wings. What made them all the more embarrassing was the presence on the spot of some hundreds of
foreign tourists, which made it impossible to pass over such
events in silence. They came as a kind of public snub, and it is
common knowledge that it is costly to lose face in the orient.

The Beijing authorities maintain that they have brought progress and prosperity to the Tibetan people, by building roads, hospitals and schools and introducing electricity and the benefits of a modern society. This is the classic line taken by all colonialist powers, and it leaves unstated the question of who profits by these changes, and whether Tibet might not have been capable of making its own adjustment to the postwar world, as its own pace and tempo. Judging by their deep-seated attachment to their own otherness, the Tibetans seem to have a different opinion, and if they persist in calling for freedom it is because Beijing has been unable to convince them otherwise. How many people are aware that it was not until July 1987 that Beijing finally recognised Tibetan as the official language of the so-called Autonomous Region of Tibet? In other words, before that time the officials and administrators who held the reins of power – Han Chinese, of course – were not even required to speak the language of the citizens in their charge; this detail says a great deal about the relations between the two societies, which although they lived next door to one another were practically unable to make themselves understood.

'The Chinese too have a right to happiness and well-being,' the Dalai Lama declaraes. 'But not at the expense of the Tibetans.' In spite of recent events, the spiritual and temporal leader of the Land of Snows keeps on insisting that for him the future remains open, and full of possibilities. Yet he is fully aware of the dangers too, and has called upon world opinion to see that the curtain of oblivion is not allowed to fall over Tibet once again.

> Let us allow a little time to go by – my proposals are intended for the long term. I think that for the moment the Chinese have had more than enough of the Tibetans. It is better to allow them to collect their thoughts in peace. We have to think of the future and see things in the longer perspective. In order to create a climate of understanding, both sides have to make an effort, and that would allow some trust to be established. As long as the Tibetan people are up to their necks in Chinese weapons and Chinese soldiers, nothing will be possible.

The problem is that as soon as we approach the Chinese to express our views and our grievances they take it as an attack against their country and immediately go on to the defensive. With the result that the Tibetan point of view does not enter the Chinese mind. That is why I speak it out in front of everybody, so that the rest of the world will hear, and know what it is.[109]

The next eruption, which happened in front of the Jokhang on the last day of the ritual ceremonial of the Great Prayer for the Happiness of All Beings, authorised by the Chinese for the third year running after a ban of over 20 years, was in the very nature of the present situation. At least, says the Dalai Lama, 'it ought to make the Chinese leaders reflect on the gravity of the situation and lead them to contemplate a solution which benefits both the Tibetan and the Chinese people alike'.

His message on the occasion of the twenty-ninth anniversary of the popular uprising, bloodily repressed, which brought about his own departure and the exile of thousands of Tibetans, is unequivocal.

During the last few months our country has suffered the most harsh repression since the era of the cultural revolution. Our people's struggle stands out from many other movements by its non-violent character. Perhaps that is why it has been harder for us to convince the world of the depth of our distress and the firmness of our resolve. Perhaps it is also why governments have ignored the justice of our cause.

What a sad indication of the state of the present-day world, to have to turn to violence in order to attract the attention of the international community! At a time when the whole world is preoccupied by terrorism and other expressions of violence, would it not be in everybody's interest up uphold the non-violent defence of legitimate causes?[110]

The Dalai Lama once again dwelt upon non-violence when we met in London in mid-April 1988. The Foreign Office has seen fit to issue a draconian requirement for discretion on all political questions, and to require him to limit his statements to purely religious or spiritual topics. The request backfired, because the press was so outraged by these restrictions that it roundly criticised this pusillanimous attitude and proceeded to give broad coverage to this visit to the United Kingdom.

Obviously it was by no accidental coincidence that on the same day when the Dalai Lama arrived in the British capital the Panchen Lama announced, to a fanfare of publicity, that if the exiled leader were to give up any idea of independence he would be welcome in China and could even settle again in Lhasa if he wished. Always provided, of course, that he accepted becoming another Chinese 'citizen', much like all the rest. It was a clever stroke of propaganda, but no one should be deceived; the Panchen Lama himself, although he is one of the nineteen vice-chairmen of the National People's Congress, is still kept in residence in Beijing, under close surveillance, and is only rarely permitted to visit Tibet. A few days later the Chinese Prime Minister in person took back this unofficial offer and hastened to modify its terms severely.

None of this affects the equanimity of the sovereign of the Land of Snows. In his concern with the seething latent tensions on the edge of boiling over, he reiterates his profound belief that the only way possible is that of the non-violence which was used by Mahatma Gandhi during the struggle against the British colonial power in India:

As long as the independence movement endured, Gandhi was its figurehead. Once the goal was achieved he refused to take part in the government. I believe that it is the right way, and in any case it is the one that suits me. Personally, it is what I would like to do. In the many years I have spent in India I have kept reassuring the Tibetan people that I took the responsibility for the liberation movement. But afterwards, it will be another matter. Afterwards, with the liberation will come the quarrels and dissensions inherent in every human society, and that is normal and natural. And in that case, it is better for the Dalai Lama to keep his distance and not to interfere in the day-to-day management of affairs. On the individual level, it will be easier for me to settle differences by being neutral . . . .

Recently there has been an outburst of violence in Tibet. That is a different matter. Because of the desperate situation of the Tibetans inside the country, unfortunately it is necessary, because they must themselves express what they feel, their dissatisfaction and discontent – or else the outside world does not understand and does not find out. They have had enough of Chinese domination, and they have made that clearly known. Yet the violence was not on their side: they did seize weapons, but instead of using them they broke them. That is a just attitude.

In order to express their solidarity with the demonstrators in Lhasa, whom I very much admire, because they took to the streets at the peril of their lives, some Tibetans in New Delhi had started a hunger strike which they meant to take to its final conclusion, in other words to the point of sacrificing their own lives if necessary, in the hope of being finally heard. Once again I admire their courage, determination and willpower. But at the same time I am a monk, and in spite of everything I remain attached to the preservation of their lives. Even though I basically agree with them, there is no point in going too far when the sacrifice is useless. I could not stay silent and let them die, so I earnestly begged them to put an end to their fast . . . .

Again, the question of essentials. Some people have a different view and think that violence is the only means of being heard. I admit that there is a certain logic in that, but it is not my own. If militant activism were to spread, if the situation were to harden beyond my reach, if I no longer managed to control it and if violence gained the upper hand, it would only remain for me to renounce my commitment to carry the responsibility for the liberation movement. For me violence could not possibly be the way, it would then be too easy for the Chinese to brutally repress and ruthlessly annihilate, in every sense of the word, Tibet and the Tibetan people.

The Chinese overtures? Sometimes they seem to appear more moderate, open and tolerant, while at the same time they are being more harsh and intractable. It is still too soon to make a definite pronouncement, and you know that the situation on the spot is still tense.[111]

So how is this deadlock to be broken, how is the Gordian knot to be cut without giving way on matters of principle? 'By the middle way, naturally,' the Dalai Lama replies with a burst of laughter.

You know that I am a follower of the Madhyamika, so naturally each time and in every field I try to find the middle path, the one most fitting. My ideas and feelings coincide, but I still have to refine certain details.

I am working towards that end at present by clarifying and sharpening the proposals in my five-point plan, which remains a valid basis on which to open any possible negotiations. Tibet has the right to claim its independence. At the same time the Chinese are unwilling to give up their claims, and they are doing everything in their power to repress and quell the demand for independence. In these circumstances I find myself acting as the free spokesman for the Tibetans. That is why I profoundly think that it is worth the trouble of exploring this way, the middle way, between these two positions.[112]

As for whether the Chinese are capable of understanding this approach, the Dalai Lama smiles:

I believe so. But it takes time. Whether the Chinese accept it or not, it is the proper card to play now. It is worth trying, and it does no harm to anybody. The bridges are not burnt, and by way of my brother who was in Beijing before the end of last year, the Chinese leadership has informed me that it would like to maintain these direct contacts with me. It is true that they are quite embarrassed by these events, and that there are probably different points of view among them. But there, that's how it is.[113]

The Dalai Lama has persevered in his efforts for Tibet, but he also pays heed to his adversaries, and in mid-June 1988 he was fully aware of the possible implications of his action in putting the ball back firmly into the Chinese court. Speaking inside the European Parliament in Strasbourg, he issued a number of concrete proposals which went so far as to offer to Beijing the option of retaining control for the moment both of foreign affairs and defence, in exchange for genuine Tibetan autonomy over civil and administrative affairs – in particular religion, education, trade, culture, tourism, science and sport. The outcome would be a kind of contract of association akin to the position of Hong Kong or Taiwan, although the Dalai Lama made it clear that in the last resort it would be up to the Tibetan people themselves to decide.

In this year of the Earth Dragon, which started on 18 February 1988 by the Gregorian calendar, and is traditionally seen as an eventful year by Tibetans, the Dalai Lama gives the impression of having drawn clear conclusions from the developments of the previous months. 'In my opinion,' he declares, 'the majority of Tibetans want to be separated from China, but on the Chinese side there is no question of such a thing.' Talking to me in June 1988, during a meeting in Geneva, he asserted: 'No one is going to come to the assistance of Tibet. Yet if the present circumstances continue they will bring yet more hardship and destruction to the Tibetan people and their culture. So the logical solution is to try to find some way out of this impasse: that is my basic idea. As for the means of application, they remain to be defined.'

The Lord of the Lotus admits that some may see this move as a concession, and that some Tibetans will blame him for his moderation. In his own mind, he prefers to see it as 'an accommodation, the pursuit of compromise, a way of throwing a line to a neighbour who does not like to lose face. Unfortunately the Chinese leadership often pays too much attention to this issue, so much so that they overlook the essentials and reach the point of responding negatively because they feel embarrassed. One of the key factors in our situation is ignorance,' the Dalai Lama insists. 'The Chinese know nothing about Tibet, its history, its traditions and peculiarities. Never since the foundation of our nation in 127 BC have the Tibetans conceded their sovereignty to a foreign power. What happened after what the Chinese call the "liberation" of 1949 has been the darkest hour in our history. Yet it is time for the Beijing leadership to realise that the colonialist way of governing occupied territories is now out of date.'

It might be said that the Dalai Lama was taking one step backward in order to advance by choosing the 'middle way' appropriate to his Buddhist beliefs, and making allowances for the constraints of political reality. He goes on to add: 'In its totality Tibet – which we call Cholka-Sum, meaning

U-Tsang, Kham and Amdo – should become a self-governing democratic entity in association with China. The government should consist of a chief executive elected by universal suffrage, a bicameral legislative assembly and an independent judiciary system. And its seat should be in Lhasa.' This is a means of pointing out that the present 'Autonomous Region' as defined to suit the interests of Beijing is only a part of the historic territory of Tibet, several of whose regions have been deliberately absorbed into the neighbouring Chinese provinces.

On fundamental principles, the spokesman for his people is unyielding. Although he has made a spectacular gesture towards Beijing, he perseveres in his demand for the denuclearisation and demilitarisation of the high country, with a view to creating a zone of peace, a kind of buffer-State strong enough to bear the brunt of the various great power interests in the heart of Asia. At the same time, he sees this possible genuine sanctuary as the planet's largest natural reserve, because for him a concern for the environment is indivisible from the future course of human life. As he puts it: 'The manufacture, testing and storage of nuclear weapons and other armaments must be prohibited, as must the use of nuclear energy and other technologies that produce potentially dangerous waste products. It is necessary for a regional peace conference to be summoned, in order to ensure that Tibet becomes a true peace sanctuary through demilitarisation. Until such a meeting is summoned, and demilitarisation and neutralisation become a reality, China might have the right to keep a limited number of military installations in Tibet, but solely for defensive purposes.'

The Dalai Lama is well aware that these new suggestions will take some time to consider, and that before initiating any prior discussions the response in Beijing may well be negative at first. 'That is in the nature of things,' he accepts philosophically. 'Nevertheless, I do hope that the Chinese leaders will eventually come to give these proposals a careful examination and will take them into consideration. For my part, I feel that it is worth while making the attempt, whatever the response may be.' As it happens, he came close to the mark once more, in so far as after an initial brusque response from Beijing, a week later the Chinese began to modify their position, leaving the door open to further developments.

Yet by talking about association, is the Dalai Lama not really renouncing the full independence of Tibet? 'Renouncing is not the word,' he explains. 'For us, and for me, Tibet has always been a different country, and has never been China. That is our deepest feeling, and I doubt that it can be altered. For the future, as with any society or human undertaking, there can be changes, according to circumstances, without changing the otherness of Tibet. In certain conditions, two different and separate communities may be provisionally joined, while others may separate for various reasons. Such is human nature, and human history.'

In this finely balanced mixture of spirituality and politics, the transcendental and the everyday, personal contemplation and altruistic action, what room is there left for the monk, what game is being played by the leader of so unknown a cause? Usually the two personas merge, or at any rate overlap. According to the situation, one will give way to the other, even though in the last resort they are indissociable. But how does the Dalai Lama himself reconcile so many diverse activities? A simple lifetime must hardly be enough, it seems.

> There are so many things that interest me, so many subjects that call for attention. That is my own way of passing the time, and in any case all these aspects complement and illuminate each other.
>
> The spiritual aspect depends on your own motivation, whereas secular activity signifies working in the world. Since motivation determines all action, it is important for it to be correct. What does the activity matter: if the motivation is negative, the activity will be negative too. Conversely, when the motivation is positive, then so is the activity.
>
> It is also a good thing to make a distinction between one's own spiritual practice and the religious institution to which one may possibly be attached. The problem, when one is the head of any kind of religious institution, is that one has to conform to its rules

and to its institutional behaviour. It is not possible to follow one's own ideas in total freedom, or to express personal opinions at odds with the tradition of the institution. Fortunately for me, I am not a religious leader in that sense, rather I am a global spiritual guide who does not have to be involved in the administrative affairs or tendencies of every school: there are proper officials for that. As I see it, my essential responsibility is to attend to the purity of the institutions and to see that none of the great lines of descent is lost. Apart from that, I mainly have to concern myself with my own practice.[114]

Which is a way of saying in the same breath that the Ocean of Wisdom is not quite a master like other masters. As the incarnation of the Lord of Infinite Compassion he is deemed to have kept returning among human kind in order to act as a beacon for them. Now that the Land of Snows is no longer what it once was, and the hidden kingdom has been induced to reveal its mysteries and splendours to the foreign view, and now that it has known the hardships of the world be brutally imposed by a ruthless invader who has in a way desacralised it by wrenching it out of its dreams above gulfs of light, what will become of the succession, the transmission of the lineage of the Precious Victorious? Without the slightest hesitation he answers:

Tibet is perfectly conceivable without a Dalai Lama: it lasted for a very long time before the institution existed as such, and in theory it is completely possible. Human institutions pass, and whether they continue or not depends on the circumstances. In the absolute, Tibet, its nation, its culture and even Buddhism are quite thinkable without the Dalai Lama

For the moment, of course, the Dalai Lama is a symbol, a symbol of Tibet. That is why he is so important for the Tibetan nature and culture, and for Tibetan Buddhism too. Today, if the Dalai Lama were to die, another Dalai Lama would be sought, found and chosen in accordance with tradition. Later on, in thirty or forty years' time, I don't know: everything changes, doesn't it? When one envisages the continuity of the institution, the question that arises is that of the succession.

This leaves several possibilities to be examined, lying outside the traditional custom, of course. Before departing, for example, I could designate somebody and confer the title of Dalai Lama upon him myself. This already happens in the tradition of certain grand lamas, like the patriarch of Ganden, Tri Rimpoche, appointed for a certain number of years on the basis of seniority and for his specific qualities. And why could some sort of conclave not be considered too, as with the choosing of a Pope, in an assembly of grand lamas?

The question has been raised several times, especially since 1979. That is because at that time there were some who seemed to think that it was a topical matter, at the moment when the Chinese were doing their utmost to put it about that there was no Tibetan problem, and that the only point at issue was the Dalai Lama. They assured anyone who would listen that the Tibetans were very happy in Tibet since their liberation by the Chinese, and that the sole obstacle to their continued happiness was the Dalai Lama, whose only purpose was to restore his own authority and to regain his former privileges. According to them, this plainly signified that if the Dalai Lama returned the old system would be reinstated at once, and they could not accept such a reactionary step.

It was to spell out the situation clearly that I took care to explain that the real problem was quite different, and one had to be able to tell the wood from the trees. The question has nothing to do with the institution as such, and if pushed, I would even go so far as to say that it is not particularly my business: personally, it does not affect me. The situation is changing, and if circumstances make the historic institution irrelevant, if there is no longer any need for it, and its role in history is over and done with, then never mind, there is no harm in putting an end to it. At least that is what I think.[115]

That is a clear-cut statement of Tentzin Gyatso's personal position. However, he acknowledges that the Tibetan people themselves may not necessarily share his point of view. 'That is another matter, certainly,' he goes on.

Officially, publicly, I have given no verdict on the subject, and I don't know whether the Tibetans are ready to accept a debate about it. Recently I happen to have put forward the idea that the time was bound to come when there would be no Dalai Lama.

That too requires some mental preparation. In fact, for the time being there is no plan for the future. The draft constitution adopted a few years ago expressly provides for the situation in which the Dalai Lama finds it impossible to govern, and that is something to begin with. I am trying to make people think about the question, and to find an idea to ripen for the appropriate moment. In any case, when the time comes I will have discussions with the people most concerned, so as to anticipate the succession question and make the best arrangements for it. But you know, that is not really my personal concern.[116]

It is not at all easy to raise this most delicate of questions with Tibetans. From the humblest to the least directly concerned, inside and outside the country, and from the nearest and furthest from the focal point where the sovereign of the Land of Snows now lives, there is no disputing the unanimous view that the Dalai Lama is Tibet. No matter how hard he may try to remove himself from the issue, and to convince his fellow countrymen that it is an open question, this is one issue on which they appear to be unready to follow him.

That being the case, while a number of variations can be envisaged, no one will venture to explore them. Some may give thought to the matter, and wonder what would happen in the Dalai Lama's absence; they say then that the cause of Tibet would survive, and that they would have to reorganise and fight on. All the same, one senses that no one accepts this prospect, even as a contingency to be allowed for, and everyone agrees that without that daily presence, the comfort of that smile and that flicker of mischief in his eyes, everything would be much, much harder – exile, the constant struggle, survival, even hope, and perhaps too the return home. It appears that it is precisely the privilege of the high country that it shaped the man who remains for all Tibetans 'the Wish-fulfilling Gem'. An Indian journalist, a grandson of Mahatma Gandhi, once said of the Fourteenth Dalai Lama, and said rightly, that he was 'the gift of providence to Tibet, and the gift of Tibet to the world'.

A stubborn undertow of whispers and rumours tends to lend credence to the idea that the Dalai Lamas are finished now, and that this prediction is supported by unequivocal ancient prophecies. Tentzin Gyatso is less categorical, and states that he has no knowledge of these texts.

> As far as I know, there are no prophecies as such, specifically connected with the succession of the Dalai Lamas. There is nothing clear or definitive on the subject. All the same, on a private level it may be possible to work out certain hypotheses or to examine various deductions. For example, when I first came to Lhasa a wise scholar, a very great lama, confided to his disciples after seeing me that the Fourteenth would be a good Dalai Lama, and perhaps the last. That is what was said by a certain person, at a certain moment, and in particular circumstances. More, I cannot tell you – to my knowledge, I repeat, there is nothing more precise.
>
> But if it comes to that, there are always those who possess all the necessary qualifications to be the Dalai Lama. The incarnation of a Buddha or a *bodhisattva* continues to be manifested whatever happens, and not only in human form. Whether the title is or is not bestowed on a particular person depends on whether or not it is beneficial in the prevailing conditions. Long before the first Dalai Lama who bore that name, there were other incarnations of Avalokitesvara, the Lord of Infinite Compassion, without their having necessarily borne the title of Ocean of Wisdom. However that may be, I am not the best Dalai Lama, but nor am I the worst . . . . So that it might be a good thing for me to be the last . . . . If, for the greater good of living beings, I had to be reincarnated as, say, a bridge or an insect, as a monk who follows the Mahayana it is my duty to do it. As long as there are beings who suffer, I shall return.[117]

Prediction or not, good omens or bad, prophecy or not, the assurance is there, given by the person best qualified to make such a commitment. For the people of Tibet it is vital, and perhaps for the rest of the world also. As much as any land, and sometimes better than the rest, the land of Tibet and its inhabitants have had the power to play with time, to scoff at time. Today, for them, it is again a question of time, which arises in new and urgent terms, since here it is a matter of survival, in all the senses of the word. But the word of the Buddha attests that the decline will be temporary and the rebirth all the more dazzling.

In this perspective, there is no doubt at all that the present representative of Chenrezig among his people is a Dalai Lama at a turning point, and perhaps even a breaking point. At the turning point of worlds in conflict, and a breaking point of shattered societies, a solitary sentinel watches at the border of distant horizons. He constantly surprises, questions or overturns old habits, shifts the entrenched certainties. He peers into the future, which resembles a quest, or a question. But with what reply? In this world of appearances, where messages are in fashion, his own perfectly simple message takes on depths of brightness. His own inner peace becomes a sharing of serenity, a purified, intensely watchful power, and a total openness to other things and other people.

So is it a matter of changing the world in order to change a destiny, or of altering the gaze that watches the fairground of illusions? One is hardly possible without the other. 'Of course human society can grow better,' the Lord of the Lotus insists,

of course it can improve for everybody. Precisely by way of inner peace. To me, 'better' means more attention and courtesy to others, a more altruistic approach for a closer understanding. First of all, it must be recognised that others, all other human beings, have the same rights and the same aspirations as ourselves towards well-being and happiness, and that they are not to be considered as objects in the service of our own selfishness, to be manipulated as we please. They are our fellows, and it is proper to value them as such. Once the first knots are untied, and the first steps taken, then vision broadens, and it is possible to go further, beyond one's limits, those of society or of the self.[118]

Some reach the goal more quickly than others, and they become milestones, or landmarks, for those who try to follow.

'The beauty of Tibet is strong, elementary, sublime,' said Fosco Maraini. 'It makes no concessions, and I was going to say that it does not forgive.' Forgive what? Why? In fact, it gives. It brings a rare and different dimension to being, a fact upon which many of its people concur, whether they are accomplished wise men or pretending to be plain mortals, nomads tracking through life as others wander through vast tracts of country, following their flocks to new seasonal pastures. Somewhere, almost by instinct, they know, as others with them also know, that the world can be seen as a mandala, and in the mandala of the world, the Tibetans see at its centre a man whom they call 'the Presence'. In their view, he embodies a principle of love and light, and there are very many who find in him the everlasting source of a reason to live/ But what about the Buddhist monk, Tentzin Gyatso? What does he think of the Fourteenth Dalai Lama? And how does the Fourteenth Dalai Lama see the monk, Tentzin Gyatso?

'A good question, and funny too.' He bursts out laughing, and then he ponders for thirty seconds.

> As a Buddhist monk, Tentzin Gyatso feels a deep compassion for the Fourteenth Dalai Lama, because he sometimes finds that he has no easy life, that he has to face complex situations, and that it is not always straightforward. As for the Fourteenth Dalai Lama, when he considers and looks at Tentzin Gyatso, he has the feeling that he is doing his best, that he is striving with all his heart and doing his utmost to do well .... Will that do?[119]

And the laughter peals again.

At the heart of the mandala, there is always a light. Often there is a divinity, sometimes there may be a void, and at other times a master, a watcher or a guide. But between the symbol and the man stands the sovereign presence of the pilgrim, he who travels in all serenity towards his goal, saying that it is a long way away, but that he knows that it lies a hand's reach, or a heart's, from everyone. This is the man who says:

> Self-confidence, courage, determination and optimism are, in my view, essential in order to gain the day. If, right from the start, you tell yourself that it isn't working, if you give way to discouragement, if you adopt a pessimistic attitude, even though

what you desire is easy to obtain you will not have it, it won't work. That is how I see it. For the human community and the individual alike, hope is vital . . . .

What matters is to do one's best. Whether or not one arrives is a different question. Even if one does not necessarily achieve what one is seeking in this life, it does not matter – at least one will have attempted to shape a better society, based upon more compassion and less selfishness. I am firmly convinced of that.[120]

The wheel turns full circle, and momentarily it hangs, ready to turn again. What is a human life, trundling at the frontiers of eternity, a reflection receding into the twin mirrors of the infinity of space and the immemoriality of time? Others will come afterwards, to the frontiers of the imaginary, questioning immortality by the standards of the ephemeral. Tomorrow the horizon of time will resemble the rainbow of all lights, as precious as the hope of all lives.

In the meantime, all through the range of light, an offering of radiant joy accompanies the footsteps of a wayfaring man, and sometimes symbolises the fascination of the occult. Out of spiritual fulfilment he has made a fundamental dimension of being, in a splendid harmony of knowledge and understanding, heart and mind. It may be a rare privilege to cross the path of a *jivan mukta*, a 'living free man' as the Hindus describe those who, in their human form, have attained the supreme level of illumination, breaking the chains of appearances for ever. Tibetans say that they are bodhisattvas, those who have reached the threshold of awakening and who choose to remain among men, to alleviate the sorrows of those who are blinded by ignorance. Others consider them simply as wise men; after having unlocked the gates of perception, their vision embraces worlds where the riddle of happiness unfolds without poppy or mandragora. Beyond the limits of the expressible, their experience becomes a gift.

Back in the Buddha's holy land, in the certainty of returning to the high country of the gods, a Tibetan monk prays in the silence of dawn for the peace of the world. Here or elsewhere, without ostentation, to the steady rhythm of damarū and hand-bell, his prayer does not rise to any god: it is meditation, climbing towards the light, a changed level of consciousness, the opening of the inner eye. From far far away, from the translucent source of time, he lights a path imprinted on the trembling crest of space. Until the next ripening of time.

Glossary

ahimsa	principle of non-violence.
amban	Chinese resident in Lhasa, under the Mongols.
bodhisattva	wise man who, having reached the threshold of Illumination, renounces his deliverance in order to help the suffering to free themselves.
chörten	reliquary monument in the form of an upturned bell, Himalayan version of the Indian stupa.
dakini	female protective guardian divinity.
damarū	small ritual drum.
darshan	blessing ceremony practised by Indian wise men.
desi	regent during the minority of the Dalai Lama.
dharma	doctrine of the Buddha.
geshe	learned monk.
gompa	dwelling in solitude, Tibetan term for lamaseries and hermitages.
guru	spiritual master.
kalon	official with the rank of minister.
karma	law of cause and effect.
kashag	cabinet of ministers.
khata	ceremonial scarf, usually white.
mandala	pictorial representation of the universe, an aid to meditation.
mani	stone engraved with sacred saying.
mantra	word of power, to incantatory rhythm.
mantric	connected with mantra.
Mönlam	great annual prayer for the happiness of all beings.
pūja	ceremony of liturgical offering.
rimpoche	honorific title, generally used to address a high-ranking lama.
sadhana	ascesis or discipline to be followed with perseverance in order to make progress along the spiritual path.
sangha	the community of Buddhist monks.
stupa	Indian reliquary.

sutra	precept or aphorism in Hinduism and Buddhism.
tanka	religious painting on cloth.
tantra	method of spiritual discipline, containing the highest Buddhist teachings.
tantric	connected with the Tantras.
tsampa	flour made from toasted barley, staple food of Tibet.
tulku	reincarnation of a sage, ascetic, abbot or lama.

Notes

Except where otherwise stated, most quotations of the Dalai Lama come from personal interviews with the author, in particular in Geneva and Rikon (Switzerland); Bodh Gaya (India) in 1985; Digne and Saint-Maclou (France); Dharamsala (India), Rome and Assisi (Italy) in 1986. Lengthy extracts from these interviews were published in *Le Monde*, *La Stampa* and *The Guardian*. Other comments by the Dalai Lama are taken, with his gracious permission, from his own works: *Kindness, Clarity and Insight* (Snow Lion Publications, Ithaca, NY, 1984); *Opening the Eye of a New Awareness* (Wisdom Publications, London, 1985); and *Universal Responsibility and the Good Heart* (LTW, Dharamsala, 1985).

1   Giuseppe Tucci, *To Lhasa and Beyond*, East-West Publications, New Delhi, 1985.
2   R. P. Huc, *Souvenirs d'un voyage dans la Tartarie, le Thibet et la Chine*, Plon, Paris, 1926.
3   'Les poèmes du VIe Dalaï-Lama', translated into French by Yves Codet, *Tribu*, no. 7, University of Toulouse-Le Mirail, 1985.
4   Charles Bell, *Portrait of The Dalai Lama*, Collins, London, 1942.
5   Daniel Bärlocher, *Testimonies of Tibetan Tulkus*, Opuscula Tibetana, Tibet-Institut, Rikon/Zurich, 1982, and personal conversation.
6   Personal conversation.
7   Personal conversation.
8   W. D. Shakabpa, *Tibet: A Political History*, Potala Publications, New York, 1984.
9   Fourteenth Dalai Lama, *My Land and My People*, Potala Publications, New York, 1977.
10 John Avedon, *Entretiens avec le Dalaï-Lama*, Editions Dharma, 1982.
11 Fourteenth Dalai Lama, *My Land and My People*, Potala Publications, New York, 1977.
12 ibid.
13 ibid.
14 ibid.
15 ibid.
16 ibid.
17 Personal conversation.
18 Personal conversation.
19 Personal conversation.
20 Personal conversation.

21 Personal conversation.
22 Personal conversation.
23 Personal conversation.
24 Personal conversation.
25 Inder Malik, *Dalai Lamas of Tibet*, Uppal Publishing, New Delhi, 1984.
26 Personal conversation.
27 John Avedon, *Loin du Pays des Neiges*, Calmann-Levy, Paris, 1985.
28 Personal conversation.
29 Personal conversation.
30 Fourteenth Dalai Lama, *Opening the Eye of a New Awareness*, Wisdom Publications, London, 1985.
31 Personal conversation.
32 Thubten Jigme Norbu and Colin N. Turnbull, *Le Tibet*, Stock, Paris, 1968.
33 ibid.
34 Personal conversation.
35 Personal conversation.
36 Personal conversation.
37 Personal conversation.
38 Personal conversation.
39 Personal conversation.
40 Personal conversation.
41 Personal conversation.
42 Personal conversation.
43 Personal conversation.
44 Fourteenth Dalai Lama, *Kindness, Clarity and Insight*, Snow Lion, Ithaca, 1984.
45 ibid.
46 ibid.
47 ibid.
48 Personal conversation.
49 Personal conversation.
50 Personal conversation.
51 Personal conversation.
52 Fourteenth Dalai Lama, *Kindness, Clarity and Insight*, Snow Lion, Ithaca, NY, 1984.
53 Personal conversation.
54 Fosco Maraini, *Tibet secret*, Arthaud, Paris, 1952.
55 ibid.
56 Gompo Tashi Andrugstang, *Four Rivers, Six Ranges*, Dharamsala, 1973.
57 ibid.
58 Fourteenth Dalai Lama, *Universal Responsibility and The Good Heart*, LTW, Dharamsala, 1985.
59 Personal conversation.
60 David Bärlocher, *Testimonies of Tibetan Tulkus, Opuscula Tibetana*, Tibet-Institut, Rikon/Zurich, 1982.
61 Fourteenth Dalai Lama, *Kindness, Clarity and Insight*, Snow Lion, Ithaca, NY, 1984.

62 Personal conversation.
63 Personal conversation.
64 Fourteenth Dalai Lama, *Kindness, Clarity and Insight*, Snow Lion, Ithaca, NY, 1984.
65 Personal conversation.
66 Personal conversation.
67 Personal conversation.
68 Personal conversation.
69 Personal conversation.
70 Personal conversation.
71 Personal conversation.
72 Personal conversation.
73 Personal conversation.
74 Personal conversation.
75 Personal conversation.
76 Personal conversation.
77 David Bärlocher, *Testimonies of Tibetan Tulkus, Opuscula Tibetana*, Tibet Institut, Rikon/Zurich, 1982.
78 ibid.
79 Personal conversation.
80 Personal conversation.
81 Personal conversation.
82 Fourteenth Dalai Lama, message for the International Day of the Environment, 5 June 1986.
83 Personal conversation.
84 Personal conversation.
85 Personal conversation.
86 Personal conversation.
87 Personal conversation.
88 Personal conversation.
89 Personal conversation.
90 Personal conversation.
91 Personal conversation.
92 Personal conversation.
93 Personal conversation.
94 Personal conversation.
95 Personal conversation.
96 Personal conversation.
97 Personal conversation.
98 Personal conversation.
99 Fourteenth Dalai Lama, *Tibetan Review*, October, 1986.
100 Fourteenth Dalai Lama, *Tibetan Bulletin*, June–July, 1986.
101 Personal conversation.
102 Personal conversation.
103 Personal conversation.
104 Personal conversation.
105 Personal conversation.
106 Personal conversation.
107 Personal conversation.
108 Personal conversation.

109   Personal conversation.
110   Personal conversation.
111   Personal conversation.
112   Personal conversation.
113   Personal conversation.
114   Personal conversation.
115   Personal conversation.
116   Personal conversation.
117   Personal conversation.
118   Personal conversation.
119   Personal conversation.
120   Personal conversation.

Bibliography

Andrugstang, Gompo Tashi, *Four Rivers, Six Ranges*, (Dharamsala, 1973).

Aten, *Un cavalier dans la neige*, (Paris: Librairie d'Amerique et d'Orient, 1981).

Auboyer, J. and J. L. Nou, *Buddha*, (Paris: Le Seuil).

Avedon, John, *An Interview with the Dalai Lama*, (Littlebird, 1980).

Avedon, John, *In Exile from the Land of Snow*, (London: Wisdom, 1985).

Bacot, Jacques, *Trois mystères tibétans*, (Paris: Bossard, 1921).

Bacot, Jacques, *Milarepa*, (Paris: Fayard, 1971).

Bärlocher, David, *Testimonies of Tibetan Tulkus, Opuscula Tibetana*, (Rikon/Zurich: Tibet-Institut, 1982).

Bell, Charles, *Portrait of the Dalai Lama*, (London: Collins, 1942).

Bernbaum, Edwin (ed.), *The Way to Shambala*, (New York: Anchor Press, 1980).

Blofeld, John, *Tantric Mysticism of Tibet*, (London: Allen & Unwin, 1970).

Blofeld, John, *Les Mantras*, (Paris: Dervy-livres, 1985).

Borromée, A., Cl. Laforêt and Dagpo Rimpoché, *Le Dalai-Lama*, (Paris: Olivier Orban, 1984).

Burman, N. R., *Religion and Politics in Tibet*, (New Delhi: Vikas, 1979).

Change. Garma, *The Hundred Thousand Songs of Milarepa*, (Boulder and London: Shambala 1961).

Clifford, Terry, *Tibetan Medicine and Psychiatry*, (London: Aquarian Press, 1986).

Das, S. C., *Journey to Lhasa and Central Tibet*, (New Delhi: Skyland Printers, 1970).

David-Neel, Alexandra, *My Journey to Lhasa*, (Rider, 1927)

David-Neel, Alexandra, *Au pays des brigands-gentilshommes*, (Paris: Plon, 1928).

David-Neel, Alexandra, *With Mystics and Magicians in Tibet*, (Rider, 1931).

David-Neel, Alexandra, *The Superhuman Life of Gesar of Ling*, (Rider, 1959).

David-Neel, Alexandra, *Le Tibet d'Alexandra David-Neel*, (Paris: Plon, 1979).

David-Neel, Alexandra, *Le vieux Tibet face a la Chine nouvelle*, (Paris: Plon, 1981).

de Riencourt, A., *Le troit du monde*, (Paris: France-Empire, 1955).

Desjardins, Arnaud, *Les chemins de la sagesse*, (Paris: La Palatine, 1969).

Dhondup, K. *The Waterbird and Other Years*, (New Delhi: Rangwang Publishers, 1986).

Donden, Dr Yeshi, *Health Through Balance*, (Ithaca, NY: Snow Lion, 1986).

XIVe Dalai-Lama, *La lumiere du dharma*, (Paris: Seghers, 1973).

Fourteenth Dalai Lama, *My Land and its People*, (New York: Potala, 1983).

Fourteenth Dalai Lama, *Kindness, Clarity and Insight*, (Ithaca, N.Y.: Snow Lion, 1984).

Fourteenth Dalai Lama, *Opening the Eye of a New Awareness*, (London: Wisdom, 1985).

Fourteenth Dalai Lama, *Universal Responsibility and the Good Heart*, (Dharamsala: LTW, 1985).

Fourteenth Dalai Lama and J. Hopkins, *The Kalachakra Tantra*, (London: Wisdom, 1985)

Fourteenth Dalai Lama, *Collected Statements, Interviews and Articles*, (Dharamsala: Information Office, 1986).

Gashi, Tsering Dorje, *New Tibet*, (Dharamsala: 1980).

Goodman, M. H., *The Last Dalai Lama*, (Boulder and London: Shambhala, 1986).

Hicks, R. and N. Chogyman, *Great Ocean*, (Shaftesbury, UK: Element, 1984).

Hicks, R., *Tibet and the Tibetan People*, (Shaftesbury, UK: Element, 1986).

Huc, R. P., *Souvenirs d'un voyage dans la Tartarie, le Thibet et la Chine*, (Paris: Plon, 1926).

Jest, Corneille, *La tuquoise de vie*, (Paris: A. Métailié, 1985).

Karan, P. P., *The Changing Face of Tibet*, (University of Kentucky Press: 1976).

Khangkar, Dr Lobsang Dolma, *Lectures on Tibetan Medicine*, (Dharamsala; LTW, 1986).

Landen, P., *Lhasa the Mysterious City*, (New Delhi, 1905).

'La question du Tibet et la primaute du droit', (Geneve: Commission International de juristes, 1960).

L'enseignement du Dalai-Lama, (Paris: Albin-Michel, 1976; réédition/poche, Paris, 1987).

Les poèmes du VIe Dalai Lama, *Le Sütra de diamant*, trad. Yves Codet, *Tribu*, no. 7, (Université Toulouse-Le Mirail, 1985).

Lhamo, Richen, *We Tibetans*, (New York: Potala, 1985).

Losang, Rato Khyongla Nawang, *My Life and Lives*, (New York: E. P. Dutton, 1977).

McGovern, William M., *To Lhasa in Disguise*, (Rider, 1924).

Malik, Inder, *Dalai Lamas of Tibet*, (New Delhi: Uppal, 1984).

Maraini, Fosco, *Secret Tibet*, (London, 1954).

Massin, Dr Ch. *La Medecine Tibetaine*, (Paris: Ed. de la Maisnie, 1982).

Mele, P. F., *Tibet*, (Oxford and New Delhi: IBH Publishing, 1975).

Meyer, Dr Fernand, *La medecine tibetaine*, (Strasbourg, 1979).

Norbu, Thubten Jigme and Colin Turnbull, *Tibet*, (London: Penguin, 1972).

Norbu, Thubten Jigme and Heinrich Harrer, *Tibet Is My Country*, (London: Wisdom, 1986).

Paljor, Kunsang, *Tibet the Undying Flame*, (Dharamsala, 1977).

Pallis, Marco, *Peaks and Lamas*, (London: Cassell, 1939).

Pemba, Tsewang Yishey, *Idols on the Path*, (London, 1966).

'Présence du bouddhisme', (Saigon: *France-Asie*, février-juin, 1952).

Question de ... no. 61, Le Tibet, (Paris: Albin Michel, 1985).

Reclus, Élisée, *Nouvelle geographie universelle*, vol. VII, (Paris: Hachette, 1882).

Richardson, H., *Tibet and its History*, (Boulder and London: Shambhala, 1984).

Schlaginweit, E., *Buddhism in Tibet*, (Susil Gupa, 1863).

Shakabpa, W. D., *Tibet: A Political History*, (New York: Potala, 1984).

VIe Dalai-Lama, *La raison de l'Oiseau*, (Paris: Fata Morgana, 1986).

Snellgrove & Richardson, *A Cultural History of Tibet*, (Boulder and London: Shambhala, 1986).

Stein, R. A., *Tibetan Civilisation*, (London: Faber, 1972).

Tewari, U. N., *Resurgent Tibet: A Cause for the Non-Aligned Movement*, (New Delhi: Selectbook Service, 1983).

Tibetan Medical Centre, *Fundamentals of Tibetan Medicine*, (Dharamsala: Tibetan Medical Centre, 1981).

Tibet, the Sacred Realm, (New York: Aperture, 1983).

Trungpa, Chogyam, *Born in Tibet*, (London: Unwin Hyman, 1987).

Tsering, Rinchen Dolma, *Daughter of Tibet*, (London: Wisdom, 1986).

Tucci, Giuseppe, *The Theory and Practice of the Mandala*, (Rider, 1961).

Tucci, Giuseppe, *To Lhasa and Beyond*, (London: East-West Publications, 1985).

Tung, R. J., *Lost Tibet*, (London: Thames & Hudson, 1980).

van Geem, I., *Crier avant de mourir*, (Paris: Robert Laffont, 1972).

Wallace, B., *Life and Teachings of Geshe Rabten*, (London: Allen & Unwin, 1980).

Yeshe, Palden, La voie vers Shambhala, (Milan: Arche, 1983).

Index

7/05